Bristol folk

A discographical history of Bristol folk music in the 1960s and 1970s

Bristol folk

A discographical history of Bristol folk music in the 1960s and 1970s

Mark Jones

BFP Bristol Folk Publications

This edition published 2009 by

Bristol Folk Publications
www.bristol-folk.co.uk

ISBN 978 0 9563531 0 8

Copyright © Mark Clinton Jones 2009

The right of Mark Clinton Jones to be identified as the Author of this work has been asserted in accordance with the Copyrights, Designs and Patents Act 1988.

Cover design copyright © Mark Clinton Jones 2009

"Robert Stewart remembers…" copyright © Robert John Stewart 2009, used with permission.

All rights reserved. No part of this book may be reprinted or reproduced or utilised or transmitted in any form or by any means, electronic or mechanical, including photocopy, recording, or any information storage and retrieval system, including the Internet, now known or hereafter invented, without permission in writing from the copyright holder.

Layout and design by Bristol Folk Publications.
Printed and bound in the EU by Akcent Media.

Contents

Contents
Contents i
List of illustrations iii

Setting the scene
Introduction 1
A note on the values included in this book 5
Thanks to 6

Folk clubs in Bristol
Some background 7
Bristol's folk clubs during the 1960s and 1970s 8
The Troubadour reunions 13

Record companies and agencies
Saydisc 15
The Village Thing 17
Bristol-based artists on other labels 21
The Plastic Dog connection 21

The artists
Ian Anderson 23
Ray Andrews – Bristol's Boy Banjoist 29
Stan Arnold 30
Jo Chambers 31
John Christie – the Bard of Barton Hill 31
Keith Christmas 32
The Crofters 35
Adge Cutler and the Wurzels 37
Elecampane 43
Dave Evans 45
Frank Evans 49
Flanagan's Folk Four 51
Folkal Point 53
Kelvin Henderson 54
Hunt and Turner 56
Erik Ilott 58
Independent Folk/Cul-de-Sac 60

Bristol folk

Al Jones 61
Graham Kilsby 63
Kind Hearts and English 66
Siobhan Lyons 67
Shelagh McDonald 68
Mudge & Clutterbuck 70
Rod Neep 73
Sally Oldfield 75
Dave Paskett 78
Lindsay Peck/Friary Folk Group 79
The Pigsty Hill Light Orchestra 79
Pat Purchase 83
Pat Small 84
Stackridge 85
Bob Stewart 88
Strange Fruit 91
Steve Tilston 92
Adrienne Webber 128
Fred Wedlock 130
White on Black 133
The Wurzels 135
Nearly made it 138

'Bonus tracks': the artists remember

Ian Anderson remembers 141
Geoff Gale remembers 144
Andy Leggett remembers 145
Gef Lucena remembers 148
Rodney Matthews remembers 150
Robert Stewart remembers 151
Steve Tilston remembers 157
Keith Warmington remembers 160
Steve Webb and Al Read remember 161
Fred Wedlock remembers 162

Discographies and lists

UK Discography - original releases 164
CD discography 189
Artists booked as guests at the Bristol Troubadour, 1966-1971 192
Artists booked as guests at the Folk Blues Bristol & West, 1967-1969 193
Websites 193
References 194

Bristol folk

List of illustrations

Many of the images show folds and creases, and so on, and some were not the best of photos to start with, but in many cases, this is all there is - these are important social documents. Similarly, many of the record sleeves shown have obviously seen better days - but again, some of these are nearly 50 years old and even finding copies to photograph proved to be a challenge in many cases: finding as-new ones is probably an impossibility. Oh yes, and have fun trying to work out what's showing through from the other side of the paper on the Dogpress clippings: I could have played with technology to remove imperfections, but it's nice to see what's really there, isn't it?

Many thanks to all those who provided illustrations and/or gave permission to use images. Special thanks to Ian Anderson for opening up the fRoots Archive and for putting me in contact with significant others, Andy Leggett for materials from Preview magazine, to which he was a regular contributor on folk matters, Al Read for materials from Dogpress and the Plastic Dog Agency and Terry Brace for permission to use Plastic Dog Graphics materials.

Page 93
Top left and top right - Cover and club adverts from the Summer 1967 edition of Folk Under Cover (fRoots Archive).
Centre left - April 1967 edition of Troubadour News showing Anderson, Jones, Jackson and Noel 'King George V' Sheldon (fRoots Archive).
Bottom - 1967 flyer advertising Jo-Ann Kelly at the Folk Blues Bristol and West Club at the Old Duke.

Page 94
Top left - Flyer advertising the first Folk Blues Bristol and West night in March 1967, which led to the setting up of the club of the same name (fRoots Archive).
Top right - Further folk club adverts from the Summer 1967 Folk Under Cover newsletter (fRoots Archive).
Bottom left - Ray and Barbara Willmott, Troubadour founders, at the club's coffee bar in 1966 (fRoots Archive).
Bottom right - Ray Willmott outside the Troubadour club with the newly-married Mr. and Mrs. Wedlock and bridesmaids (Fred Wedlock).

Page 95
Top left - Troubadour programme for April 1967 (fRoots archive).
Top right - June 1971 Dogpress advert for the Troubadour - the last advert before the club was closed (Al Read).
Bottom left - Flyer advertising the second Troubadour Reunion concert, which took place on March 6th, 2004.
Bottom right - The first Village Thing label design, which incorporated an idealised view of Clifton as a village - see following page for Andy Leggett's original illustration.

Page 96
Top left - Original sketch of an idealised 'Clifton Village' by Andy Leggett, which, redrawn, was used for the Village Thing label (Al Read, used courtesy Andy Leggett).
Top right - May 1971 Preview advert for the Village Thing agency (Andy Leggett).
Centre right - Rodney Matthews' new logo for Village Thing (fRoots Archive).
Bottom left - 1970 Village Thing flyer advertising Ian A. Anderson and Wizz Jones' LPs (fRoots Archive).
Bottom right - Front cover of Village Thing's bi-annual Bumflet agency brochure for Autumn 1971 (fRoots Archive).

Page 97
Top left - Back cover of Village Thing's Autumn 1971 Bumflet (fRoots Archive).
Top right - The April 1971 Dogpress, which celebrated the linking up of the Plastic Dog and Village Thing agencies. From left to right are Terry Brace, Maggie Holland and Al Read, with Ian Anderson behind (fRoots Archive, used courtesy Al Read).
Centre left - February 1972 Preview advert for the graphics wing of Plastic Dog (Andy Leggett).
Bottom left - Gef and Genny Lucena of Saydisc in 1969, seen at home with their mono Ferrograph tape recorder - this [probably] 1959 recorder evidently exhibited less wow and flutter than the later ones (Gef Lucena).
Bottom right - October 1971 Dogpress advert for the Village Thing agency, this was the first advert to use the new Rodney Matthews logo (Al Read).

Page 98
Top and centre left - Further pictures from the photoshoot for the April 1971 Dogpress cover. The top photo shows the junction of Park Street and Park Street Avenue in the background (Al Read).

Bristol folk

Bottom left - Rodney Matthews' logo for Saydisc's Matchbox label (Terry Brace).
Bottom centre - Village Thing button badge. Plastic Dog manufactured button badges as part of its operations, with most designed by Rodney Matthews (fRoots Archive).
Bottom right - August 1973 What's On In the West Country advert for the Bristol Folk Cruise.

Page 99
Top left - Anderson, Jones, Jackson (appearing here in reverse order) at the Old Duke in King Street. The whistle player is Terry Silver, from the Backwater Jook Band (fRoots Archive).
Top right - Ian Anderson at the "Freak House", 2 Grove Road, Redland in 1967. The National guitar cost £2, bought from the hairdresser next door (photo Joe Gedrych: fRoots Archive).
Centre left - Ian Anderson with Adrian Pietryga from the Deep Blues Band (photo David Harrison: fRoots Archive).
Centre right and bottom left - Ian Anderson recording for Saydisc at Frenchay in 1968. Note the lack of shoes to prevent extraneous noise from the wooden floor (photos David Harrison: fRoots Archive).
Bottom right - John Turner and Ian Anderson at the Troubadour in 1970 (fRoots Archive).

Page 100
Top - Ians Hunt, Anderson and Turner, that last of whom was known as "Heavy Drummer", at the Pilton Pop Folk & Blues Festival - otherwise known as Glastonbury - in September 1970 (photo Joe Gedrych: fRoots Archive).
Bottom - The Troubadour set and friends at the Pilton Pop Folk & Blues Festival. Sounds journalist, Jerry Gilbert is front left, partially obscuring Ian Hunt, behind whom are Maggie Holland (in hat) and Ian Anderson (in shades). Ian Turner is centre right, in shades and furry waistcoat, next to Pat Roche (whose daughter, Chloe Herrington is in space rock group, Chrome Hoof). Behind these is Tim Hodgson, manager of the Troubadour. Far right is Al Stewart, who had played the Troubadour the night before. Parts of Melody Maker journalist, Andrew Means, can also be seen between Ian Hunt and Ian Turner (photo Joe Gedrych: fRoots Archive).

Page 101
Top left - The Troubadour set at a photo shoot for Ian A. Anderson's Royal York Crescent LP in 1970. The Pigsty Hill Light Orchestra's Andy Leggett is to the left with dog (Joe Gedrych: fRoots Archive).
Top right - Stickers promoting Ian A. Anderson's second and third Village Thing LPs (fRoots Archive).
Centre left - A break in recording sessions for Ian A. Anderson's A Vulture Is Not a Bird You Can Trust at Rockfield in 1972. From left to right, Ian Hunt, Anderson, Kipps Brown, Pique (Pick) Withers (on floor), Pat Moran and Pete Descindis. Brown, Moran, Withers and Descindis were four-fifths of progressive rock band, Spring. Withers was later a founder member of Dire Straits (fRoots Archive).
Centre right - Hot Vultures button badge (fRoots Archive).
Bottom left - Ian A. Anderson at Rockfield, 1972 (photo Martin Wise: fRoots Archive).
Bottom right - Hot Vultures: Ian Anderson and Maggie Holland in 1975 (photo Dave Peabody: fRoots Archive).

Page 102
Top left - Keith Christmas with headband (fRoots Archive).
Top right - Keith Christmas at home from the May 1972 edition of Preview (photo Keith Morris: Andy Leggett).
Bottom left - Keith Christmas at the De Montford Hall on (possibly) 20th May 1971 (photo Keith Morris: used courtesy Clare Morris/Keith Morris Archives).
Bottom right - The Crofters on the Pill Ferry in 1965, Gef Lucena on the left and Martin Pyman on the right and Pill Creek in the background (photo Graham Kilsby: detail from the Crofters' first Saydisc EP sleeve).

Page 103
Top - The Crofters at Coates cider factory in Nailsea (detail from the Crofters' second Saydisc EP sleeve).
Bottom left - the original Wurzels line-up in 1966 from a Western Daily Press Wurzels special (Jonathan Conibere, used courtesy of Northcliffe Media Limited).
Bottom right - Adge Cutler promotional photo from the HTV special, "Adge Cutler - the First Wurzel", broadcast May 4th 1974 (Jonathan Conibere: used courtesy ITV West).

Page 104
Top right - Programme for the 1967 Scrumpy and Western shows (Andy Leggett).
Top left - Programme for the 1968 Wurzelrama shows (Andy Leggett).
Centre and bottom left - 1978 Elecampane promo flyers (Andrew Stephens, used courtesy John Shaw).
Centre right - The pre-Dave Evans line-up of Canton Trig in the February 1973 Preview (Andy Leggett).
Bottom right - 1971 Village Thing Flyer for Dave Evans' first LP, The Words In Between (fRoots Archive).

Page 105
Top left - Dave Evans, possibly at the 1972 Cambridge Folk Festival (photo Joe Gedrych: fRoots Archive).
Top right - Dave Evans as seen on the back sleeve of Elephantasia (photo Dave Borthwick: fRoots Archive).

Bristol folk

Second row left - 1972 Village Thing promotional sticker for Dave Evans' Elephantasia LP (fRoots Archive).
Second row right - Dave Evans live at the Stonehouse in Bristol, 1972 (photo Joe Gedrych: fRoots Archive).
Bottom three illustrations - Kicking Mule promotional photographs of Dave Evans taken by label owner, Stefan Grossman (courtesy Stefan Grossman).

Page 106
Top left - Frank Evans at Wraxall Manor (detail from the 1972 Saydisc LP, In an English Manner).
Top Right - Flanagan's Folk Four, from left to right, Mike Flanagan, Richard Lee, Pat Spearing and Andy Leggett (Andy Leggett).
Centre right - 1962 (probably) and about as important as it gets in some respects: a 17-year old Geoff Gale reflected in the window of Jennings Music in Soho with one of the the very first consignment of Fender guitars to be sold in the UK (Geoff Gale).
Bottom left - Geoff Gale in his workshop in Worcester Terrace, Clifton (Geoff Gale).
Bottom right - 'Mahavishnu' Geoff Gale from a photoshoot for the March 1979 edition of Sound International magazine with one of his prototype guitars (photo Tim Bishopp: Geoff Gale).

Page 107
Top left - Agency photo of Kelvin Henderson, circa 1978.
Top right - Ian Hunt at the September 1970 Pilton Pop Folk & blues Festival (photo Joe Gedrych: fRoots Archive).
Centre left - 1971 Village Thing promotional photo of Hunt & Turner (fRoots Archive).
Bottom left - Advert for Bristol's hippest gents outfitters (even Peter Banks from Yes is known to have bought clothes here!) from the September 1971 edition of Dogpress. Ian Hunt, centre, is apparently naked, though with tastefully-positioned guitar (Al Read).
Bottom right - Al Jones with Elliot Jackson at the Troubadour in 1966 (fRoots Archive).

Page 108
Top left - The Alligator Jug Thumpers, comprising Cliff Brown, Andy Leggett and Al Jones, (presumably) somewhere in Devon in early 1967 (Andy Leggett).
Top right - 1973 Village Thing promotional sticker for Al Jones' Jonesville LP (fRoots Archive).
Centre left - Poster for a gig at St. Peter's Hall, Henleaze, Bristol, on Valentine's Day, 1968. The Pink Coffee Blues Band included bassist, Kevyn Jones, who later joined Kind Hearts and English.
Centre right - Tony Bird of Kind Hearts and English (Geoff Gale).
Bottom left - Huw Gower, seen here with the Graham Smith Combo at the Hotwells Festival (circa 1976), who played on early Kind Hearts and English demos and on their first LP. Geoff Gale is on bass - the guitar being played by Gower was built by Gale (Geoff Gale).
Bottom right - A post-KH&E Tony Bird with Looney Tunes at the Ashton Court Festival, circa 1977 (Geoff Gale).

Page 109
Top left - Shelagh McDonald publicity shot from 1967/8 (fRoots Archive).
Top right - Shelagh McDonald publicity shot from 1971 (fRoots Archive).
Bottom - Shelagh McDonald and Keith Christmas on August 16th 1970, during a break in recording McDonald's second LP, Stargazer (photo Keith Morris: used courtesy Clare Morris/ Keith Morris Archives).

Page 110
Top left - Mudge and Clutterbuck (Dave & Tim) with John Turner at the Troubadour circa 1968 (Andy Leggett).
Top right and centre middle - Dave Mudge, taken on one of the folk cruises along the River Avon on board the Kingstonian in the summer of 1967 (photos Joe Gedrych: fRoots Archive).
Centre left - August 1967 Troubadour News showing a (presumably Roneo copier-ravaged) picture of Dave Mudge (fRoots Archive).
Centre right - Rod Neep in photo booth, 1973 (Rod Neep).
Bottom right - Rod Neep, later 1970s publicity shot (Rod Neep).
Bottom centre - Western Daily Press article from April 1973 reporting Rod Neep's arrival in Bristol (Rod Neep, used courtesy of Northcliffe Media Limited).
Bottom right - November 1966 Troubadour News showing Sally Oldfield and Ian Bray (fRoots Archive).

Page 111
Top left - The Alligator Jug Thumpers in 1966: Cliff Brown, Quentin Williams and Barry Back (Andy Leggett).
Top right - The Pigsty Hill Light Orchestra at the Troubadour in the October 1969 edition of Airframe: from left to right, Andy Leggett, Dave Creech, Barry Back and John Turner (Andy Leggett).
Centre left - 1970 Village Thing flyer advertising the first two Village Thing LPs by the Pigsty Hill Light Orchestra and Sun Also Rises (fRoots Archive).
Centre middle top - June 1971 Dogpress advert for a Pigsty Hill Light Orchestra gig at the Granary Club. Support

Bristol folk

was by fellow Village Thing duo, Strange Fruit (Al Read).
Centre middle bottom - The Rodney Matthews pig, which originally illustrated a poem about the "snot garden up your nose" in the Pigtales booklet. The illustration was later used on the rear of the Pigs' 1976 LP (Terry Brace).
Bottom left - Publicity photo of the Pigs, which was later used on the rear jacket of the Pigtales booklet: from left to right, John 'Wash' Hays, Dave Creech, Andy Leggett and Dave Paskett (fRoots Archive).
Bottom right - December 1971 Dogpress advert for the second Pigs LP, Piggery Jokery (Al Read).

Page 112
Top - Rodney Matthews illustration of Stackridge and the Pigsty Hill Light Orchestra, from the December 1972 edition of Preview, advertising the forthcoming Treasure Island pantomime (Andy Leggett).
Centre left - Pigsty Hill Light Orchestra promotional photo, 5th December 1976: from left to right, Jon 'Wash' Hays, Dave Creech, Robert Greenfield and Richard Gould (photo Keith Morris).
Centre right - Pat Small at the Troubadour circa 1968 (fRoots Archive).
Bottom - The West Country Three 1968/9 with Pat Small on the left (fRoots Archive).

Page 113
Top left - The Westlanders with Mike Evans, later of Stackridge, on the left (fRoots Archive).
Top right - Stackridge line-up with Paul Anstey in place of Crun from the June 1971 edition of Preview: from left to right, Anstey, Billy Bent (with dog), Andy Davies, James Warren, Mike Evans and Mutter Slater (Al Read).
Centre left top - Andy Davies from the March 1971 issue of Dogpress (Al Read).
Centre left bottom - Christmas message from Stackridge from the December 1970 issue of Dogpress (Al Read).
Centre right - Advert for the first Stackridge LP from the September 1971 issue of Dogpress (Al Read).
Bottom - Rodney Matthews promotional picture of Stackridge Doing the Stanley (Terry Brace).

Page 114
Top left and right - Strange Fruit at the Troubadour shortly before it was closed in 1971 (fRoots Archive).
Centre left top - Advert for the Strange Fruit single in the July 1971 edition of Dogpress (Al Read).
Centre right - 1971 Village Thing flyer advertising Steve Tilston's An Acoustic Confusion (fRoots Archive).
Bottom three - Steve Tilston on the main outdoor stage at Cambridge Folk Festival, July 1972. Note the Village Thing sleeves (Wizz Jones and Ian A. Anderson) pinned to the canopy (photos Joe Gedrych: fRoots Archive).

Page 115
Top left - Adrienne (Webber) (fRoots Archive).
Top right - Adrienne Webber in the December 2nd 1970 edition of the Bristol Weekly News (Andy Leggett, used courtesy Northcliffe Media Limited).
Centre left - Just married! Mr. and Mrs. Wedlock exit from St Mary Redcliffe church through a processional arch of guitars. Left side: Big Brian; Pat Spearing; Roger White; Tim Clutterbuck. Right side: Dave Mudge; John Turner; Andy Leggett (obscured); Pat Small (Fred Wedlock).
Centre right - Fred Wedlock from the September 1972 edition of Preview (Andy Leggett).
Bottom - Another wedding shot. Left side: Aj Webber; Barry Back; Big Brian; Pat Spearing (front); Tim Clutterbuck (top); Roger White. Right side: Pat Small; Dave Mudge(top); Andy Leggett; John Turner (Fred Wedlock).

Page 116
Top left - 1971 Village Thing flyer advertising Fred Wedlock's The Folker (fRoots Archive).
Top right - 'Apology' from the November 1971 issue of Dogpress (courtesy Al Read).
Bottom left - October 1971 Preview Advert for Fred Wedlock's The Folker LP (Andy Leggett).
Bottom right - Fred Wedlock at the Stonehouse, 1972. Guess the song (photo Joe Gedrych: fRoots Archive).

Page 117
Top left - White On Black from the November 1972 issue of Preview (Andy Leggett).
Top right - Advert for White On Black's Saydisc LP from an unidentified issue of Dogpress (Al Read)
Centre left - White On Black; from left to right, Jon Knowler, Suzi Lawrence and Sue Franklin (fRoots Archive)
Centre right - Agency advert for White On Black and Erik Ilott (complete with misspelled surname) from the August 1973 edition of What's On in the West.
Bottom left - The final line-up of Adge Cutler and the Wurzels shortly before Adge's death in 1974: from left to right, Cutler, Tommy Banner, Tony Baylis and Pete Budd - the last three carried on as The Wurzels after Adge's death. Publicity photo for the HTV special, "Adge Cutler - the First Wurzel", broadcast May 4th 1974 (Jonathan Conibere, used courtesy of ITV West).
Bottom right - Remaining detail from Decanter publicity photo showing Sarah Bale and Richard Gould (Rod Neep).

Page 118
Top row - Almost the Country Blues EP (Ian Anderson with Elliot Jackson); Royal York Crescent (Ian A. Anderson);

Bristol folk

A Vulture Is Not a Bird You Can Trust (Ian A. Anderson).
Second row - Singer Sleeps On as Blaze Rages (Ian A. Anderson); Anderson, Jones Jackson EP; Banjo Maestro (Ray Andrews: cassette-only issue).
Third row - Ladies Man (Stan Arnold); Showstoppers for the Intelijunt (Stan Arnold); Fable of the Wings (Keith Christmas: apologies for the battered condition of the sleeve - this is one of the best condition copies seen in 30 years of collecting).
Bottom row - Pigmy (Keith Christmas); The Inverted World (Mike Cooper: Ian Anderson); Pill Ferry EP (The Crofters).

Page 119
Top row - Drink Up Thee Cider EP (The Crofters); The Ballad of the Severn Bridge EP (The Crofters); When God's On the Water (Elecampane).
Second row - The Further Adventures of Mr. Punch (Elecampane); The Words In Between (Dave Evans); Elephantasia (Dave Evans).
Third row - Sad Pig Dance (Dave Evans); Take a Bite Out of LIfe (Dave Evans); Stretching Forth (Frank Evans).
Bottom row - In an English Manner (The Frank Evans Consort); Noctuary (Frank Evans); Soiree (Frank Evans).

Page 120
Top row - ...for Little Girls (Frank Evans); Folkal Point; Carrion On (Hot Vultures).
Second row - The East Street Shakes (Hot Vultures); Up the Line (Hot Vultures); Magic Landscape (Hunt & Turner).
Third row - Shipshape and Bristol Fashion (Erik Ilott); Sounds of the Sea (Erik Ilott, Michael Aspel, etc.); Independent Folk.
Bottom row - Jonesville (Al Jones); Album (Shelagh McDonald); Stargazer (Shelagh McDonald).

Page 121
Top row - Sheep EP (Dave [Mudge] + Tim [Clutterbuck] with the Downsiders); Heading for the Sun (Rod Neep); Isambard Kingdom Brunel (Old Pete & John Christie, 7" LP).
Second row - Water Bearer (Sally Oldfield); Easy (Sally Oldfield); The Sun in My Eyes (Sally Oldfield, 7" single).
Third row - I Still Dream About Your Smile (Dave Paskett); Pasketry (Dave Paskett); Pigsty Hill Light Orchestra Presents! (Pigsty Hill Light Orchestra).
Bottom row - Piggery Jokery (Pigsty Hill Light Orchestra); The Pigsty Hill Light Orchestra; Blues and Gospel (Pat Purchase, CD).

Page 122
Top row - Children of the Sun (Sallyangie); Children of the Sun (Sallyangie, reissue); Stackridge.
Second row - Friendliness (Stackridge); The Man In the Bowler Hat (Stackridge); Extravaganza (Stackridge).
Third row - Mr. Mick (Stackridge); Do the Stanley (Stackridge); Tomorrow We Part (Bob Stewart & Finbur Furey).
Bottom Row - The Wraggle Taggle Gypsies O (Bob Stewart); An Acoustic Confusion (Steve Tilston); Collection (Steve Tilston).

Page 123
Top row - Songs From the Dress Rehearsal (Steve Tilston); Volume One EP (Fred Wedlock); Virtute et Industrial EP (Fred Wedlock).
Second row - The Folker (Fred Wedlock); Frollicks (Fred Wedlock); Fred Wedlock's Homemade Gramophone Record.
Third row - Fred Wedlock's Greatest Hits; The Oldest Swinger In Town (Fred Wedlock and Chris Newman); West Country Three Sing the Hits of Peter Paul and Mary.
Bottom row - White On Black; Bristol Fashion (unknown artists, one-sided EP); Bristol Folks (Various artists).

Page 124 - various artists LPs and EPs
Top row - Ragtime Piano; Blues Like Showers of Rain; Listen Here!.
Second row - The Great White Dap EP; Men and the Sea; Clogs.
Third row - Club Folk Volume 1; Club Folk Volume 2; Matchbox Days.
Bottom row - Us; Sounds of Bristol EP; Guitar Workshop.

Page 125 - various artists LPs
Top row - Rave On; Contemporary Guitar Workshop; Irish Reels Jigs Hornpipes and Airs.
Bottom - Detail from the insert from the Crofters' Pill Ferry Saydisc EP.

Page 126
Top - Detail from the insert from the Crofters' Drink Up Thee Cider Saydisc EP.
Bottom - Detail from the insert from Fred Wedlock's Volume One Saydisc EP - the first record released by Saydisc.

Bristol folk

Bristol folk

Setting the scene

Introduction

Bristol has long been an important city, second only to London in terms of maritime trade until supplanted in that category by Liverpool. As a major industrial centre Bristol boasted numerous coal mines, glass-cones, factory chimneys, brass furnaces and pottery kilns, many of which encroached into the very heart of the city. By the end of the Second World War most of this industry was either gone already or was otherwise in serious decline: although the docks were still busy, trade was not what it had been a century before.

Bristol made the national news rarely in the 1960s and the 1970s: the major stories in the 1960s were the opening of the Severn road bridge in 1966, the devastating floods of 1968 and the first successful test flight of Concorde from Filton in 1969 – the last of these even became the subject of a Giles cartoon; the main stories in the 1970s were the 'Bristol 600' celebrations in 1973 commemorating 600 years of the 'City and County of Bristol', followed with near-impeccable timing by Bristol losing its county status. A couple of years later, the opening of the Royal Portbury Dock with both the Queen and the Royal Yacht Britannia in attendance brought the return of the national news cameras and a certain amount of parochial pride. That was it really, until the St. Pauls riots in the early 1980s reminded the rest of the country that Bristol was still here. A highly-biased and selective view of the city during those years, but for someone growing up in the 1960s and 1970s, Bristol seemed sleepy and quiet, moving at its own pace and with its own agenda. These were the only events that seemed to stand out amongst a backdrop of Vietnam, the Investiture, John and Yoko, the Apollo programme, Monty Python, Decimalisation, Princess Anne and Captain Mark Phillips, the EEC, power cuts, the Yom Kippur war, Cyprus, the Sex Pistols and the Jubilee.

To go back a bit, as the 1950s and 1960s progressed, there were still scars left by the blitz and the opportunity was taken to sweep away much of the old, to create a brave new world of high rise blocks and ring-roads that finished some of the work started by Hitler. On the positive side, the remaining central slums were cleared, but on the less positive side, some important buildings were lost along the way, such as the historic and irreplaceable shot tower in Redcliffe – not to mention the Ship Inn on the same street. In the midst of rebuilding the city, and no doubt as an antidote to the rigours of post-war austerity, youth got on, as it always does, with the important business of enjoying itself. In various cellars, attics and back rooms, first jazz, then folk and blues clubs sprouted and Bristol discovered that here was something else in which it could excel.

Bristol's jazz heritage is adequately covered in Dave Hibberd's *Recollections of Jazz in Bristol – My Kind of Town*[1] but I became frustrated when trying to find any sort of record of folk music in Bristol. After a fair amount of procrastination I thought, okay, if there's no

Bristol folk

book on Bristol's folk music heritage, then I'll write one. Which brought the first major problem: what exactly *is* folk music? Well, both Louis Armstrong and Big Bill Broonzy have been attributed as saying, "All music is folk music. I ain't never heard a horse sing a song"[2], which isn't exactly helpful. In the end it didn't really matter because I decided not to make too much distinction between folk, blues, gospel, ragtime, country, a spot of jazz and even a modicum of progressive rock. This was mainly because I wanted the resulting book to appeal to as wide a variety of people as possible – and perhaps even make some money to compensate for all those dreary trips on overcrowded First Great Western trains to look up odd back copies of the Melody Maker and the like in the British Library. Anyway, I hope that most readers can agree that most of the artists included can be classed as folk artists without too much argument, or at least can be seen to have been inspired by traditional music of one sort or another – whatever 'traditional' might mean.

That dealt arbitrarily with the first problem, but the next problem was what exactly would I mean by *Bristol* folk? Should I limit the book to those born and bred within the city – or county – limits or should I allow some foreigners in? I finally decided to interpret Bristol folk as anyone working in the broadly-defined genre, who at some point in the two decades in question used Bristol as a permanent base for their musical meanderings. Somehow, a group based in Clevedon in north Somerset also found itself included, but as that particular group survived numerous bouts of proofreading before the anomaly was spotted I decided that they could stay. After all, Clevedon does have a Bristol postcode.

There is just one thing. I was far too young to see any of these people playing at the time, so what did I think gave me any sort of special knowledge for writing this book? Well, this was why this book is subtitled a *discographical history*. I know most of what I know because, as a record collector of some years standing, I have always made a point of picking up records with any sort of local interest – at least, when they've been cheap enough. At some point in the last thirty-odd years I have owned, borrowed or otherwise heard almost every record released by the musicians covered in this book.

The only real drawback to making this a discographical history is that those who did not release records do not necessarily get a mention. This, although a limiting factor, did mean that the book was more likely to get finished: trying to include every person who played on the Bristol folk scene during the period in question remains, probably, an impossible task. Many of those who didn't make records in their own right get a mention where they played with those who did, so hopefully not too many people are missed out by using this approach. Another reason for this approach is that part of the book's target audience is the growing global record collecting fraternity, many of whom have discovered Bristol's rich folk heritage via the Village Thing and Saydisc labels. It is this global market, with eBay at its core, which has caused the values of many of the records mentioned in this book to soar. Ten years ago, you could pick up most of these records for a few quid in Plastic Wax[3], but the Internet in general, and eBay specifically, have changed the rules – Bristol's folk scene has gone global with many of the remaining copies of records now selling to overseas collectors on the few occasions that they are offered for sale.

Bristol folk

Over the years I have got to know quite a few of those playing on the folk scene during the time covered by the book, so some of the gaps in my knowledge have been filled up with anecdotal material, some of it publishable – you know what musicians' libidos are like – and some of it possibly even reliable – you know what musicians' memories are like. The first source of *reliable* information was Andy Leggett, who luckily is an archivist by nature. Having found my Saydisc and Village Thing discography website a few years ago (now at www.VinylAttic.com) he kindly provided me with several records, various anecdotes and numerous music paper clippings. So, to some extent, he was responsible for kick-starting this book. I was going to write it anyway, but it's nice to be given a prod when you've long since decided that you'll start the book mañana.

Since getting started, I have received a great deal of encouragement, numerous corrections and asides and a great deal of extremely useful content and other help from both Gef Lucena and Ian Anderson, who also have large archives and good memories. After this, things started to snowball as more and more people got to hear about the book. In alphabetical order, Tony Bird, Sue and Tim Brine, Keith Christmas, Henry Davies, Colin Evans, Dave Evans, Dave Fuller, Maggie Holland, Graham Kilsby, Rodney Matthews, Rod Neep; Chris Newman, Dave Paskett, Al Read, John Shaw, Robert John Stewart, Steve Tilston, Mike Tobin, Keith Warmington, Steve Webb, Fred Wedlock and Mike West have all helped with error-trapping, filling in the gaps and supplying me with reminiscences and/or other materials. What has surprised me is the enthusiasm that has been shown for this project by those who were there and their willingness to help. Even with all the help, there will still be mistakes and these, of course, are down to me or to my being daft enough to believe the music press.

What did take rather more energy than anticipated was the task of gaining permission from copyright holders to include pictures of the record sleeves in this book. This turned into a project in its own right, and the process almost doubled the time taken to get this book to print. In several instances, despite in-depth research, copyright owners of several long-defunct, small, local record labels proved to be unknown or to be deceased with next of kin's whereabouts (or even existence) unknown. In these instances, I have reproduced the sleeves and would welcome contact from the copyright holder, if any exists, so that I can credit these few sleeves in future editions. Where copyright holders were identified, all those involved with small, independent record labels gave ready permission to reproduce record sleeves, with yet more enthusiasm shown for the book. Of the majors, Universal's Sanctuary imprint proved to be extremely supportive, granting permission to use sleeves from the many old record labels now owned by them. RCA proved to be the oddest company to deal with – the obviously recent 'graduette', to whom an equally-bemused call-centre operative directed me, didn't seem to know what 'records' were, let alone what 'record sleeves' were and seemed to be convinced throughout that I was trying to license use of the RCA logo for some sort of franchise: it is not very often that I give up, but sometimes life is just too short. The two RCA sleeves in question do not appear in the book. EMI proved to be the most frustrating company to deal with. After about three months of to-ing and fro-ing, they decided that I would have to pay £1,000 plus VAT to reproduce fifteen Adge Cutler/Wurzels sleeves (i.e. rather more than the projected profit margin of this book). This figure dropped mysteriously, and by return of email, to £750 plus VAT after I turned the offer down. To

Bristol folk

paraphrase one particular contributor to this book, being charged £1,000 seems somewhat excessive for offering to advertise a record company's product for free. No EMI-owned images appear in this book.

Meanwhile, to get back to the text, the artists are listed in alphabetical, rather than chronological, order and those who start at the beginning and read through to the end will find a certain amount of repetition. This is deliberate and has been included so that the reader can dip into the book, looking first at the artists that specifically interest them, rather than having to start at the beginning and work their way through sequentially. The aim has been that each section should be self-contained, though you'll get a richer picture – and the occasional sense of déjà vu – by reading the whole lot. There are also some parts that contradict each other, and you can make of this what you will – it might be down to some musicians' memories of the same event differing or it might be down to inaccuracies in sources from the music press – or it might easily be down to my misinterpretation of either of these. Contradictions have been left for you to make of them what you will.

The book also looks at the two main local folk-friendly record companies, Saydisc and Village Thing: it also discusses the agency side of Village Thing and its hook-up with the rock-oriented Plastic Dog agency. Saydisc and Village Thing were responsible for releasing a great deal of music by Bristol-based folk musicians – and for those who want to delve deeper into all things Bristolian and West Country, Saydisc recorded much more for posterity, from school concerts to steam locomotives to mechanical music to change ringing to wildlife sounds to tales from Cotswold characters to … well, in the interest of brevity let's just say that the words 'eclectic' and 'comprehensive' fit the bill. The overall picture is completed by a look at Bristol's folk clubs, of which there were a surprisingly large number.

So have a look in your record collection or scour the car boots and last few remaining junk shops to see if you can find some of the glorious records discussed within and give them another listen. Some of the best folk-based music in the world has come out of Bristol … and if you can't be bothered to spend years hunting down the records, can't afford the hefty price tag now attached to many of them, or if you are young enough to be wondering quite what an LP is, a good deal of the music discussed within is now available on CD, much via Ian Anderson's Weekend Beatnik label and Gef Lucena's resurrected Saydisc label, and/or for download, though mostly the music has been remastered for digital ears, so you don't get quite the same as you do on the vinyl originals. Although there is a CD discography included, this book doesn't otherwise mention CD reissues unless there is a specific reason to, but discusses the original vinyl releases because, whatever anyone says:

It is always best to listen to recorded music in the distribution format for which it was originally recorded. Discuss.

A note on the values included in this book

The specific values included in this book are values that records have been seen to sell for on eBay in the last few years. Those records selling for lots of money on eBay have generally been in near new condition, with the sleeve and any inserts in near new condition too. If you have got copies of any of these records just remember that you are not necessarily sitting on a gold mine: a well-played copy of any of the Village Thing LPs with a sleeve that has one or two light creases or edge scuffs will sell for only a fraction of the price mentioned here. For example, a near perfect copy of Dave Evans' *Elephantasia* sold on eBay shortly before I started work on this book for almost £60, but a near perfect copy of the record in a sleeve that had a small price sticker tear sold a week later for only £4. It's easy to find records in perfect condition – that's one of the reasons that the sleeve is there – but it is not easy to find sleeves in perfect condition, and that is what heavy-duty collectors are paying big money for. Also remember that eBay is a fickle market place. Just because a record has sold for a certain price once, it doesn't mean that it will sell for the same price again. It all depends on the good, old economic laws of supply and demand – in other words, on just who is willing to pay what for which record this particular week.

Where I have given an estimate, this is the sort of amount that I would expect to pay for a near perfect copy. If you have any of these records that you want to sell, remember that dealers will *at best* only offer around 20% of the full value: usually they will offer much less because they have their overheads to pay and a need to make a viable profit. Every record they buy is speculation and they might have to hold on to a record for several years to get a worthwhile return, hence generally only offering a small amount up front. You might be lucky and find something much cheaper at a car boot sale, or you might find that I've not placed the price high enough. Basically, the second-hand record market is a funny beast and the moment that any set of values is printed, it is immediately inaccurate. Let's just say that the values here are a *guide* to what you might expect to have to pay for one of these records in near-perfect condition rather than what you might get if selling, unless you really do know how to play the second-hand record market … caveat venditor.

Before I forget, much like share prices, record values go down as well as up. As generations die off, interest in old musical genres and formats plummets – in the 1980s, certain rock and roll records sold for silly, large amounts, but nowadays, many of these same records are carboot fodder at £1 a go. All records will, I suppose, go the same way as the wax cylinder and the 78, though there will still be some of us silly, old buggers collecting them – and then burning them on to CD and transferring them to iPod so that we can actually get to listen to them once in a while.

Thanks to…

Ian Anderson; Iain (Jethro) Anderson; Stan Arnold; Tony Bird; Terry Brace (RIP); Sue and Tim Brine; Keith Christmas; Jonathan Conibere; Henry Davies; Colin Evans; Dave Evans; Kevyn Fortey-Jones; Dave Fuller; Geoff Gale; John Garrad; Stefan Grossman; Gordon Hale; Liz Hannam; Maggie Holland; Sue Kearley; Graham Kilsby; Andy Leggett; David Lord; Gef Lucena; Rodney Matthews; Clare Morris; Rod Neep; Chris Newman; Bristol Evening Post/Northcliffe Media Limited; Dave Paskett; Al Read; John Shaw; Joe Stead; Andrew Stephens; Robert John Stewart; Steve Tilston; Mike Tobin; Keith Warmington; Tim Wearen; Steve Webb; Fred Wedlock; Mike West; Sil Willcox; Paul Woods.

… and for permission to include record sleeves …

Gef Lucena (Saydisc, Matchbox and Village Thing); Ian Anderson (Village Thing); David Lord/Robert John Stewart (Crescent); Mike Tobin and Angel Air's Peter Purnell (Stackridge); Stefan Grossman (Kicking Mule); John Shaw (Dame Jane); Colin Evans (Blue Bag); Steve Tilston (Cornucopia); Fred Wedlock (Pillock); Alan Robinson (Red Rag); Richard Ellen (Plant Life); Dave Paskett (Think!); Bristol's City Museums, Galleries and Archives (Men and the Sea); and last, but not least, Simon Lindsay of Sanctuary/Universal (B&C, Peg, Transatlantic, Bronze and Marble Arch).

... and for help with the technical side of things ...

Ian Anderson and John Garrad both contributed to a level well over and above the call of duty. Thanks to them I am now immersed in the 'joys' of QuarkXPress and have even started my own publishing company. Now, I wasn't expecting that when I started out on this project over a year ago ...

Folk clubs in Bristol

Some background

The British folk revival was born in the early 1950s, headed by musicians such as Ewan MacColl. The revival prompted many musicians to form folk clubs, many of which were hotbeds of Socialism, a political stance that fitted easily alongside the promotion of folk as a peoples' and, predominantly, a worker's music: indeed, Bristol's first folk club was based at the Communist Club at Lawford Gate, though the cheapness of hiring the room might have been a factor in deciding on location. Politics aside, many clubs promoted some form or another of research to rediscover the roots and branches of Britain's indigenous folk music and folk music throughout the world. Ironically, one of the pioneers of the British folk revival was American, Alan Lomax, who had relocated to the UK in the early 1950s. Both he and his father, John, were well-known for their US Library of Congress recordings of American music in the field. So it was that many British folk revivalists came to be just as much at home with an old blues as they were with *Blow Away the Morning Dew*. Many were more at home with the blues, which led by degrees to the British blues boom of the mid-1960s and the odd, late 1960s country blues offshoot in which Bristol-based musicians played such a part – but we're running ahead a bit here.

Why was it that British folk music needed to be researched and revived? There are several linked reasons, and all of them oversimplifications. On one hand Britain had undergone intensive industrialisation over the previous two centuries, which had caused a mass movement of labour from the country to the growing urban centres, where folk song was replaced in the urban psyche by music hall, parlour song and other popular styles: folk researchers suggested that the oral tradition of passing on song was near-dead by the end of the 19th Century[4]. Then the First World War decimated a whole generation, reducing living folksong even further: an oral tradition of song requires people to pass it on, people to pass it on to, and the heart left to sing it. Also, there was no systematic attempt to preserve folk song for future generations – but after all, how do you preserve something that is not static and therefore cannot be written down, or if written down makes that one variant the exemplar? There was a handful of evangelists, such as Cecil Sharp, Gustav Holst, Ralph Vaughan Williams, Percy Grainger and the like, who hunted down songs around the country, Sharp famously collecting folksong from Somerset on a bicycle on several occasions between 1903 and 1916[5]. However, even these collectors altered metre and pitch, changed words and edited out verses that they considered too rude or suggestive for polite society.

> Many of the words and phrases noted were a little too explicit for Edwardian sensibilities, or at least for publication and thus Sharp … often "had to soften the words". In particular, any mention of illegitimacy, women enjoying sexual pleasure or promiscuity has been erased from the songs in their published versions.[6]

Sharp made arrangements of songs that he collected and what emerged tended to be pretty-pretty, though innocuous arrangements, ready-made for the programmes of light music concerts and folk dance orchestras. Grainger arranged one of Sharp's collected pieces and the resulting *Country Gardens* became a very big 'hit' – though this was seen by Sharp as almost a debasement of folk music and he is cited as regretting having let Grainger use the piece. Although the likes of *Country Gardens* did very well, as did other classical composers' use of folk themes in their compositions, few recordings were made of British folk song sung by genuine country singers either in the field or in the studio in the first half of the 20th Century[7]. Whereas in America folk music remained popular and acceptable, though often remaining so on only a regional basis, indigenous folk music in Britain was considered somehow rustic or vulgar, good enough for children to sing – from heavily-censored collections – at school and useful in film scores as a clichéd audio mnemonic to let you know in which part of the British Isles the film was set. It was not until the folk revival of the 1950s, that companies such as Topic began to release authentic British folk music as a core policy.

By the early 1950s many people had worked out that Owen Brannigan, Richard Lewis and Kathleen Ferrier, although making popular and accomplished recordings of British folk song, were not quite the real thing. Real folk song did not have stirring orchestral arrangements conducted by Sir Malcolm Sargent and they were not sung in wonderfully-modulated tones, complete with massed choirs to join in with the remaining rumbustious bits. Also in the post-war years the in-strict-tempo stranglehold of orchestrated country dance music and the massed accordions and bagpipes of Scottish and Irish dance music continued their false, if highly popular, pre-war idea of folk music being predominantly something to accompany organised dance, as evinced by the order of the wording in EFDSS – the English Folk Dance and Song Society. The middle class had hi-jacked folk music and made it into something they wished it to be and this 'recreation' of a utopian past could provoke unfortunate parallels with the epic myth-making of pre-war National Socialist Germany[8]. Not surprisingly, it was also the middle class that started to make the rediscovery and transmission of traditional folk music acceptable, this time not by sugaring it up, or watering it down, but by underpinning the whole with a respectable academic ethos. So it was, to get back onto the point, that folk clubs sprang up throughout the country, the first in Bristol being, in Gef Lucena's words, "… a pretty informal affair that Dave Creech ran at the Communist Club in Lawford Gate (off West St, Old Market)"[9]. Many more followed.

Bristol's folk clubs during the 1960s and 1970s

Bristol boasted an enviable roll-call of folk clubs in the 1960s and 1970s. The best-remembered clubs are the Bristol University Folk & Blues Club, which, with the largest audience space and budget, could pick and choose from the biggest names on the international folk scene, the Troubadour, which made its name through presenting top quality local and national artists, with a bias toward contemporary folk, and the Bristol Ballads and Blues, which also presented top quality local and national artists, but with a more traditional bias. Other clubs with various policies came and went – as Robert Stewart explains:

Bristol folk

> In Bristol the twin streams of contemporary and traditional folk were embodied by two successful folk-clubs, the Troubadour in Clifton, and the Bristol Ballads and Blues in dockland. Other venues, such as the thriving acoustic blues or ultra-traditional clubs, had special interests that came and went as the folk-scene ballooned and then collapsed. The Troubadour Club tended strongly towards the American contemporary influence, while the Ballads and Blues, at the Bathurst pub, tended towards American and British and Irish traditional. I say "tended towards", because the boundaries were extremely flexible at this most creative time in Bristol ... While Bristol University had a huge following drawn from an ever changing student audience base, plus the benefit of university funding, the Troubadour and the Ballads and Blues, both relatively small venues, had the largest creative influence on the Bristol folk scene, balancing the contemporary and the traditional streams of inspiration between them. [10]

In the early 1960s the Bristol Ballads and Blues Club met at The Old Duke, King Street, on Saturday evenings and in 1963 this was joined at the Old Duke by the Bristol Poetry and Folk Club, which met on alternate Friday evenings. Both these clubs later moved to The Bathurst Hotel, on Bathurst Basin and shortly afterwards Gef Lucena, of the Crofters folk duo, took over the running of the Poetry and Folk Club when the original committee broke up. Also on hand was the Bristol Folk Song Research Society, based at 66 Park Street, which had Martin Pyman, the other half of the Crofters, as its Secretary. Of the Park Street address, Gef Lucena explains:

> The significance of 66 Park Street was that that was the address for music store Churchill and Son Ltd where I ran the record department for c. 3 years before starting Saydisc in 1965 – Churchills was owned by Mickleburghs which led to the ultimate recording of Roy [Mickleburgh]'s collection.[11]

Although the Old Duke is now globally associated with jazz, it also played an important part in Bristol's folk scene. Apart from the Ballads and Blues and Poetry and Folk clubs, it also played host to the Folk Tradition Club, formed in 1967 by Dave Searle and Pete McNab[12], and also to Ian Anderson's Folk Blues Bristol and West, which moved in from the Troubadour[13]. These clubs provided an outlet for local, national and even international musicians. The Folk Tradition Club had quite a diverse mandate – apart from music sessions the club also organised lectures, special recitals and Mummers plays. The Bristol Ballads and Blues also had a very eclectic approach, as Robert Stewart explains:

> This was Bristol's longest running folk club, situated at the Bathurst pub, located beside Bathurst Basin in dockland. The Ballads and Blues was loosely based on a London folk club, started by MacColl and Seeger, who created the ubiquitous model of "floor singers" and "guest artists" used by hundreds of British folk clubs. Ballads (traditional British) and Blues (traditional American) were mixed with new contemporary songs from the very early days of the folk revival in the late 1950s, all the way into the late 1970s when the original folk scene expired ...[14]

Another club, Ballads and Broadsides, with its feet firmly in the traditional camp, originally met in Hotwells and later on moved up the hill to the Lansdown in Clifton. Of this club, Ian Anderson says:

Bristol folk

Angela Carter, later famous novelist, and Paul Carter her husband, an early director of Topic Records, ran a very traditional club [which] opened in 1964 as Ballads & Broadsides at the Bear Hotel, Hotwells [and] later moved to the Lansdowne in Clifton. It stated in the Folk Directory that its policy was "British traditional" and it had a fearsome local reputation for being hardline. I think it ran [until] about 1967 and probably the later Folk Tradition club then took its place.[15]

Meanwhile, in 1966, just off Richmond Hill in Clifton, the Broadside Folk and Blues Club opened in Frederick Place. Also known as Miranda's, this was run by Mike Evans, violinist with the Westlanders and later with Stackridge. Other than folk-specific clubs, there were at this point other folk-friendly venues: Ian Anderson remembers that these, "… included a coffee house in Whiteladies Road called the Pam Pam, where Al Jones, myself and others had residencies - round about the time of the short-lived club at Mirandas off Park St…"[16]

By far the biggest folk club in Bristol, however, was the Bristol University Folk & Blues Club: as Ian Anderson says, "Although … in the Students Union this was open to the public, had the biggest guests, huge audiences (up to at least 500!), and was a real learning ground for many local artists."[17] The club was located at the Victoria Rooms, along with the rest of the Students Union, until the opening of the newly-built Anson Rooms in Queen's Road. Many of those who did floor spots at the club later played at the Troubadour.

The Troubadour was opened in Waterloo Street in Clifton by returning Australian émigré, Ray Willmott, on Friday, 7th October, 1966 and the first act to play was Anderson, Jones, Jackson. Andy Leggett says of the Troubadour:

> According to my diary, the Clifton Troubadour opened on Friday the 7th Oct '66. I first attended and became a member on the following evening … I'm not exaggerating when I say it was a significant moment in my life. That night I met Ian Anderson, Al Jones, Fred & Sue Wedlock, Roger White, and Bob Stewart among others.[18]

Ian Anderson remembers a couple more people who were regulars at the Troubadour at various points over the next few years:

> Other Troubadour residents around then included Norman Beaton who I think was at the Old Vic Theatre School and later starred in Desmond's on TV. He was one of the first Troubadour residents, popular enough to be given a Wednesday night residency in his own right within a month or two of the club opening. A bit later on, around 1970, "Wizz" Langham (nickname inspired by Wizz Jones) was a regular, who later got more (in)famous as Chris Langham, the recently disgraced actor.[19]

Robert Stewart remembers the care with which the Troubadour ensured that it did not step on the toes of other folk clubs:

> In the early days of the Troubadour, I can remember Ray Wilmott, the owner, being concerned that on Saturdays he should not book an artist who clashed, or competed somehow, with the Ballads and Blues. Meetings were held to scrutinize the BBB advance guest list, as at that stage, shortly after opening, Ray had little knowledge of

folk artists ... as it turned out both clubs were full no matter who they booked and the Troubadour stormed onwards to field an impressive and influential list of performers.[20]

In 1967 Ian Anderson started the Folk Blues Bristol and West club, which met the first Sunday of every month at the Troubadour. This became so popular that he was forced to move the club to the Old Duke before later moving again to the Full Moon on Stokes Croft. Anderson remembers:

> In early '67 we'd started some monthly blues nights at the Troubadour which had been so packed and successful that we'd had to move them to the Old Duke in King Street. We were the first country blues club in Britain, just before this became a big national boom – talk about being in the right place at the right time![21]

The music press also recognised that a club with a specific policy of booking country blues artists was something new when the country blues boom hit nationally. For example:

> ... the Folk Blues Bristol and West ... was the first to really feature country blues music as a policy[22] ... The first country blues specialist club was Ian Anderson's Folk Blues Bristol and West club which featured Ian, Elliott Jackson and Mike Cooper. "The audience was up to 200 a night when I left," says Ian ...[23]

Another club was Folk Under Cover. This met in the premises that had been used by Bristol's first folk club. Of this club, apart from its interesting acronym, Ian Anderson remembers:

> This was co-run by Kelvin Henderson and ran in 1967 (at least) at The Celler (sic), 10 Lawford Street, Oldmarket, which was noted in the [Western Daily Press] as being "the premises formerly occupied by the YCL" which I think was Young Communist League. Kelvin and the club launched a magazine called Folk Undercover which ran for I think only 3 issues in 67...[24]

In 1968 another folk club was opened at the Swan Hotel in Stokes Croft. The extremely short-lived Biafra Jug Band played there and Keith Christmas was booked at one point for the now miniscule-sounding fee of 17/6 (87½p). By 1971 the surviving folk clubs had been augmented by the White on Black Club at the Arts Centre on King's Square, the Folk House, the Crown and Dove Folk Club and, to service the growing Caribbean community, the Bamboo Club.

The mini-country blues boom, the home-grown singer-songwriter and traditional folk scenes kept the established folk clubs busy into the start of the new decade. However, making a living on the club circuit was becoming harder, for both clubs and performers. This was mirrored around the country with crowd-pullers moving into the rock concert arena, playing support to popular bands and demanding bigger wages, rather than playing for (often not quite) expenses on the folk club circuit. In mid-1971, following problems related to the financial expectations of the new owner, the Troubadour was closed – just after it had been advertised that the club was to gain a drinks licence: throughout its life, the Troubadour had been an alcohol-free venue. Both Ian Anderson and Troubadour owner, Peter Bush, put their opposing views on the closure via an article in Bristol's *Pre-View* arts and entertainments magazine. The article was confrontationally titled "DEATH of a folk club – whose fault?" but all it really did was to highlight the tension between the worlds of music and commerce. The importance of the club was summed up thus:

> The loss of the Troubadour can't just be assessed in terms of the weekly entertainment it provided. Above all, the club was a social centre – and an inspiration and springboard for countless young artists.[25]

By the time the Troubadour closed in 1971, the roll-call of folk clubs in Bristol was still quite impressive: the Ballads and Blues was still going strong, and indeed lasted until the late 1970s; the Ballads and Broadsides club was still going, though by now it met on Saturdays at the Lansdown in Clifton; the Bristol Fashion Folk Club met on Sundays at the Swan Hotel on Stokes Croft; the Old Barn Folk Club met Fridays at the Crown and Dove; the University Folk/Blues Club met on Thursdays in the Students Union on Queen's Road, but was now open to Union card holders only; the White on Black Folk Club was still at the King's Square Arts Centre, meeting on Thursdays – and being a member of this club later allowed you entrance to the Toby Folk Club in the Red Lion in West Pennard, Somerset; the Polytechnic & Redland College Folk Club met on Thursdays in the Common Room at Redland College; St. Matthias College Folk Club met fortnightly on Tuesdays at the college in Fishponds; Folk on Tuesday met at the Folk House, oddly enough on Tuesdays; and the Beeches Club met Wednesdays at Filton Technical College. The Folk Tradition Club had moved briefly to the Crown and Dove, during which time the club's 200 members were swelled to around 7,000 members because of an associate membership scheme with The Folk Song Club, Cheltenham, The Folk Singers' Club, Swindon, The Wessex Traditional Folk Song Club, Bournemouth, and the Traditional Music Club, Nottingham. These Monday sessions moved again early in the year to the Nova Scotia on Cumberland Basin, where folk singing still continues.

Nowhere really filled the gap for contemporary folk left by the closing of the Troubadour and premises were sought for another club in Clifton Village. The quest was given press in the August 1971 edition of Dogpress and concluded:

> The venue problem is not acute. We have several possibilities which mean a club will open somewhere this autumn. BUT … everybody would prefer that it was in the peaceful, creative atmosphere of "Clifton Village" and therein lies the problem.

Nothing was immediately forthcoming, but a successor finally appeared on 20th March 1972 when the Bunch of Grapes pub on Newfoundland Road – nowhere near Clifton – opened the Stonehouse folk club, which usefully had its own entrance on Milk Street. Andy Leggett, who provided write-ups on the local folk scene for *Pre-View* magazine, described the soon-to-open Stonehouse Club thus:

> For people who like their folk music laced with contemporary jazz and blues, there will be a new Monday night club. It opens early in March at the "Stonehouse" connected to the "Bunch of Grapes", Bond Street.[26]

Colin Irwin of the *Melody Maker* provided national exposure for the club, pointing out that there were some similarities between the old and the new:

> Alas, the Troubadour is no more. But folk lives on in Bristol ... The Stonehouse, which meets on Mondays behind the Bunch of Grapes in Newfoundland Street is modelled vaguely on the old Troubadour ... it has become a popular central point for artists to drop in ...[27]

As the 1970s progressed, the Old Barn Folk Club moved from the Crown and Dove to the Bathurst Hotel and one or two other folk clubs came and went, such as the Granary's New Grain Folk Club, which opened for a few months in 1975: unfortunately, the sound of glasses chinking on the bar tended to drown out the singer. Also in 1975, Steve Tilston and Keith Warmington opened another folk club at the Bathurst Tavern overlooking Bathurst Basin. Several folk clubs closed as well, the Beeches Club's demise was reported in the same edition of *Pre-View*[28] that reported the opening of the Stonehouse, though it then seemed to reopen with barely a hiatus.

The Stonehouse carried on until both pub and club were demolished in 1982 to make way for the Spectrum Building, a speculative office block, which has been underutilised almost ever since its completion: perhaps the building nearly thirty years later of Cabot Circus opposite – smack on top of the site of the Western Star Domino Club, whilst I think of it – will alter this. The Folk House, meanwhile, is still going strong and there is still a folk club at the Nova Scotia. The Crown and Dove was demolished long ago, whilst the Bathurst Hotel/Tavern, now named The Louisiana, is still a live music venue. A growing number of pubs and bars now operate 'open mike' nights, which seem to correspond to the earlier floor spots, so 'folk' music still lives in Bristol.

Before closing, it is worth putting Bristol's folk scene into a wider perspective. Bristol was blessed with equally committed and talented jazz, rock and classical scenes, and these all fitted within and without the more general arts scene. There was a great deal of interaction and crossover between poetry, theatre, the arts and music, with musicians like Bob Stewart being extremely active in several areas within Bristol's thriving performing arts scene. Projects were often funded by such organisations as the BBC, the British Arts Council and South West Arts, and theatres and arts centres represented other, non-folk club venues, for folk music.

The Troubadour reunions

The Troubadour, probably thanks to its close association with the Village Thing label, produced more home-grown – or at least recently-imported and firmly-replanted – recording artists than any other Bristol folk club. This is probably the main reason that there is more source material on the Troubadour than on any other Bristol folk club and why many could be forgiven, after a brief Internet search, for thinking that the Troubadour represented the *whole* Bristol folk scene – after all, it did get a mention in one of Al Stewart's more memorable songs, *Clifton in the Rain*. The other thing is that the Troubadour, despite closing

Bristol folk

in 1971, won't quite die: the great affection and sense of nostalgia that has remained over the years for both the Troubadour and the scene that revolved around it led to two reunion concerts in the new Millennium by various club regulars.

The first Troubadour reunion was at the QEH Theatre in Clifton on 9th November 2002. It was organised to commemorate the thirtieth anniversary of the closure of the club, although in the event the reunion actually took place just over 31 and a half years after the club had closed. Still, that slight mistake aside – and it's the thought that counts – the concert saw performances by Kelvin Henderson, Ian Hunt, Adrienne Webber, The Westlanders, Pat Small, Al Jones, Anderson Jones Jackson, Keith Christmas, Mike and Mitch, Fred Wedlock and the Pigsty Hill Light Orchestra. In 2003 a double CD, *Waterloo Street Revisited*, was issued with performances by all.

The concert was such a success that a second reunion concert was organised in 2004, this time at the Redgrave Theatre in Clifton on 6th March. Mike and Mitch acted as comperes and did a short set. They were followed by (in what order I can't remember) Beggars Opera, Adrienne Webber; Fred Wedlock, Keith Christmas, Nick Pickett, Steve Tilston, Maggie Holland and Ian Anderson. Anderson and Holland also performed several songs together along with Ben Mandelson, all of whom had been in Tiger Moth. The evening finished with a loud, echo-plexed, electric performance by Ian Hunt and guest. Pat Small and Al Jones were billed though they didn't play on the night; there was also an unbilled artist who was accompanied by her son. Pre-orders were taken for a possible CD to commemorate the evening, but no CD was issued this time around because of both recording problems and copyright issues.

Record companies and agencies

Saydisc

Gef Lucena formed Saydisc Specialised Recordings in May 1965, with himself, his father, Lauri, and Roy Mickleburgh as directors. In 1968, Gef Lucena's wife, Genny, became a director and Saydisc carried on as a limited company until about early 1971, when it became a partnership of Gef and Genny Lucena. Some of the earliest Saydisc recordings were of local folk, blues and jazz musicians, including live recordings from The Ship Inn[29], in Redcliffe Street, which was soon demolished, along with the world's first lead shot tower, to make way for road widening. Saydisc also recorded and released records of local events and sounds, such as musicals staged by local schools, change ringing from St. Mary Redcliffe, steam engines from south Gloucestershire, transcriptions of jazz, ragtime and cakewalks from old cylinder recordings in the Mickleburgh collection and much, much more. The first release was an EP by Fred Wedlock and the first LP, released shortly afterwards, was a compilation of local folk musicians called *Bristol Folks*.

In 1968 Ian Anderson and Mike Cooper suggested that Saydisc should start a label called Matchbox to release country blues by both American and British musicians. The first LP was recorded at the Meeting House, Frenchay, by Gef Lucena in March and April 1968 and was called *Blues Like Showers of Rain*.

> Mike Cooper and I had suggested Gef Lucena of Saydisc in Bristol start a blues label called Matchbox, and when its first compilation LP Blues Like Showers of Rain came out in July 1968, everything went silly … John Peel, then as now, the first to spot something good happening at the roots, played it every week on Night Ride and had most of the artists guesting.[30]

It was released in July 1968 and included Anderson, Cooper, Dave Kelly, his sister, Jo Anne Kelly, the Panama Limited Jug Band, Simon and Steve[31], and the Missouri Compromise, who were all guests at Anderson's Folk Blues Bristol and West club. The first Matchbox LP gained a lot of exposure for the label and also helped to draw a hardcore of blues and jazz fans who recognised that the label was not just concerned with presenting new music and re-releasing otherwise hard to find music, laudable in itself, but also that they were committed to flying the flag to the extent of getting known and respected experts to write minutely-detailed sleeve notes: records were also sensibly programmed, rather than presenting a hotchpotch of back catalogue as many of the bigger labels seemed content to do. In short, Saydisc and Matchbox releases were quality items put together by people who were knowledgeable and enthusiastic about what they released. Early releases included recordings by Blind Boy Fuller, Kokomo Arnold, Cripple Clarence Lofton, Furry Lewis, and Peetie Wheatstraw, often recorded from the only known remaining 78 rpm recordings. On the home front, Matchbox released a now rare LP by Ian Anderson and Mike Cooper, titled *The Inverted World*, on which each musician had one side each. There was also an obscure follow-up to *Blues Like Showers of Rain*, with several musicians from the first volume, including a lightly disguised Mikel Kooper, now signed to Pye: this sold poorly compared to the first, having just missed the main thrust of the mini-country blues boat.

Saydisc and Matchbox continued to release obscure veteran and vintage recordings by American blues and jazz artists, including manufacturing and distributing Johnny Parth's Roots label. They also started to release current folk and 'old-timey' country-based music, licensing LPs from specialist American labels such as Ahura Mazda, Rounder and Kanawha. In the early 1970s David Wilkins[32] of Valley Recordings came on board as a recording engineer and Saydisc branched out in another direction with the Amon Ra label, which presented classical and chamber music played on authentic instruments – one of the earliest labels to do this as a policy. Much of the Matchbox and Roots content was repackaged and reissued in the 1980s in the Matchbox Bluesmaster series. Gef Lucena's memories on some of these labels run as follows:

> The two [Ahura Mazda] albums we released were pressed and printed in UK from US metalwork and amended artwork. AMS-SDS 1 was Scott [Dunbar of Lake Mary] … AMS 2003 was Harmonica Williams with Little Freddie King. The choice of label name, Ahura Mazda, was entirely coincidental with our choice of Amon Ra for our classical label. The former being the godhead of the Zoroastrians and Amon Ra the dual Egyptian god (Amon the ram headed god of Thebes conjoined at the horns with Ra the sun god of Heliopolis) … As regards the provenance of our Roots series, these all used Austrian metalwork and most used Austrian printed sleeves with our sticker appended. The larger selling titles had UK printed sleeves from Austrian printing film. We … started our own Matchbox Bluesmaster Series with Johnny Parth supplying the masters and Paul Oliver doing the notes.[33]

Throughout the 1970s Saydisc continued releasing well-researched LPs of rare jazz and blues, but started to move in a more mainstream direction, though admittedly a decidedly left-field mainstream direction. There were LPs by barbershop groups, choirs, forays into world music and even an LP of parlour poetry by Kenneth Williams – and on the heavy metal front there were more recordings of church bells, steam locomotives and several outings for Lyndon Baglin's euphonium.

The quality of the records was also an issue of prime importance with Saydisc and they were one of the first small, independent labels to routinely press all their records to classical standards using the highly-regarded Nimbus pressing company, which was located just across the River Severn in Monmouthshire. To the ultimate end of musical fidelity, Saydisc was the first small independent to cease releasing albums on vinyl, moving to the new CD format. Certainly Saydisc can be seen to have been a trend-setter in many areas and although other labels, such as Cornwall's Sentinel Records, have been run on similarly committed lines, no other label has ever touched Saydisc for breadth and depth of vision, commitment to fulfilling that vision and, ultimately, achievement of that vision to the extent that it ended its days providing music and, via Music Education Consultant, Christine Richards, written teaching materials for *Listen To This!* Key Stages 1, 2 and 3 for UK schools, as well as a Comparative Religions pack. After retiring in 2000, Gef Lucena resurrected the label and to date has reissued around 215 CDs from the Saydisc, Village Thing and Amon Ra catalogues, including releases by several of the musicians discussed in this book.

The Village Thing

> We've got ourselves lumbered with being a West Country record company, which we've never set out to be ... It just so happens that there's been more good artists living in the West Country than anywhere else for a while.[34]

Ian Anderson, now well-known as the editor of fRoots magazine, and currently gigging with Blue Blokes Three, was a country blues singer from Weston-super-Mare. He moved to Bristol in the mid-1960s, playing floor spots at the usual folk clubs. When the Troubadour opened, he gained a residency and later started the Folk Blues Bristol and West club. Various artists who played the club were recorded for a Matchbox label LP, titled *Blues Like Showers of Rain*. After the success of the LP, Anderson, Jo Anne Kelly and Mike Cooper all found themselves with deals with major labels. Anderson, however, had various problems with his record companies and wistfully bemoaned the state of the music industry as regards the humble artist. Along with local musician, John Turner, he talked about taking their recording careers into their own hands. Of the birth of Village Thing, Anderson explains:

> By late '69, Al Jones was also back in Bristol and we were all living in the rather disreputable flat above the Troubadour. In those days, after late nights at the Troubadour, we were in the habit of taking our hangovers and whichever girlfriends or club guests had stayed the night across to Splinters coffee house in nearby Clifton Down Road. Over strong coffees and Sally Lunn teacakes one day, John [Turner] and I were wondering what would be the best for the Pigsty Hill Light Orchestra's recording career and for my own future one. We'd already started using the term "Clifton Village" for the area around Waterloo Street, Princess Victoria Street and The Mall and we dreamed up this concept of an agency and record label where we could all be in complete control of our own destinies without the interference of uncomprehending "suits". So our concept was this… thing… this… ahah! The Village Thing! Born December 1969.[35]

The agency side of things quickly got off the ground and as early as April 1970, Village Thing was advertising in the music press[36] that Ian Anderson, Keith Christmas, Pigsty Hill Light Orchestra, Sun Also Rises and Ian Hunt were all available for bookings from the Troubadour's 5, Waterloo Street address (reachable on 0272-36543). The record label was run by John Turner, Ian Anderson and Saydisc's Gef Lucena and although based in Bristol was intended to be national in outlook and distribution. Village Thing was virtually a cottage industry, with a certain amount of incestuous activity going on: musicians happily played on each others' albums and even got involved in design – the label was based on a drawing by the Pigsty Hill Light Orchestra's Andy Leggett: this was an idealised view of Clifton as a village – and the term 'Clifton Village', which started off being used by various musicians and artists, is now in common use for this part of Clifton – and overused by Estate Agents to justify silly prices. Leggett also painted the sleeve for the Sun Also Rises' LP, for which he got a free copy of the album. Of the first clutch of releases, Anderson explains:

> The Pigsty Hill Light Orchestra became our first album, and Cardiff duo Sun Also Rises, who'd blown everybody away with spots at the Troubadour, became our second, both released 18th September 1970. Mine came up next, along with guitar legend Wizz Jones who had also fallen out of United Artists and had a half-begun album which we completed in Bristol, both released November 13th. In between we put out a promotional EP *The Great White Dap*, and on 25th November we promoted a London label launch at the Country Club, Haverstock Hill, with the entire label roster. We were off and running.[37]

The artists signed to both agency and label gigged around various parts of the country, with the names Pigsty Hill Light Orchestra, Keith Christmas, Shelagh McDonald[38], Ian A. Anderson and Hunt & Turner appearing all over the gig pages of the music press. Village Thing also promoted regular concerts at the Victoria Rooms, with 'name' artists such as Steeleye Span, Al Stewart, Stefan Grossman and the Rev. Gary Davis, most of whom used Village Thing artists as support acts.

By the third LP on the label, Ian A. Anderson's *Royal York Crescent*, released in November 1970, Bristol's Plastic Dog organisation had become involved and the record was issued with a Plastic Dog sleeve design. Ian Anderson's memories of this period run thus:

> The label was being successful and so was the agency, representing not only our recording artists but other noteworthy Bristol-based names like Keith Christmas, Al Jones, Mudge & Clutterbuck and the wonderful Shelagh MacDonald. All this was being run out of the flat in Royal York Crescent. By then, John Turner had moved out and I'd married Maggie Holland, and it all got a bit much having the business in our flat. So in April 1971 we teamed up with Al Read, Terry Brace and designer Rodney Matthews of the fast growing Plastic Dog organisation who had an office above a gents' outfitters at 77 Park Street with a spare back room. The label also signed a production/ distribution deal with Transatlantic Records, which eventually proved to be Village Thing's downfall – another story.[39]

On Village Thing's link-up with Plastic Dog, Al Read adds, "[In] April 1971 … Village Thing shared the Plastic Dog offices at 77, Park St. [and in] Dec. 1971 … Plastic Dog and VT amalgamated."[40] Plastic Dog published the *Dogpress* magazine each month: this basically advertised forthcoming attractions at the Granary rock club, padded out with record reviews, silly poems, adverts for local shops and a rather dubious feature called *Groupie of the Month*. The cover of the April 1971 edition commemorated, "… the coalition of Plastic Dog and Village Thing", with a photo on the cover of Al Read and Terry Brace of Plastic Dog with Ian Anderson and Maggie Holland of Village Thing – or as December 1971's third anniversary issue of Dogpress described it, "Alan looking smug, Terry looking lecherous, and Ian & Maggie looking married …" From April 1971 onwards, not surprisingly,

Bristol folk

Dogpress featured a larger proportion of adverts for Village Thing than hitherto, plus a page of local folk news titled, "The Village Dog's Plastic Thing".

Apart from the link-up between Bristol's premiere rock and folk agencies, there was also a great deal of cross-fertilisation between Bristolian rock and folk musicians. For instance, it was not surprising to see the Pigsty Hill Light Orchestra's Andy Leggett guesting with Rodney Matthews' progressive band, Originn[41] at the Granary and some of these rock musicians, in turn, also played on Village Thing releases – drummer, Matthews, and John Merrett, Squidd's bassist, played on Hunt & Turner's LP and on Dave Evans' LP, *Elephantasia*, the latter of which also included Squidd's keyboard player, ex-Cathedral schoolboy, Steve Swindells. Ian A. Anderson's *A Vulture Is Not a Bird You Can Trust* included most of Monmouthshire-based progressive band, Spring, who were friends of the Plastic Dog crowd.

With Rodney Matthews and Terry Brace of Plastic Dog working on many of the sleeve designs, Village Thing LPs became almost immediately identifiable. Matthews' illustrations were of gloriously caricatured people or creatures, and the label itself was modified by the inclusion of Rodney Matthews' yokel logo, complete with straw sticking out of its mouth.

> We've finally got around to adopting a new logo … instead of our tatty old letraset. Needless to say it was designed by kind Uncle Rodney who has also produced some pretty amazing sleeve designs for various items in the pipeline.[42]

Button badges were made with the new logo design and these are now quite rare. Early 1971 also saw new artists signed, as Anderson remembers:

> Ralph McTell pointed Steve Tilston at the Troubadour and us, who pestered us until we took him on (actually it didn't take much pestering). Tilston moved to Bristol and brought Dave Evans, who also stayed and became one of our favourites. Local folk hero Fred Wedlock was a natural for us: his album *The Folker* provided perfect national press publicity when the line "Prince Phillip is The Queen in drag" to the tune of the National Anthem so offended the ladies at the EMI pressing plant we used that they refused to press it until changed – and there's no such thing as bad publicity! All these releases did well, with Tilston and Evans getting great critical success, press and radio, and Fred Wedlock selling particularly promiscuously. And so it went …[43]

However, not long after the link-up with Plastic Dog, the Troubadour, after two years of failing to live up to the financial expectations of its new owner, was arbitrarily closed, an event that was to lead to Ian Anderson and Maggie Holland leaving Bristol and taking the administrative side of Village Thing with them. Ian Anderson explains:

> Not long after the agency merger, disaster struck when Peter Bush closed the Troubadour. The lively scene centred around it imploded, quickly reduced to people sitting in the pub across the road generally backbiting about whoever wasn't there at that point. Everything soured, and within the year, Maggie and I decided to head for somewhere fresh. She originally came from Alton in Hants, and 20 miles up the road

was a very lively scene centred on Farnham, Surrey, itself within easy striking distance of London. We moved there in 1972, taking the label admin with us and at the same time setting out as a new duo, Hot Vultures. That was the last of my seven year association with Bristol, and Farnham was where I lived for the next 16 years.[44]

Most subsequent LPs were still recorded in Frenchay, many with the usual cohort of local musicians, but with the move away from Bristol, the label started to issue a greater proportion of LPs by national, and even international, names. As Anderson says:

> ... a particular coup came about through me meeting and becoming friends with legendary American banjo player and songwriter Derroll Adams while touring in Belgium (where I'd also met Tucker Zimmerman whose self-produced album we licensed and released in the UK). Derroll, who came to Europe with Rambling Jack Elliott in the late 1950s and stayed, famously appearing in the drunken hotel room sequence in Bob Dylan's *Don't Look Back* film ... We brought him over to Frenchay and recorded the *Feelin' Fine* album with Wizz Jones and Belgian star Roland Van Campenhout, then brought him back to tour when it was released. That got us a lot of kudos (not to mention people like Rod Stewart and Long John Baldry turning up at his folk club gigs!) ...[45]

Production and distribution of Village Thing LPs had been taken over by Transatlantic in July 1971, thus promising the chance of wider distribution in the UK, but sales were never that heavy, even after EMI started to distribute the label along with Transatlantic from October 1971. Most releases averaged 2,000 sales with Fred Wedlock as the highest seller with approximately 20,000 per album. The commercial pressures put on the label by Transatlantic caused Village Thing to shut down and, apart from some delayed new releases, the whole catalogue was deleted in 1974, except for the Wedlock LPs, and back catalogue items were sold off by Village Thing at 99p each from Saydisc's Inglestone Common address. So it was that the Melody Maker, unbeknown at the time, reported both the last set of long-delayed Village Thing releases and, effectively, the label's demise in the same article.

> Village Thing will be selling off their earlier records for 99p until they run out. This is because their distributors Transatlantic Records, have decided to delete a number of the early releases ... Village Thing have bought them and will be making them available by mail order. The albums involved are Pigsty Hill Light Orchestra, Steve Tilston, Ian A. Anderson, Dave Evans, Wizz Jones, Hunt and Turner, Sun Also Rises, Tucker Zimmerman and Al Jones ... This month the label is releasing albums by Noel Murphy, Wizz Jones and Chris Thompson, all of which have been held up for a considerable time.[46]

The Chris Thompson LP became an instant collector's item when, reputedly, only 101 of the 1,000 press run made it to the shops with the rest destroyed by Transatlantic. In a write-up of the Noel Murphy LP, the Melody Maker commented that this was to be, "The last Village Thing record with Ian A. Anderson at the helm ..."[47] though it turned out to be the last Village Thing LP altogether. Fred Wedlock survived the demise of the label and his two LPs remained available well into the 1980s via Saydisc, which switched its distribution from Transatlantic to Lugtons.

Bristol folk

With its interesting cross of folk, blues, ragtime and jazz musicians with a smattering of progressive rock musicians it is no wonder that some of the Village Thing LPs have become classics of their genre, whatever that genre actually is. Most are described as 'acid folk' or 'psych folk' and are now highly collectable, with some of the LPs selling on eBay for up to and over £100 each at time of writing.

Bristol-based artists on other labels

Not all the output of Bristol-based artists was via Saydisc or Village Thing. Adge Cutler and the Wurzels released records on EMI's Columbia and Starline labels and CBS. The post-Adge Wurzels released records on EMI. Ian Anderson released records on Liberty and Fontana, with the Hot Vultures LPs appearing on Red Rag and Plant Life. Al Jones recorded for Parlophone and had material issued on RCA Victor and B&C's Peg label. Graham Kilsby was signed to EMI before moving to the US and gaining a certain amount of fame in Nashville as Tony Graham. Keith Christmas records were issued on RCA Victor, B&C and WEA's Manticore label. Kind Hearts and English recorded for DJM. Shelagh McDonald recorded for B&C and also had material issued on its Peg imprint. Bob Stewart recorded for Argo, Crescent and Broadside. Steve Tilston recorded for Transatlantic before issuing an LP on his own Cornucopia label. Fred Wedlock was signed to EMI via their One-Up imprint, but otherwise issued records on his own Pillock label. Erik Ilott and Ray Andrews appeared on Ilott's Folk'sle label. Elecampane appeared on their own Dame Jane label. Dave Paskett recorded on his own Think! label. Independent Folk and Jo Chambers recorded for the GWR and Firebrand labels respectively. In fact, there are too many to mention here – why not read the book and find out who recorded for whom!

Just one thing – we're on a boundary, but Stackridge, who recorded for MCA and Rocket, also need inclusion. Stackridge was undoubtedly a rock band but there were folk elements in both songs and act. Those trying to explain their style have described it as pastoral or rustic rock. After all, there was a violinist from the bone-fide folk group, The Westlanders, who moonlighted with Fred Wedlock, a bassist called 'Crun' after the *crunberry* – whatever that is – and a vocalist called Mutter, who sang in a West Country accent, danced odd yokel dances, thrashed rhubarb stalks, clanged dustbin lids and played flute on songs about such things as purple spaceships and 400 year-old farm workers in Somerset. Their guitarist played on John Lennon's *Imagine* and *still* plays Bristol pubs, such as the Coronation Tap in Clifton Village.

The Plastic Dog connection

Plastic Dog developed from a group of musicians from various Bristol bands, such as the Franklin Big Six, Picture of Dorian Gray, East of Eden and Barnaby Goode. They began by organising musical events at the Dug Out Club, just off Park Row. In 1968 these events became too successful for the limited space so the Plastic Dog nights, as they were known, moved to the Old Granary[48], which was a jazz venue at that point. Plastic Dog evolved into a music and graphics agency. The graphics side comprised Terry Brace and Rodney Matthews, the latter of whom later became one of the world's foremost popular fantasy artists. They started to design sleeves for the Village Thing label in late 1970, the first being for Ian A. Anderson's *Royal York Crescent*, issued in November. Over the next couple of years some excellent Rodney Matthews illustrations appeared on the label. Brace and Matthews fulfilled the same function for Saydisc from late 1970 or early 1971: the first sleeve design was for the Matchbox issue, *Little Brother Montgomery 1930-1969*. Of the work for Saydisc, Matthews later said that they always paid promptly[49].

Matthews also undertook some private commissions for the Lucena's, which are in his glorious early 1970s 'naïve' style. On the record side the Saydisc work was mostly one of arranging supplied photographs and sleeve notes and creating an attractive layout rather than one of creating original artwork, and the real gems for Saydisc were Matthews' sleeve illustrations for several 7" LPs presenting Bristol humour and dialect, one of which showed the Three Wise Men waiting at a local bus stop. There were also a couple of uncharacteristic portraits of classical composers by Matthews for Saydisc's Amon Ra label, which is ironic because one of Matthews' tasks when a student at the West of England College of Art in 1961 had been to design a notional record sleeve for Stravinsky's *Rite of Spring*.

The Village Thing agency linked up with Plastic Dog in April 1971. Both continued to be run separately because they were aimed at distinct audiences, even after they were fully amalgamated in December 1971. Steve Webb[50] joined to concentrate on the folk side and the VT agency organised nationwide appearances by artists signed directly to them as well as organising UK appearances for international artists, such as Stefan Grossman. Plastic Dog, meanwhile, was geared to booking bands to the Granary, the Winter Gardens in Malvern and a few other venues. Rodney Matthews later said that they had concentrated more on the folk side of their operations[51].

Village Thing artists, Strange Fruit and Hunt and Turner, had already started playing support slots at the Granary before the merger and now appearances of Village Thing acts at the Granary increased, the Pigsty Hill Light Orchestra and Strange Fruit, especially, becoming regular visitors. In 1975, Sundays at the Granary were set aside for folk music in the New Grain Folk Club, though this was a fairly short-lived experiment thanks to unfortunate acoustics, which meant that the bar was more audible than the musicians – which is the reason why Muddy Waters went electric in the first place, possibly in unknowing anticipation of he and his toupee being booked to play the Granary in 1968.

The artists

Ian Anderson

> I have a sneaking suspicion that with all the pop music I heard in my youth plus the blues phase, plus the stuff I have been listening to since, in terms of the 1970s I'm probably closer to a folk singer than people who are dragging up long forgotten traditional forms. I'm just playing a mixture of what everybody else hears.[52]

Much could be written about Ian Anderson, mainly because over the years he made sure that his voice was heard: certainly he was often derided in the 1960s and 1970s music press for raising his head above the blues and folk parapets and daring to challenge the assumptions of audience and musicians alike. In later years he continued to be heard as editor of the influential and successful *fRoots* magazine. Anderson discovered the blues in post-Austerity Weston-super-Mare, where he became a member of the Backwater Jook Band. He then moved to Bristol and started to play floor spots around the local clubs. Of this period, Anderson says:

> After I'd left home and moved to Bristol in 1965 (when I was 18), I still kept in touch with people back in Weston-super-Mare as I went "home" most weekends that year. We had a band there called the Backwater Jook Band, led by Terry "Beetle" Wiltshire on guitar/ vocals – he'd been in a skiffle group who had appeared on BBC TV's *6-5 Special* in the late '50s – with Alan Iggulden (guitar, piano), Adrian Bastin (banjo), Terry Silver (soprano sax, tin whistle), Bob Summers (washboard, harmonica) and myself (oildrum bass, kazoo), with sometimes Tim Clutterbuck (guitar, jug), Cliff Mormon (guitar, harmonica, jug) and Jim Smith (trombone). The core group appeared twice on local TV – TWW's early evening local news magazine *TWW Reports* – in December 1965.[53]

In the early to mid-1960s there was an annual tour by visiting American blues and folk artists and Anderson attended the 1965 tour when it reached Bristol.

> A really life-changing event for me was 23rd/24th October 1965. On the 23rd, the annual American Folk Blues Festival tour came to the Colston Hall, where I saw the legendary Mississippi Fred McDowell play slide guitar, which I'd never seen anybody do live before. It blew me away, and somehow I'd had a "lightbulb" moment, realising that to do it the guitar was open tuned to a chord. I went back to my flat, figured out from the key on one of his records what the chord must be, looked around for some piece of metal tube and spotted a brass curtain rail so took a hacksaw and liberated 2" of it! I stayed up all night working out how to play his *Highway 51 Blues*, rang in to my job and pulled a sickie, slept all day, got up and practised some more, and in the evening of the 24th went up to the University Folk Club where the guest was Phil Ochs. I was given the best floor spot, last before he came on, and finished it with my new slide guitar party piece. As I walked off through the audience with applause ringing, Phil Ochs was coming up to play and as he passed me he said "Great, man!" At that point,

receiving such praise from a big star, I decided then and there that I was going to make it as a professional musician!⁵⁴

Anderson hooked up with harmonica player, Elliot Jackson, and, a little later, with guitarist, Al Jones. The trio was known as Anderson, Jones, Jackson, and they were the first group to play at the newly-opened Troubadour club in Clifton. They made an EP for the Saydisc label, which was issued in December 1966. In 1967, Anderson began the Folk Blues Bristol and West Club at the Troubadour: this was the first country blues club in the UK and it was so successful that it had to be moved to the Old Duke in King Street. Anderson, Jones, Jackson, not surprisingly, had a residency at the club.

In 1967 Al Jones left for the London blues scene and Anderson made another EP for Saydisc, this time with just Eliott Jackson. This was called *Almost the Country Blues* and, like the first EP, it is extremely rare. Meanwhile, Folk Blues Bristol and West was making a name for itself on the national circuit, not least for the quality of various local acts. One of those who played regularly was Mike Cooper, a country blues guitarist from Reading. He and Anderson suggested to Gef Lucena that Saydisc, which was by now releasing LP compilations of early blues, ragtime and jazz recordings taken from such sources as wax cylinders, old 78s and pianola rolls, should start a specialist label called Matchbox to, "… document the growing English country blues scene as well as re-issuing old 78s."⁵⁵ Lucena agreed and the Matchbox label was launched with an LP called *Blues Like Showers of Rain*, which included performances by both Anderson and Cooper.

The national blues scene was currently undergoing something of a reinvention, with homegrown country blues coming into the ascendant, and the LP was picked up on by John Peel, who played tracks from the LP on his *Night Ride* programme and invited several of those playing on the LP up to London to record sessions. Anderson was one of these and he recorded his first BBC session shortly after he had left Bristol for London. The fruits of his time in Bristol also saw release during this period: *The Inverted World* with Mike Cooper was made up of tracks from Anderson's *Almost the Country Blues* and Cooper's *Up the Country Blues* EPs, augmented by several further recordings, with each musician getting one side of the LP to themselves.

In London, Anderson was signed to Sandy Roberton's September Productions and proceeded to make an LP, *Stereo Death Breakdown*. Of this period, Anderson says,

> I was approached by producer Sandy Roberton ... he had a deal with Chappell Music whereby he got studio time and they got the publishing on the records. He liked my idea of a trio with harmonica and bass guitar to make things more lively. Elliot Jackson wasn't up for a pro music career, so I rehearsed with Chris Turner, from London's Missouri Compromise, and co-opted Bob Rowe from Bristol's Deep Blues Band who moved to London too. On a Saturday in November 1968, we went into the studio, inviting pianist Bob Hall, singer Annie Matthews, and three of the Panama Limited Jug Band to join us. Five hours and a fair amount of drink later, we'd recorded all of Stereo Death Breakdown, mostly in first takes!⁵⁶

Bristol folk

A deal was organised by Roberton with Island to release the LP and Anderson was involved in a photo shoot that led to his appearing very prominently on the sleeve of the Island sampler LP, *You Can All Join In*, along with the other Ian Anderson and the rest of Jethro Tull plus a host of musicians from Free, Fairport Convention, Spooky Tooth, Traffic, Clouds and Nirvana. Anderson's band toured to promote the forthcoming LP, appearing at the Granary in Bristol on 5th May 1969, playing support to jazz-rock band, Heaven: they also played at the Folk Blues Bristol and West club, which was now being run by Elliot Jackson. Unfortunately, there was a certain amount of hassle going on behind the scenes that forced Island to drop the LP, as Anderson explains:

> The legendary Guy Stevens, then doing A&R at Island Records, licensed Stereo Death Breakdown for February 1969 release. But fate did its bit after the Island artist roster assembled in Hyde Park to be photographed en masse for the cover of their soon-to-be No.1 sampler album, You Can All Join In. Another Island band, Jethro Tull, featured a musician with the same name as me, and their management threw a wobbler about the confusion that might be caused, so under pressure Guy had to organise me a swift transfer. Andrew Lauder at Liberty/UA came to the rescue and the delayed Stereo Death Breakdown came out in May 1969, unfortunately missing all the tour dates and pipped to the post by Mike Cooper and Jo-Ann Kelly's debuts. But Crazy Fool Mumble made the Top 30 on Liberty's Son Of Gutbucket sampler, so technically it remains my greatest hit … By the time [the LP] eventually came out I'd already had enough of London, so hopped it back to Bristol and moved into the flat above the Troubadour.[57]

Stereo Death Breakdown is incredibly rare and the only way that most people will get to hear anything on vinyl is to find a copy of the *Son of Gutbucket* compilation LP, which included one track from the LP. The Melody Maker, meanwhile, gave the LP a positive two line write-up, which said, "Things work well and there is some lively playing …"[58]

In 1969, after a year's hurly-burly on the London blues scene, which included organising and playing on a UK tour for Mississippi Fred McDowell, Anderson returned to the more sedately-paced Bristol, where he lay low, playing occasionally at the Troubadour.

> … Ian's periodic diatribes on aspects of the folk scene have caused a few raised eyebrows, and he bravely took what could be termed a sabbatical – and stayed right away from the folk clubs for a year. During this time he strove to carve his own niche on the folk scene under his own terms…[59]

In November 1969, following another brief sojourn in London, where he was handled by Blackhill Enterprises[60], Anderson reappeared without most of his previous country blues trappings – or as Anderson put it, "a wholesale change of musical direction which ruffled a few feathers on the blues scene"[61].

> Ian Anderson, prolific country blues revivalist for the past seven years, has resurfaced after several months underground, as Ian Anderson the folk singer … "well, there was only ever one tune, and you can do a lot more with a shotgun … All the best people who rode through the blues boom have progressed. With my last album, "Stereo Death Breakdown," I reached the ultimate in that style."[62]

Bristol folk

Anderson and fellow Troubadour resident, John Turner, now set about starting the Village Thing agency and record label. However, although putting together his own record label, next up on the record front was an LP for Fontana, *Book of Changes*, which had already been recorded but not yet issued. The LP, which included Turner, Keith Christmas and Al Jones, was released on 31st March 1970 and belatedly received a short review in the June 13th edition of Sounds, basically admitting nothing more than the fact that it existed and that it was worth a listen, though for various reasons connected to distribution not many people ever did get a listen. Anderson explains:

> I was contracted to make one more album for Chappell Music, with whom Sandy Roberton was no longer involved. I recorded it all in another brief session in early autumn '69, only to find that Chappell licensed it to Phillips, instead of Liberty with whom I'd had a good relationship. Phillips arranged a cover photo session, and when they sent the sleeve proof it was the most awful thing I'd ever seen: truly embarrassing. By then back in Bristol again, I got straight on the train to London and went to see Phillips whose response was "What's it got to do with you? You're only the artist!" I went back to Bristol, hopping mad. As far as I was concerned, I'd had it with major labels. When the album, Book Of Changes, came out on Fontana in March 1970, I got my revenge because it was the week Phillips changed to computerised distribution, which was a complete disaster. Several weeks' worth of their releases, including mine, got lost without trace. Poetic justice!

If Anderson's sleeve notes on *Singer Sleeps On As Blaze Rages* can be trusted, *Book of Changes* sold a total of 209 copies, and is consequently impossible to find.

Anderson started to record his next LP at Village Thing studios during July and August 1970 with Gef Lucena engineering. Prior to the LP's release, Anderson was booked to play a local festival being organised by dairy farmer, Michael Eavis. So in September 1970 the Troubadour set went down to Worthy Farm, just outside Pilton, in deepest Somerset. The *Pilton Pop Folk & Blues Festival*, as it was originally billed, is now better known as the Glastonbury Festival. The Troubadour contingent was very much in evidence with both Anderson and Ian Hunt playing alongside Stackridge, Marsupilami, Originn and faded pop idol, Wayne Fontana, of Mindbenders fame. The Kinks were billed as headliners, but dropped out. A letter and two photos from Anderson were published in Mojo Magazine[63], one of which shows almost exactly the same set of people as were to appear on the rear sleeve of Anderson's first Village Thing LP. The other photo shows the obligatory onstage jam session with Anderson, Hunt, Maggie Holland, Keith Christmas, Al Stewart and Ian Turner. According to Anderson, "... in a sad attempt to drum up Woodstock spirit in jaws of immense apathy, I think we were caterwauling Country Joe's Feels Like I'm Fixin' To Die Rag."[64] Anderson was never paid for his performance at Pilton!

Meanwhile, Anderson's first LP for Village Thing, *Royal York Crescent*, was released in November 1970. On the LP, Anderson was joined by Maggie Holland, Ian Hunt, John Turner, Ian Turner (known as Heavy Drummer), Andy Leggett, Pete Siddons and Cardiff duo, Sun Also Rises.

Bristol folk

Anderson's next LP, *A Vulture Is Not a Bird You Can Trust*, was recorded at Rockfield studios in South Wales during September 1971, part-engineered by the studio's owner, Kingsley Ward. Apart from Ian Hunt, John Turner and Keith Warmington, Anderson used some of the musicians from the progressive band, Spring, who were living and working at Rockfield. The band had just lost its original bass player and was rehearsing with new bassist, Pete Descindis, just prior to breaking up for good. So it was that organist and Mellotron player, Kipps Brown, drummer, Pick/Pique Withers (later of Dire Straits) and Descindis all appeared on the LP. The album gained mostly good reviews from the nationals, though a write up in the local *Pre-View* magazine went for the jugular with the only real praise being for Rodney Matthews' sleeve design[65], provoking Anderson to write a strong letter, which was published in the February 1972 edition. To put things in a 21st Century context, the same magazine 'slagged off' Nick Drake's current album as well.

Things were changing on the Bristol folk scene, however. The Troubadour closed in mid-1971, shortly after the Village Thing agency had linked up with Plastic Dog. If the closure of the Troubadour wasn't shock enough, Anderson decided to leave Bristol for Surrey, where he had recently been impressed by the still lively folk scene.

> Only a year ago Ian was the nearest thing to a publicity officer that the Bristol folk scene had. After the Bristol Troubadour closed down ... year things began to cool down in Clifton Village circles ... The move coincides with developments within the Village Thing Company. The agency side of things has now been taken off Ian's shoulders and the recording and promoting side Ian reckons he can maintain from anywhere.[66]

Once Anderson and Maggie Holland had moved away from Bristol, the Village Thing label itself became less parochial in output, releasing LPs by Tucker Zimmerman, Tight Like That, Lackey and Sweeney, Derroll Adams, New Zealander, Chris Thompson, and folk scene stalwart, Noel Murphy. Anderson's final album for his own label was issued in late 1972 and was called *Singer Sleeps on as Blaze Rages*. As for the title, Anderson explains:

> [After leaving my job to go professional] I took the statutory month that I was legally entitled to on the dole, then signed off … I signed off on the Friday, and on the Monday was involved in a mishap – my flatmate dropped a smouldering cigarette end in his waste paper basket when leaving for work and I was awoken by the fire brigade shouting at me to get out fast. The front page of the Bristol Evening Post carried the great headline *Singer Sleeps On As Blaze Rages* over a report saying how I'd been awakened by the fire brigade while sleeping late after travelling back from a gig the night before. Somebody in the Troubadour audience who worked in the dole office told me that this had been spotted and queried: if I hadn't signed off correctly I'd have been busted. It taught me the lesson of the Bob Dylan line "to live outside the law you must be honest" ...[67]

The LP was recorded half at Rockfield and half at Village Thing and included performances by Belgian harmonica player, Roland Van Campenhout, whom Anderson had met on a Belgian tour, Maggie Holland on guitar, Pete Siddons on bouzouki, Mike Cooper on guitars and Mike Moran, from Spring, on vocals. The LP also included Cooper's band, the Machine

Bristol folk

Gun Company, which comprised Les Calvert on bass & organ, Ian Foster on drums and Bill Boazman on guitar. The Rockfield influence was obviously beginning to make itself felt with song titles such as *Shirley Temple Meets Hawkwind*.

With his move away from Bristol, Anderson also began to disassociate himself from his earlier LPs – to the extent of locking the master tapes for his three Village Thing LPs away and refusing all offers to reissue them. Village Thing had organised a distribution deal with folk label Transatlantic in 1971, which seemed to bode well but was really the death knell for the label – Transatlantic had greater expectations and made greater demands than the label could cope with. The final LP for the label was by Troubadour regular, Noel Murphy, and was called *Murf*. It was recorded at the Friends Meeting House in Frenchay between 7th and 12th January 1974, though it was several months before the record saw release.

Anderson and Maggie Holland now formed Hot Vultures, a duo that was able to call on the talents of a formidable pool of musicians. Unfortunately, because Holland didn't get to record in her own right during the time that she was in Bristol she doesn't get as big a mention as she warrants – a victim of this book's ground rules; as Ian Anderson says:

> Maggie came to Bristol as a student, was Bristol Uni Folk Club organiser 70/71 and a regular floor singer at the Troubadour. We got married in 71: when we left Bristol she became first the bass player in Hot Vultures with me, then got better and better as a singer/guitarist/banjo player as we evolved into the English Country Blues Band. Eventually in the '80s she went solo after we divorced and has made a lot of records, had songs recorded by Martin Carthy, June Tabor and others.[68]

Hot Vultures' first LP, *Carrion On*, was released in 1975 in Belgium on the EMI Bestseller label, with Al Jones on guitar, John Pilgrim on washboard, Dave Peabody on harmonica and Dave Griffiths[69] on mandolin: it was issued a little later by Red Rag in the UK. The second LP, *The East Street Shakes*, was released in 1977 and included Martin Simpson on guitar and banjo, Simon Mayor on mandolin and fiddle with Hilary Jones and Raggy Farmer on vocals – with photos by Dave Peabody. The final Hot Vultures LP was called *Up the Line*, released in 1979. It included Simpson from the previous LP, plus Pete Coe on melodeon and Chris Coe on hammered dulcimer.

In 1979 Anderson started the magazine *Southern Rag*, which over the years developed into *fRoots*. On the music side he and Maggie Holland formed the English Country Blues Band and Tiger Moth, which metamorphosed – probably the correct word in the circumstances – into L'Orchestre Super Moth, a wonderfully eclectic global-Morris-come-influences-too-numerous-to-mention conglomeration ... but this is in the 1980s and beyond.

As for the records, all bar those by the Hot Vultures come under one heading – valuable. The first two Saydisc EPs were limited pressings of 99 copies each and could easily sell for £60 or more should they ever turn up for sale. *The Inverted World* with Mike Cooper has hit the £100-plus mark as have the Liberty and Fontana LPs, in the latter case £100-plus probably meaning more like £200-plus. (Breaking news: there are rumoured to be one or two white label test pressings of *The Inverted World* LP in plain white sleeves, which could easily change hands for around £200.) The *Son of Gutbucket* Liberty sampler should be around £10 whilst the *Blues Like Showers of Rain* compilation will happily sell for up to £60. The three Village Thing LPs have recently been seen to sell on eBay for anything between £16 and £105: even an 8-track copy of the final Village Thing LP will cost you around £10. Of the two Village Thing 7" records, you might be lucky enough to find Anderson's *One More Chance* for about £10, though you'll have to pay around £20 to get the *Great White Dap* Various Artists EP in its picture sleeve. As for the Hot Vultures LPs, you should be able to find these for around £10 to £15 each, with US copies of the third LP available, still sealed, in different sleeve design, for around £8.

Ray Andrews – Bristol's Boy Banjoist

Ray Andrews, was born in 1922, the son of a banjo playing ex-seaman. He first learned banjo from his father, who had been self-taught, and later learned classic banjo style from Harold Sharp, a member of the Bristol Banjo, Mandolin and Guitar (BMG) Club, learning and playing the tunes of the day from manuscript and banjo magazines. His first stage appearance was as a balancing act with his father in the mid-1930s, though with his banjo he later won a talent contest at the Theatre Royal in 1937, becoming known as Bristol's Boy Banjoist. He played the music halls and variety venues around Bristol and appeared regularly in variety concerts until the outbreak of war in 1939. He took his banjo to war, playing throughout North Africa and Italy. After the war, Andrews played again with the Bristol BMG Club, which had been suspended during the war, and with various members played pubs and clubs around Bristol throughout the 1950s and 1960s.

The BMG Club folded in the early 1970s and Andrews played informal sessions in pubs, joining the Swingers, with whom he played working men's clubs, such as the Temple Meads Railwayman's Club, and Irish clubs, such as the Holy Cross Club in Southville. He also started to accompany Erik Ilott, playing at the Folk Tradition Club. Ilott was asked to record a tape of Shanty music associated with Bristol for the launch of H.M.S. Bristol. This led to the recording of the *Shipshape and Bristol Fashion* LP, with banjo by Andrews, which was released by Ilott's Folk'sle label in 1973. The duo continued to play together and in the late 1970s Ilott recorded Andrews for a cassette-only issue called *Banjo Maestro*, also on Folk'sle. Unfortunately, much of the music was poorly recorded in the first place and, to make matters worse, poor quality tape was used for its only issue.

In the 1980s, Andrews was included on a cassette-only issue called *Alongside Bristol Quay*, which featured traditional music from the Bristol area, and he continued playing, now with traditional Irish fiddlers, the Moran Brothers, as well as continuing with solo performances and teaching. Andrews died in 1987 leaving a wealth of privately recorded tapes, most of which look as though they will never see the light of day.

The Erik Ilott LP is becoming hard to find and is starting to sell for around the £30 mark if it includes the booklet. The Banjo Maestro cassette, however, is almost impossible to find, though, because it is unknown on the collector's scene it does not have a high collector's interest and is more likely to be found in a local charity shop for 50p than on eBay. Rod Stradling's Musical Traditions has released a CD, *Classic English Banjo*, which includes seven tracks from the cassette along with other recordings from the 1970s and 1980s: the cassette tracks were transferred from the only known copy, owned by ex-Elecampane member, John Shaw. The CD includes a comprehensive booklet, which is worth the money alone, covering the lives of both Andrews and, through association, Erik Ilott in great depth, as well as discussing the history of banjo music in the UK and Bristol – an absolutely fascinating glimpse into a past long lost, though well within living memory of many of those reading this book.

Stan Arnold

Stan Arnold was resident in Downfield Road in Clifton throughout most of the 1970s and did the usual rounds of folk clubs. His act was a mix of traditional and self-penned songs with a lot of comedy patter, not just between songs but often in the middle. Songs would stop abruptly as Arnold dealt mercilessly with hecklers – who he'd encouraged in the first place anyway.

His first LP, *Ladies Man*, was recorded live in folk clubs at Beckenham and Amberley and was issued in 1973 on Joe Stead's Sweet Folk All label. It has a wonderful sleeve showing Arnold in long, dirty mac, standing outside a ladies toilet. Comedy-based LPs tend to pall after a few plays, but this one is still surprisingly listenable, probably because of the way in which Arnold plays his audience along, which can be heard to excellent effect on *Drunken Sailor*. Also, the LP switches occasionally away from comedy – Arnold's own songs on this album are generally poignant, little love songs, full of emotional trivia and gawkily sung, which somehow endears you to the song – even the one about the hairy mouse, I suppose. Certainly they wouldn't work half as well if Ian Matthews or Al Stewart had decided to cover them, though Shep Woolley did cover Arnold's *Southsea Love Song*, which probably tells you a lot about *his* act. *100 Yards* from the LP was reputedly issued as a single, though this is not verified.

In 1975 Arnold was signed by the Red Rag label, which reissued *Ladies Man*. Early copies distributed by the Red Rag were old Sweet Folk All copies with Red Rag stickers added. Arnold produced an LP for label-mates The Calico String Band and, a couple of years later, was again recorded in a solo performance at the Coach House in Farningham. The record company seems to have sat on this recording for a while and it finally appeared in late 1979[70] as one side of *Showstoppers for the Intelijunt*. The live side is incredibly vulgar and also incredibly funny and every collection should have a copy – if only for the extended musical sketch about Bristol Royal Infirmary, where Arnold's Ennio Morricone-style guitar meets hecklers head-on in widescreen 'put-down' comedy. Side two, however, presents the recently-formed Stan Arnold Combo, complete with Bristol newcomer, Steve Payne, previously with Rosie Hardman's band, on electric guitar. It was recorded in Mushroom Studios on West Mall and at Sound Conception in St. Pauls and, whilst it has its moments, it doesn't really compare to the Combo's excruciatingly funny live stage act – actually, just how do you go about putting a cheesy hand-jive onto record?

The Combo played Bristol venues such as the Docklands Settlement and the Granary, as well as playing nationally, and in the early 1980s they appeared on the *David Essex Showcase* TV talent show, playing *Do You Like Rock and Roll?*, coming second and, in Arnolds words, " … getting loads of points."[71] They also played on local BBC TV show, *RPM*, which was presented by a then very young Andy Batten Foster. At time of writing, these performances are available on *YouTube*. The Combo broke up in the early 1980s and Arnold took a job in a Bristol-based advertising agency.

Arnold's two LPs are fairly common, attesting to his popularity on the live scene, and shouldn't set you back more than £8 each. The original copy of *Ladies Man* (white or yellow labels) is harder to find that the reissue (red labels), but it doesn't seem to affect the price – though you might have to pay more for an original copy with stickers added by the new label. The only real rarity is the single, but even that shouldn't cost more than £3 once you find one, presuming that it really exits, that is.

Jo Chambers

Jo Chambers wrote feminist songs and made an LP called *Every Woman Will Be Free* in 1979 on the local, independent, Firebrand label. The LP was recorded at Mushroom Studios, in West Mall, Clifton, and pressed by Lyntone. The catalogue number would tend to suggest that Firebrand was part of the same company as Great Western Records. Copies have sold on eBay for up to £50, the higher-end prices paid by Japanese private folk label collectors. However, interest in this LP now seems to have faded and recent copies have tended to achieve a more modest £5 or so. The brevity of this article is due to nothing other than a complete inability to find anything out about the artist or even to find a copy of the LP during preparation of this book. Any information whatsoever would be welcome.

John Christie – the Bard of Barton Hill

There is far too little John Christie material: this amounts to two songs covered by the Wurzels and three songs by Christie himself. Christie specialised in writing gently-amusing songs about local celebrities and events, with more of an affinity with the music hall than with folk music per se. The songs included some 'Bristolese', but to a much lesser extent than in the songs of Len 'Uke' Thomas or Adge Cutler, with Christie's own delivery being in a gently-lilting, sing-song Bristolian accent, described by David Waine, then the Station Manager for BBC Radio Bristol as, "[not] quite a Caruso'l not a Nellie Melba'l – sort of inbetween, with that infectious power that drove Cabot all the way to America'l."[72]

Christie played around Bristol in a trio with his son and daughter and his recording life started when he was asked to collaborate with Radio Bristol presenter Peter Lawrence, better known as Old Pete, on the *Morning West* and the *Pete and Eva'l* shows. Lawrence had written a few ditties and Christie set them to music. This exposure on Radio Bristol caught the attention of the Wurzels, who recorded *Cabot Song* on their *Golden Delicious* LP, released in April 1977: the Wurzels' version is titled *Cabot Song (Big 'Ead)*, the addition alluding to some of the lyrics within.

Christie recorded *The Cabot Song* himself later that year. A 7" LP, titled *Isambard Kingdom Brunel and other comical saga'ls from our area'l*, was produced by John Turner and released by Saydisc. Christie accompanied himself on Yamaha Organ and Logan String Synthesiser and apart from *The Cabot Song*, the record included *Isambard Kingdom Brunel* and *Inventions*, all understated gems, which acted as musical interludes to three of Peter Lawrence's humorous monologues.

Only one further Christie composition was recorded during the 1970s – I would be very happy to be proved wrong – and this was the low-key *Willie Freise-Greene*, about the Bristol-based photographic pioneer. This was recorded by the Wurzels and was the stand-out track on their *Give Me England* LP, released in December 1977 just in time for the lucky Christmas market.

The Saydisc 7" LP, playing at 33⅓ rpm, was the last record the company released in this odd format and it tends to sell for between £5 and £8. The two Wurzels LPs should be easily picked up for a similar amount. Just one thing, did Isambard Kingdom Brunel *really* drink ginger beer and, if so, just how did John Christie find out when L. T. C. Rolt never mentioned this particular peccadillo?

Keith Christmas

Keith Christmas joined Bristol's folk set whilst a student in the School of Architecture at Bath University[73], and if you want to know how being a writing and gigging musician fits in with being a student, listen to Christmas' song, *Examinations Rag*, on Fred Wedlock's *The Folker*[74]. In these early years Christmas was described as, "...perhaps the most aggressive and heavy acoustic guitarist in Britain"[75], which was possibly a stylistic left-over from his pre-guitar days as a drummer.

In-between studies Christmas fitted in a regular gig schedule and was signed to Sandy Roberton's September Productions after he introduced himself to Roberton at an Al Jones gig. Christmas' first LP, *Stimulus*, was released in 1969 on RCA Victor along with albums by other September Productions signings, Liverpool Scene, P. C. Kent, Synanthesia and Steeleye Span[76]. Christmas was backed by ex-soul group, The Action, who had recently turned progressive and changed their name to Mighty Baby, and Gordon Huntley, from Matthews Southern Comfort, played pedal steel guitar. Whilst recording *Stimulus*, Christmas played acoustic guitar on sessions for David Bowie's first Mercury LP, which initially sank without trace, despite including Bowie's recent hit *Space Oddity* – the LP was later reissued by RCA Victor as *Space Oddity*, which, as Bowie was by then a 'superstar', sold in truckloads. As a consequence of these sessions, Christmas played at a free concert that Bowie set up to promote the album in Beckenham Park, near to his arts workshop.

In early 1970, a live version of *The Ballad of Robin Head* appeared on the September Productions compilation, *49 Greek Street*, which was named after the address of Les Cousins club in London. Christmas' track was recorded at Leyton Senior High School's 'Folk for Christabel' concert on December 6th 1969[77]. Shortly before his next LP, *Fable of the Wings*,

Bristol folk

was recorded in 1970, Christmas invited fellow Bristol resident, Shelagh McDonald, to play a few of her songs during one of his gigs. Sandy Roberton was at the gig and he signed her immediately, promising studio time for recording. By this time, Roberton had hooked up with Lee Gopthal's B&C label and so now had a single outlet for his artists. The sessions for *Fable of the Wings* included Mike Evans[78] and Ian Whiteman from Mighty Baby, plus Pat Donaldson and Gerry Conway from Fotheringay. Troubadour regular, Bob Stewart, played psaltery[79], Southmead lad, Keith Tippett, at this point hot property on the London free jazz scene, played piano and Shelagh McDonald sang on *The Fawn*. These same sessions produced McDonald's first album as well, which is covered in her own section.

Despite playing the folk clubs, Christmas was happy to play in a more rock-oriented setting, as can be heard in the rock feel of much of *Fable of the Wings* and the more 'blowing' style of parts of his next LP, *Pigmy*. Christmas said, "If a guy's not in a band, he's classified as a folk singer, but my stuff is more widely accessible to audiences that are into groups. The best gigs tend to be those where I appear with bands …"[80] This affinity with the rockier side of things had led to his recording informally in 1970 with Bristol acid rock band, Magic Muscle - he can be heard playing electric guitar on the retrospective[81] *The Pipe, the Roar, the Grid* LP. This LP was issued as a very limited edition on the now very collectable Five Hours Back label. The Magic Muscle involvement was only to be expected because Christmas was living at their squat in Cotham at the time: the photograph on the front of *Fable of the Wings* was taken in a coach house in the garden.

The next LP was given the working title of *Conversation Peace*, but was renamed as *Pigmy* when issued. Christmas had now gained his BSc and wanted to concentrate full time on music, which at this point included supporting the Who, King Crimson and Ten Years After. He also planned to put a full band together around Magic Muscle's Adrian Shaw. A live review of the time describes Christmas' performance thus:

> Keith's performance is very free and experimental, his stage act quite unplanned, totally natural and engaging, his songs bluesy, wistful, melancholic, sometimes fast and furious sung in an intense tenor and usually followed by long passages of instrumental improvisation – hammering-off riffs with guitar in open tuning.[82]

To return to *Pygmy*, there were, on the one hand, simple and sumptuous songs, lifted by string and choral arrangements by Robert Kirby, who is now famous for his earlier work with his Cambridge University contemporary, Nick Drake. The other hand showed Christmas in jamming mode, with more than a passing nod at Magic Muscle. The sleeve showed Christmas sitting by the bank of the Kennet and Avon Canal in Bath, rolling a cigarette: judging by the smiley photo on the rear of the sleeve, we can make a few guesses about what type of cigarette it was.

Having finished university, Christmas started a commune in a farmhouse near Vobster on the Mendips. Originally, the commune had included several London-based musicians, but this set-up doesn't seem to have lasted long and Christmas asked Magic Muscle to move in to help cover costs. Prior to this, Christmas' record label B&C had gone out of business as a record label and although some of Roberton's artists had their LPs reissued on the nascent Mooncrest label, Christmas' LPs were not amongst them. In fact, Roberton told Christmas that no-one would be willing to sign him, so instead of hustling away in London on his own behalf, Christmas settled down to life in the commune.

> I was dropped unceremoniously by Sandy Roberton after the release of Pygmy in 1972 and the ugly collapse of B&C records with (apparently) huge amounts of money going missing ... instead of going to London to try and get a deal for myself I simply believed [Roberton] when he said nobody wanted to sign me and I rented Newbury farmhouse near Mells to start a Grateful Dead type of band-commune with some London musicians (Terry Stannard, later of Kokomo on drums and a bass player called Stan!) ... It folded fairly quickly and I then managed to persuade all of Magic Muscle to come out there and help me pay the costly £50 pm rent![83]

In late 1971, Christmas was involved in recordings with Dave Mudge, though these were abandoned due a combination of Mudge's well-known inability to 'get things together' and illness. In 1972 Christmas played at the end of tour party for Hawkwind's *Space Ritual* tour on which Magic Muscle had been support band and this marked the end of the Bristol connection, really. Even before the release of *Pigmy*, Christmas had been quoted as saying, "My days of folk clubs are over…"[84] and he soon moved from playing the folk, college and festival circuit to supporting major bands, such as Roxy Music, Barclay James Harvest and Emerson, Lake and Palmer, on their tours. He also toured with the band Esperanto and sang on their *Dance Macabre* LP.

Meanwhile, in 1973 ELP formed their own label, Manticore, and Christmas signed with them. ELP must have looked upon this with some delight because, despite Sandy Roberton's prediction, Christmas had recently been voted amongst the top six international artists by music journalists at *Sounds*. From Christmas' point of view, ELP was one of the top grossing bands around and signing with their label offered the potential of a wider audience through overseas tours and record releases: B&C had mainly concentrated on the UK market because, as a UK-based distribution company first and foremost, that was where their distribution expertise was.

The first Manticore LP, *Brighter Day*, issued in 1974, was produced by ELP's lyricist, Pete Sinfield. The sound on the title track seemed to be dominated by the ex-King Crimson contingent who played on the sessions – especially Mel Collins, whose horn arrangements turned parts of the LP into a jazz-rock extravaganza, similar to parts of Pete Sinfield's own recent ex-King Crimson-heavy Manticore LP. A single from the sessions was issued of the R&B classic, *My Girl*, which picked up a fair amount of airplay but didn't trouble the charts. A different version of *Brighter Day* was also issued on single and this should annoy completists because it is quite hard to find. Worth noting is that the American version of the LP had an altered track listing to incorporate *My Girl*. The American version was released in 1975, marketed through Motown, presenting a certain amount of incongruity between associated genres.

The second Manticore LP, *Stories From the Human Zoo*, and the single taken from it, *The Dancer*, were even further away from Bristol, literally, being recorded in the US. This was the last album that Christmas issued until some extremely rare, limited edition cassettes in the late 1980s. The overall feel of the album was more R&B than folk, though perhaps an LP with Steve Cropper and Donald 'Duck' Dunn, from Booker T. and the MGs, couldn't help but sound a tad more American than British. Soon after this, Manticore ceased to release any new product and all LPs, except those by ELP and PFM, were deleted in the UK, though US copies of *Brighter Day* were available as deletion imports in the UK until about 1984, when the last few copies dried up.

Christmas subsequently formed several bands, playing around London and at festivals, including a solo set in the folk tepee at Glastonbury in 1981, eleven years after his first, unbilled, performance at the festival. The Pete Sinfield connection led to Christmas writing English lyrics for Angelo Branduardi's *Life Is the Only Teacher* in 1979 – Sinfield had done the same job on Branduardi's previous LP, *Highdown Fair*. In 1987, after a hiatus from the music scene, Christmas reappeared on the Bristol and Bath scenes with a flurry of gigs, including one upstairs at Crockers, at this point an excellent venue for local folk and jazz. Christmas is still gigging and releasing albums and is regarded as one of Britain's grand old men of folk.

Of the five LPs released between 1969 and 1976, *Stimulus* is extremely rare and is likely to set you back about £100, *Fable of the Wings* and *Pigmy* are a little less expensive and you might be lucky enough to find them for less than £60 apiece, though the inclusion of the highly-collectable Shelagh McDonald on *Fable of the Wings* is pushing the price of that one up sharply. The two Manticore LPs should prove easiest to find and shouldn't set you back more than £10 each – American copies a bit less. Of the singles, *My Girl* and *The Dancer* tend to sell for less than £5, but *Brighter Day* can cost you anything up to £10. Although issued in the 1980s, the Magic Muscle LP is made up of recordings made in the early 1970s so is worth a quick mention. It was issued in a very limited edition and, with insert, will cost up to £30. The title, *The Pipe, the Roar, the Grid*, alludes to the band's water pipe and its subsequent effect on perceived reality.

The Crofters

The Crofters comprised Gef Lucena and Martin Pyman and they hold the distinction of being the first people to record and release an Adge Cutler song, pipping Cutler to the post by a year. Lucena had been an active jazz, folk and blues fan and musician for many years and the Lucena's house in Frenchay had been a magnet for like-minded people since the late 1950s. Pyman, meanwhile, was the Secretary of The Bristol Folk Song Research Society, based at 66, Park Street.

The Crofters were regulars at the Bristol Ballads and Blues and Bristol Poetry and Folk Clubs, both of which met at The Old Duke, in King Street. Lucena took over the running of the Poetry and Folk Club after both clubs had moved to The Bathurst. The Crofters also played on local radio and TV, and on one of these sessions sang a song in Russian, accompanied by balalaika, though in more normal moments they were keen to discover and maintain a written archive of more local folk songs.

Gef Lucena, his father, Lauri, and Roy Mickleburgh, put together Saydisc Specialised Recordings in May 1965 and started to record aspects of the local music scene as well as mechanical music from the Mickleburgh collection. Bev and Richard Dewar, Anne Mavius, Patrick Small, Graham Kilsby and Paul Evans, all regular performers at the two clubs at the Bathurst, joined the Crofters on Saydisc's first LP, issued in late 1965. The LP was called *Bristol Folks*, subtitled *folk songs old and new sung by Bristol singers*, and was limited to a pressing run of 99 copies to preclude payment of Purchase Tax, which kicked in on pressing runs of 100 and over. The Crofters had two songs on the LP and the sleeve notes had the following to say:

> The Crofters play, between them, twelve or so instruments, but only the guitar of Martin Pyman is heard on this record. Both Martin and Gef Lucena sing on both tracks – the first of which is the Somerset version of "Geordie", a song which dates from 1600 and then the Scots song "Tramps and Hawkers" in its original form. The strong tune has often been adapted to modern folk songs.

One of the artists on the LP, Graham Kilsby, was a press photographer by day and began to take photographs for various Saydisc sleeves, including that for The Crofters' first EP, *Pill Ferry*, which shows The Crofters on the aforementioned ferry[85] with Pill Creek in the background. The misnaming of Adge Cutler's song as *Pill Ferry* is interesting, because this version preceded Cutler's own recording of his song, which was titled *Pill, Pill* on release. The EP included a typed insert informing the public at large of The Crofters' intention to record an EP of local songs, and for interested parties to send their contact details on the insert – consequently, finding copies with the insert is difficult. It also stated that one of the tracks on the EP was to be Adge Cutler's *The Great Nailsea Cider Bet*, but this track never appeared and, according to Lucena, "I think Adge had such a title in the pipeline, but have no recollection of it ever having been finished"[86].

The second EP was made up entirely of Adge Cutler songs and was titled *Drink Up Thee Cider - The Crofters Sing Adge* and was issued in late 1966 with another Graham Kilsby photo on the cover. This showed the band at Cutler's old workplace, Coates Somerset Cider Factory in Nailsea. Apart from the title track, the EP included *Casn't Kill Couch*, *Champion Dung Spreader* and *When the Common Market Comes to Stanton Drew*. Pete 'Henry' Davies played string bass, which predicted the future in that Davies later joined the Wurzels as both musician and musical director. The Crofters were concerned with playing folk music in an authentic style, so perhaps these country-tinged recordings of the songs provide a glimpse of how Cutler himself performed them as a solo singer, though as Gef Lucena says, "Adge did comment that we sang them too fast!"[87]

The Crofters appeared in a local TV series called *The Cider Apple* with Cutler during 1966. The series comprised six episodes and included Bath-based singer, Chas Upton, London-based singers, such as Steve Benbow, and even a guest star appearance by Larry Adler. Chas

McDevitt and Shirley Douglas appeared and were impressed by the Crofters to the extent that they asked them to play on their next LP, of which Gef Lucena says:

> Chas McDevitt and Shirley Douglas [appeared] in the TWW 'At the Cider Apple' series and as a consequence asked The Crofters to back them with their arrangements of 'The Cattle Smock' (Martin guitar, Gef on treble recorder), 'The Tailor's Breeches' (Martin guitar, Gef on tenor mandola, both on chorus), The Seeds of Love (Gef on kalimba - nee mbira) and The Sweet Nightingale (both vocal on chorus).

The LP was titled *Chas McDevitt and Shirley Douglas Sing Sixteen English Folk Songs* (Columbia SX 6082, 1966) and it made reference to both *At the Cider Apple* and the Crofters in the sleeve notes – copies crop up fairly regularly and you shouldn't have to pay much more than £10 for one.

The last Crofers record was called *Ballad of the Severn Bridge and Other Songs*, the other songs being *As I Walked Out One Morn*, *The Butter Churning Race* and *Buttercup Meadows*. The title song was commissioned for an ITV documentary on the opening of the bridge and was a traditional tune with new words by Lucena. On *The Butter Churning Race* the duo was accompanied by Pete Davies on sousaphone, Dave Emmett on trumpet, plus 92 year-old Daniel Jeremiah Wainwright on bass drum; on *Buttercup Meadows* Tessa Schiele played French horn. The sleeve notes were written by "Dr. Dorian Mode", who was either a figment of someone's music-fuelled imagination or, if real, had parents with a sense of humour and, probably, an awful childhood. The sleeve notes, after explaining the songs, say:

> These four songs are a sample of the modern approach to "non-commercial" folk music writing and presentation. Another facet of the Crofters' music will be featured in a future L.P. of traditional and historic folk songs ...

However, this EP was the final record released by The Crofters and no LP was issued – any Crofters LPs you might see are by a different group. At this point Saydisc was starting to organise, record and release more and more records and the Crofters got put to one side because of the time involved in the day-to-day operations of running a record company. As for values, the compilation LP, *Bristol Folks*, is by far the rarest and because it is currently unknown on the collector's scene, assigning a value is difficult, but it could easily run to three figures. The three EPs crop up occasionally in the Bristol area, though not as frequently as they used to. The first two are the more collectable because of their inclusion of Adge Cutler songs and, if complete with their inserts, should set you back at least £15 apiece, whilst the last should set you back about £10.

Adge Cutler and the Wurzels

Adge Cutler was born in Portishead in 1930 and brought up in Nailsea. Adge, a contraction of Alan John to A.J. and the phonetic pronunciation thereof, briefly joined the family business when he left school at the age of fourteen, but not before a spell as a market gardener. He later undertook his military service and on being demobbed spent periods working for Coates Cider in Nailsea and labouring in Wales. Early on, Cutler noticed that all the singsongs in local pubs involved songs from foreign parts, such as *I Belong to Glasgow* and *Maybe It's Because I'm a Londoner*. There weren't any songs about the West Country, so Cutler started to write them, anecdotally writing *Drink Up Thy Zider* as early as 1957. In this pursuit, Cutler was influenced by Bristolian singer and entertainer, Len 'Uke' Thomas, 'the Bard of Bedminster Down', a banjo-playing member of the Bristol Banjo, Mandolin and Guitar Club, who wrote and sang songs such as *Wassfink Of 'Ee, Den*[88] and *Thee Bissn't Gonna Get'n Out Of I*.

In 1960 Cutler became road manager for Acker Bilk's Paramount Jazz Band, a job he held for several years. A contemporary of Adge's at school in Nailsea remembers going for a pre-concert pint at the Artichoke, opposite the Colston Hall, and found himself hailed by Cutler, who was also in the upstairs bar. During their conversation it was suggested that being road manager for Acker Bilk and the band must be an exciting life, to which Cutler pointed out that his main role was to stop the band from getting too drunk before the gig, which generally involved scouring the local pubs, as he was now doing, and making sure that everyone got on stage in time and in a fit state to play. Cutler had written several songs by this time and on occasion would sing them with Acker's band. Q. Williams wrote:

> Adge Cutler is remembered at the Crown and Dove singing, with Acker's band, numbers like "Drink up Thee Cider" and "Scrumpy-Drinkin' Brickies from Home" (a parody of "Cakewalking Babies").[89]

The Bilk family was also involved in property development and, on their behalf, Cutler moved to Spain to work in tourist property development at, as it turned out, just the wrong time. He lasted a year before returning to the UK, initially to London, where he lived at 82 Solent Road in West Hampstead.

Cutler began performing his songs up and down the country and on West Country radio and TV. He had his own radio show on the BBC West of England station in March 1966 and later that year appeared on TWW, Bristol's local TV station, in a programme called, appropriately enough, *The Cider Apple*, which comprised six episodes and featured other local acts. He also performed, usually unaccompanied, in pubs and clubs around the country, charging £5, plus expenses, playing at venues as diverse as Liverpool's Cavern Club and the Bristol Ballads and Blues. In the mid-1960s, Cutler found himself in the odd position of being unsigned himself, but seeing others record and release his songs: The Crofters recorded *Pill Ferry* – as it was then named – in late 1965, followed by a whole EP of Adge's songs the following year, and Fred Wedlock recorded *Virtute et Industrial* in 1966.

Back in Bristol and living in a top floor flat in Pembroke Road, Clifton, Cutler met with John Miles in June 1966 and he ended up managing both Cutler and the post-Adge version of the Wurzels for 21 years. Miles got in touch with Bob Barrett, an EMI house producer, who booked a recording date for Abbey Road 2 studio[90] so that, in effect, Cutler and his currently non-existent band could audition for EMI. Cutler put together his band from the various talents available on the local jazz scene. The original line-up consisted of Reg Quantrill on banjo, John Macey on double bass, Reg Chant on accordion and Brian Walker

Bristol folk

on Tuba, or *Wurzelphone* as Cutler referred to it. Quantrill had started off in the 1950s jazz group, Cassey Bottom and this group made two records in 1953, recorded by Stan Strickland from the record shop in Denmark Street[91]. Quantrill then moved up to London, where he played with the Crane River Band, the Storyville Band and the Mike Peters Band. Back in Bristol he joined the Stainer/Collett 7, playing guitar, and revived Cassey Bottom, which this time around included future Wurzel, John Macey on bass. Cutler knew Quantrill well and had often sat in with the Stainer/Collett 7, singing his early compositions.

Before moving on to Cutler's audition for EMI, his urgent need for a band led to one amusing complication. Cutler chatted with Cliff Brown, who had been the drummer with the Chew Valley Jazz Band and was now with the Okeh Rhythm Kings, about having an upcoming audition with EMI and no band to take with him. Brown was left with the impression that Cutler had asked him to form a backing band and consequently he put together a band comprising himself, Q. Williams and Barry Back. They got as far as rehearsals before being told that Cutler already had a band. They decided to stay together as the Alligator Jug Thumpers and Cutler later invited them to appear in his *Scrumpy and Western* shows, where they closed the first half.

Meanwhile, for the first recording session, John Miles decided that the band should make some sort of impact at EMI, so he arranged some suitably rustic clothing and accoutrements, including hats, neckerchiefs and jerkins as worn by Somerset farm labourers at work in the field. The band stopped on their way up to London to change into these clothes and made a predictable stir when they got out of their van at EMI's studios looking like a group of agricultural labourers up for Smithfield, complete with milk churn and bales of straw, which they proceeded to unload with unnecessary noise. This recording session introduced them to Bob Barrett, who is rightly famous for recording some of EMI's more eclectic artists, as well as succeeding in making excellent on-location recordings for such luminaries as Reginald Dixon. The Wurzels' association with Barrett was to last beyond the end of the 1970s, and even beyond their time with EMI, but at this point they didn't have a contract. Half way through the recording of the demos[92] EMI's Chairman came down to find out what the earlier commotion had been about and asked to listen to the tapes at the end of the day. The upshot was that Adge Cutler and the Wurzels got a recording contract on Columbia, the same label as Cliff and the Shadows.

A likely reason for Cutler being signed was that EMI had recently had success with Allan Smethurst, the Singing Postman, who wrote and sang songs in the Norfolk dialect. His single, *Have Yew Gotta Loight, Boy?* won the Ivor Novello Award for best novelty song in 1966 and made a lot of money for Parlophone, who took over distribution of the record from the small, Norfolk-based Ralph Tuck label. In Cutler, here was more of the same, another writer and singer of comic songs, this time about the West Country and sung in a Somerset accent. EMI had a reputation for signing and marketing novelty acts, and it can be assumed that Columbia's executives thought that, with Adge on the books, they would have a serious rival for Parlophone's Singing Postman – inter-label rivalry within EMI was not unknown.

Bristol folk

Barrett wanted to make an album but was concerned that the studio wasn't the right setting, so the record was recorded live at *The Royal Oak*, in the High Street of Cutler's home town of Nailsea. With Cutler already a local celebrity, a home-based recording was guaranteed to generate the right sort of atmosphere. The recording took place on November 2nd and *Drink Up Thy Zider* and *Twice Daily* – the latter complete with censorious bleep over the word "*u*g*r" and an airplay ban by the BBC – were issued as a single in December 1966. Originally issued in the West Country, sales were so promising – reputedly it was the best selling single in Bristol for ten weeks – that it was issued nationally and it entered the UK singles chart on February 2nd, peaking at number 45 and remaining on chart for a week. This bettered the Singing Postman's record, which had been a regional hit but had not been a 'regional breakout' when given national promotion and distribution. Cutler's record didn't receive any kind of award but, like Smethurst's single, it did outsell both the Beatles' and the Rolling Stones' latest records locally. Meanwhile, has anyone else noticed how similar the tune of *Twice Daily* is to the blues tune *Beedle Um Bum*.

The LP was issued in early 1967 and was titled *Adge Cutler & the Wurzels* with the legend *Recorded live at the Royal Oak, Nailsea, Zummerzet* so that a national audience would know what to expect. What they got was a set of mostly tried and tested songs from Cutler's solo days, confidently and humorously performed so that it also connected with a non-West Country audience. The LP entered the UK album charts on March 11th, reaching number 38 and staying on chart for four weeks, so it beat the Singing Postman's first LP on that score as well. The LP was quickly followed by the *Scrumpy and Western* EP, which helped to promote the current shows of the same name: it's worth noting that the vocal lead-ins to the songs on the EP are different to those on the same songs on the LP, even though the songs are identical takes. Q. Williams said of this time, "Adge had been developing his comedy music steadily and was working with the late Norman Beaton, the Dewar Brothers, Adrienne Webber and Derek Brimstone. The folk scene had arrived."[93]

Shortly after this, Columbia put out another single, *The Champion Dung Spreader*, backed with *When the Common Market Comes to Stanton Drew*: the a-side is a live recording, but the b-side is clearly a studio recording, possibly from the 1966 demo recordings. Two further singles were released during 1967, the non-LP, live-recorded *I Wish I Was Back on the Farm* was backed with the studio-recorded *Easton-In-Gordano* and this was followed by two non-LP tracks, *All Over Mendip* – a different version of which cropped up again on the band's 1969 LP – backed with the risqué *My Threshing Machine*, the latter being released in October 1967, most likely to promote the second LP. None of these, however, worried the UK singles charts.

Talking of the second LP no sooner had the dust settled on the first LP that a second was recorded, again using the winning formula of recording at the Royal Oak, though without Brian Walker, who had left by this time. The recording was not without incident: more people turned up than the pub could allow in and one of those turned away lobbed a brick through the window, which can be clearly heard on the subsequent LP. The LP, *Adge Cutler's Family Album*, was released in 1967 and, although not denting the charts, did well enough for EMI to want to record another LP. However, the band was getting too popular to play such a small venue as the Royal Oak, so the Webbington Country Club was used for the *Cutler of the West* LP, which was released in 1968.

There had been some upheavals within the band prior to the recording of the third album and only Cutler and Reg Quantrill now remained from the original line-up. Pete Davies, better known as Henry[94], leader of Henry's Bootblacks, joined on double bass, tuba and violin whilst the accordion spot was taken in November 1968 by a foreigner, Scotsman Tommy Banner, on the recommendation of Acker Bilk's bass player. *Cutler of the West* is the best LP that Cutler made and every collection should have a copy – the jokes were still fresh, and Banner's presence on piano as well as accordion helped to add more variety. Two singles were also released during 1968, one was made up of the non-LP tracks *Don't Tell I, Tell 'Ee* – which was later cleaned up and used on the 1972 compilation LP of the same name – and *Faggots Is the Stuff*, whilst in August, *Up the Clump* was backed with *Aloha Severn Beach*. These last two songs were studio recordings and are different versions to those released on LP[95]. Henry Davies, having put together some rudimentary brass parts for the recording sessions was rather shocked to find some of Britain's most 'heavyweight' jazz musicians lined up in the studio waiting to play along to them. It sounds as though it was a very enjoyable session for everyone!

The last LP was released in 1969, also recorded at the Webbington – according to the credit on the front sleeve at any rate – and was called *Carry on Cutler!* Henry Davis had left and had been replaced by Tony Baylis, from the Temperence Seven and Bob Kerr's Whoopee Band amongst others. Davies had not disappeared entirely and was acting as musical director for the band. Davies later said of his time with the Wurzels, "The music of the Wurzels was fun but of insufficient content to satisfy me"[96].

Meanwhile, there was a certain amount of cheating going on during the making of this album, as those scrutinising the sleeve and labels discovered. Far from all being recorded at the Webbington, some of the recordings were made at the *White Buck Inn*, in Burley in Hampshire and two of the songs had earlier publishing dates - *All Over Mendip* had a publishing date of 1967 and *Aloha Severn Beach* had a publishing date of 1968. As both of these had previously been issued on singles in those years then EMI was probably merely faithfully crediting the original publishing dates of the songs[97]. However, it is possible that EMI was using up odds and ends for this LP, dubbing in laughter to make studio recordings of some songs sound like live recordings: *Down On the Farm* sounds suspiciously like a studio recording with canned laughter from a live gig added. As to which of the remaining tracks were recorded where, the inclusion of two drummers, with track credits provided, makes it possible to make a guess at which tracks were recorded at which venue – you have a 50/50 chance of getting it right and a 100% chance of never knowing whether you guessed right or wrong. In September a single, consisting of *Ferry to Glastonbury* and *Saturday Night at the Crown*, was released to promote the LP. The a-side was lifted straight from the album, but the b-side was a cleaned up version of the album track.

No new LPs were released, though Columbia put out a single, *Poor, Poor Farmer*, backed with *Chitterling* in May 1971. Both songs were included on the 1972 budget issue LP, *Don't*

Bristol folk

Tell I, Tell 'Ee, which also included several of the earlier single-only songs plus a couple of favourites and one otherwise unavailable track, a 1972 published recording of *I'd Love To Swim In the Zuider Zee*[98]. When this last song was recorded is unclear, and from a close listen this might be a studio recording, slotted into previously-recorded live banter from Adge. This is easily possible because this LP was cleverly programmed and dubbed so that it sounded like one seamless performance. That this is done so successfully is what starts to make one suspicious about the provenance of some live tracks on the earlier LPs too. However, even if some were studio recordings, they were at least, by the sound of them, recorded 'live' in the studio.

Sales of both albums and singles had been generally becoming more disappointing since 1968 and EMI quietly dropped the band. However, in May 1972, very close to the release of the *Don't Tell I, Tell 'Ee* compilation, CBS signed the band, via Chicory Tip's producer, Roger Easterby, and issued what turned out to be a one-off single, rather than the looked-for crossover hit. It comprised *Little Darlin'* and *Mother Nature Calling* with the a-side being a near straight remake of the original 1957 hit by the Diamonds. The single came in a picture sleeve and was issued in various non-UK territories, including, oddly, Japan.

The band remained as popular as ever on the cabaret and club circuit with nothing much of note happening until early 1974, when Reg Quantrill left after nine years with the band. He was quickly replaced by Pete Budd, who had been leader of the local rock and roll outfit, Pete Budd and the Rebels. The band continued to gig and appeared in the local TV series, *The Great Western Musical Thunderbox*, which also featured Fred Wedlock. Sadly, this was amongst Adge Cutler's last appearances. He was killed on May 5th 1974 when his MGB overturned on a roundabout outside Chepstow as he drove home to Tickenham from a gig in Hereford. He is buried in Nailsea. The CBS single was reissued on the Santa Posta label after Cutler's death in 1974 and Columbia put out a reissue of *Drink Up Thy Zider* as a tribute. Cutler's death was, oddly, the spur that the band needed to get back to recording – they renewed their acquaintance with Barrett and EMI and made an LP that featured several previously unrecorded Adge Cutler songs. The LP sold modestly but, undeterred, the Wurzels carried on and ended up with a number one in the UK charts, but we'll hear more of the Wurzels later on.

As regards the records released by Adge and the Wurzels, the first LP is fairly easy to find, as is the first single and neither should set you back more than £2 at a carboot or £5 on eBay. However, original copies of the other three LPs, which, like the first, all appeared in flipback[99] sleeves, are harder to find and will probably set you back about £10 each. However, beware later stereo pressings minus the flipback sleeve, or indeed, any pressing that has an EMI logo or two on the label. These should set you back no more than £5 at most. An original copy of the *Don't Tell I, Tell 'Ee* compilation with flipback sleeve goes for about £8 or £9, though reissues of this and other compilation LPs released during the 1970s should be about £5 each. The only exception is the late 1970s reissue of *Don't Tell I, Tell 'Ee* in a different sleeve and with extra tracks added: this is harder to find than the original and could cost anything up to £10. The singles are a different matter: all apart from the first are very hard to find, and can easily set you back £10 each, as can the *Scrumpy and*

Western EP in picture sleeve. The first single has also been discovered as an acetate and this has been valued at around £70. Sheet music was also available for some of the singles and this too is becoming fairly pricey, with *at least* a £10 price tag should you find any.

Elecampane

Elecampane was formed in 1972, named after the dandelion-like plant that grows in Britain, Southern Europe and all the way up to the Himalayas. The plant was well-known to have antiseptic properties and, more in keeping with music and musicians, was the base ingredient of absinthe. The group, meanwhile, is best remembered for its theatrical performances, but it originally started out as a normal folk-rock group, as John Shaw explains:

> ... we started out as a straightforward electric folk group (in the Mr. Fox/Albion Country Band style of the times), but within a very short time (a few months at most) moved into blending this with theatrical shows ... the first one we did, and the one which set the pattern for the future, was our musical "electric mummers' play" – "The Amazing Death and Resurrection of Tommy the Ploughboy".[100]

The group billed themselves as 'The Greatest Little Show on Earth' and played the folk circuit, arts centres and folk festivals. The line-up was Dave Byrne on vocals, electric and acoustic guitars and descant recorder, Chris Lyons on vocals, drums, bongos and tambourine, Daphne Miller on vocals, descant and tenor recorders, John Shaw on vocals, electric bass, acoustic guitar and electric dulcimer and John Taylor on vocals and piano accordion. All had previously been involved in various folk and Morris dancing clubs, with some being involved in the formation of the Bristol Mummers in 1967, and both John Shaw and David Byrne had previously appeared along with other members of the Folk Tradition club on an LP titled *Men of the Sea*, which was recorded to coincide with a marine archaeology exhibition at Bristol Museum in 1971. In Elecampane the musicians' various roots were well in evidence and their performances were based on the idea of the traditional travelling fair, in that they should be "flamboyant, exotic and fun"[101].

In early 1975, the group released *When God's on the Water* on their Dame Jane label. The majority of the LP was traditional, though it also included John Shaw's *The River*, Robin Williamson's *Water* and Tom Paxton's *A Sailor's Life*. The significance of the record label and the ODJ catalogue number are obvious if you happen to be a fan of Mummers plays. If, like most, you have only a nodding acquaintance with this historical theatrical form, Dame Jane was a witch, who is introduced thus in one version of The English Folk-Play:

> (Enter The Old Witch)
> Here comes old Dame Jane,
> Comes dabeling about the Meadow,
> Comes Jumping about, to show you such sport;[102]

In Mummers plays, it is elecampane that brings St George back to life – and Elecampane's performances brought jaded folk audiences back to life by presenting almost end-of-the-pier type shows – in fact, one of their shows was called *Weston Rock*: promotional posters

Bristol folk

showed the now destroyed Weston Pier. Other shows included *A Canterbury Tale*, *The Greatest Little Show from Earth* (a play on the band's catchphrase), *Doctor Elektron's Travelling Fair* and *Wally the Wonderhorse or "Roll Over Ursula Birdhood"*!

In 1978 the group recorded their second LP, *Further Adventures of Mr Punch*. The line-up included Dave Byrne, John Shaw and Chris Lyons. Daphne Miller had married in the meantime and appeared under her new name of Grant. Newer members were Katrina Rock, who sang and played descant recorder, English concertina and guitar, and Chris Lovegrove, who sang and played keyboards.

That same year, Elecampane appeared at the Bristol Folk Festival, which took place at Hanham Mills between 23rd and 25th of June, 1978. They played on Friday 23rd as part of what was billed in the official programme as a "Bristolian Session". This series of sets on the main stage also included other Bristol-based acts – Beggars Opera, Tuppence, Erik Ilott, Pat Small, Good Jelly, Dave Paskett and the Pigsty Hill Light Orchestra. Many of those appearing got to play more than one set and Elecampane played again on the Sunday on the other main stage. John Shaw provides some insight into just what it was that made the group so entertaining:

> In my time with the band … the "front man" on stage was our drummer Chris Lyons, who among other things was a superb morris dancer. He was also into all sorts of 70s rock music, including glam-rock. One feature of his solo morris jig that we all fondly remember, is that when he pulled his morris handkerchiefs out of his pockets, raising them high and shaking them out with a flourish, clouds of sparkle dust fell through the air from them.[103]

Shaw left the group in late 1979 and Elecampane continued into the 1980s, during which time Dave Byrne produced two LPs by Dr. Bowser's Brown Bowel Oil Band – *A Good Run for Your Money* in 1981 and *Not to Be Sniffed At* in 1985[104]. Also in the very early 1980s, a project that had its genesis in 1971 finally came to fruition. After the *Men of the Sea* LP had been issued, various members of the Folk Tradition club had planned to record an LP of traditional music from Bristol. It was, however, another 11 years before the cassette, *Alongside Bristol Quay*, was issued in 1982. John Shaw explains:

> … a number of people from the Folk Tradition club were trying to develop a project of an album of traditional songs and tunes from Bristol, mainly gathered by myself from various archive sources. An entrepreneur … put us in touch with Arthur Radford[105], with the idea that Mr. Radford would record it with a view to licensing it to Bill Leader (of the Leader and Trailer record labels). Some of us, including Bob Stewart and myself met Mr. Radford and Bill Leader one evening to discuss this. However we … pulled out of the project. Nothing further happened with these recording plans until we recorded the "Alongside Bristol Quay" cassette at Dave Byrne's Launderama studio in 1982. This was a self-produced project.[106]

In the late 1980s, Elecampane released their final album, which was available on cassette only. John Shaw explains:

... after my time with the band they released one more album – on cassette: "Swings and Roundabouts" … One side of this was devoted to "Dr. Elektron's Travelling Fair". The line-up at this time was: Dave Byrne, Daphne Grant, plus Chris Ellicott (keyboards, recorder, vocals) Debbie Ellicott (vocals, mandolin, percussion, guitar, whistle) Vincent Johnson (recorders, dulcian, vocals) Steve Vernon (vocals, bass, guitar). The album had been recorded over quite a period of time, and included contributions from members who had come and gone over the years: Chris Lyons (drums, vocals) John De Pulford (dulcian) Shep Robson (bass, vocals) Mark Strawbridge (bass, guitar).[107]

Dave Byrne and John Shaw are still involved in similar productions to those staged by Elacampane. One show at the Granary in Frome, to commemorate the 200th anniversary of the Battle of Trafalgar, resulted in the following comments from reviewer Pete Minall, who, in his youth, had roadied for Elacampane.

Shantymen Dave Byrne and John Shaw have to be publicly applauded for yet another triumph! Who would have thought they could have matched the success of Cecil Sharp's Big Night Out last year. Once again, they projected visual images on to the stage to help the narration flow with ease … Dave and John have been massively influential over the years in their meticulous research and presentation of many folk events. This stems from their days together in Elecampane, the most influential folk theatre band to have graced the Festival circuit over the years.[108]

The two LPs appear rarely and occasionally sell for £100 or more, though £30 or so is a bit more realistic for the second LP, perhaps more if it still includes the booklet. Some unplayed copies recently cropped up on eBay from a folk collector in Gloucestershire who had bought a couple of boxes of unsold stock from the band many years ago. That was probably your last chance to bag a bargain! The *Men of the Sea* LP, meanwhile, was credited to "Stan Hugill and the Folk Tradition" with accompaniment and vocals from various members of the Folk Tradition club. Although presumably over a thousand copies were sold by Bristol Museum, it is surprisingly rare and hardly ever surfaces: £20 or so should secure one should one turn up.

Dave Evans

I fell in love with the guitar in 1955 when I first heard Big Bill Broonzy … Made my first guitar in 1968 and it earned my living from '71 until '78.[109]

After leaving school, Dave Evans spent five years travelling the world with the Merchant Navy then enrolled at Loughborough Art College in 1963. Whilst there he ran a folk club and ended up living in the same house as Steve Tilston. Tilston encouraged Evans to write his own songs, a task that Evens evidently found unduly onerous, and they played local folk clubs together. After leaving college, Evans spent three years running a pottery, which he described as mind-numbing: after the initial bout of creativity in making the original design, he was stuck with repeating himself over and over – Evans said that at least with a song, he could make it different each time so that it didn't become stale[110]. Evans also built guitars and in 1968 he built the one which he used until 1978. After closing his pottery Evans moved first to Devon, to work in another pottery, and then, in late 1970, to Bristol, where his friend Steve Tilston was now spending much time.

Evans came up ostensibly to play on sessions for Tilston's first LP, which took place in February and March 1971, but never got around to returning to his job in Devon and moved into Bristol's City Road area instead. Evans proceeded to make a bit of a splash on the Bristol music scene and was quickly signed to Village Thing. He was recorded at Ian Anderson's Royal York Crescent flat in July 1971 and the subsequent LP was titled *The Words In Between*. The LP included Pete Airey[111], Adrienne Webber and Strange Fruit's Keith Warmington, and soon after release Evans was regularly playing in a trio with Airey and Webber. Meanwhile, a local review of the LP concluded thus:

> Evans and second guitar Pete Airey get some good things going in the manner of Jansch and Renbourn and there is also a little help from a young lady called Adrienne on vocals. But it's only when Keith Warmington joins in on harmonica on the tracks "Sailor" and "City Road" that the album rises above melancholia. Cheer up, Dave.[112]

To which Evans recently responded, "Never read that review, but melancholia? I don't think so."[113] Oddly, the Daily Mail picked up on both Steve Tilston's and Dave Evans' debut LPs, as Evans explains:

> … here's a funny thing – I seem to remember a guy called Mike Cable … of the Daily Mail … who voted "*The Words in Between*" & Steve Tilston's "*An Acoustic Confusion*" amongst the top ten LP's of the year … I can't remember if he placed us above or below John Lennon's "*Imagine*" …[114]

It wasn't just the Daily Mail that picked up on *The Words In Between*: BBC DJs, Bob Harris and John Peel, also picked up on it and played tracks from the album on their respective Radio One shows. Both Peel and Harris booked Evans for radio sessions and these led to further solo radio sessions, including a *Sounds of the Seventies* session on 6th July, plus sessions with Canton Trig, who Evans had joined, and even some spots on The Old Grey Whistle Test. As Evans remembers:

> I remember appearing on 7 *Sounds of the Seventies* sessions – one with John Peel & six with Bob Harris including one with Canton Trig … Also, I appeared three times on the *Old Grey Whistle* Test – the first time was in a minuscule London studio with Bob Harris about three feet to my left. I had to play & sing to this camera which had Bob's auto-cue in blue on a white background … "Thank you very much Dave Evans", it read, "So nice to have him on the show – and now we have a real treat…" And the treat was standing six feet away to the right of the camera – Lou Reed was swaying there & one of his eyes was blinking & blinking …[115]

Meanwhile, back in Bristol, the Troubadour had just closed down and of this venue, Evans commented, "… the Bristol Troubadour … was a good testing ground for other people's reaction and it was a good testing ground for trying out new material."[116]

Bristol folk

Evans' second LP, *Elephantasia*, was recorded in June 1972 at Kingsley Ward's Rockfield Studios, near Monmouth, and at Village Thing in July. Keith Warmington again played harmonica and Evans was also joined by three-quarters of Bristol progressive rock band, Squidd. Steve Swindells played some lovely piano whilst John Merrett and Rodney Matthews respectively played some perfectly-understated bass and percussion. Matthews also designed the wonderful sleeve. Evans promoted the LP on local television when he was one of the featured musicians on *Stackridge, Squidd and Co.*, broadcast on BBC 1 on 25th July.

In August 1973, the Melody Maker reported that Evans had joined Canton Trig, replacing Graham Smith, who had joined Magna Carta[117]. The other members of Canton Trig were Dave Fuller on guitar, his brother Andy on percussion and Rob Spensley on guitar and keyboards. They had originally come over from the Channel Islands specifically because of the reputation of the local scene and because of the proximity of the Village Thing agency. Plastic Dog, who now ran the agency, handled both management and agency duties for the band. The group had recently backed Steve Tilston on a BBC *In Concert* programme and had backed and supported Al Stewart on two tours[118]. Partly on the basis of this exposure, but mostly on the basis of a great deal of talent and some stunningly pretty songs in the CSN or Heron mould, Canton Trig recorded several BBC sessions and got a record deal with Bradleys.

The band recorded two songs as choices for the b-side of their first single, but Bradley's owner, Stuart Slater, knew which song he wanted recorded for the a-side – it was a Dave Fuller song called *Miss Karen Mutch*, written about a girl who had left him. According to Plastic Dog's Al Read, "It was a masterpiece and the bands arrangement with the four part harmonies and superb musicianship made it a certain chart success in every way."[119] However, because of the personal nature of the song Fuller refused to record it for a single, despite having already recorded it for at least one BBC session:

> ... persuasion, threat and bribery would not make him change his mind. Stuart Slater tore up the record contract, Plastic Dog dropped the agency and management, I lost a lot of money I didn't have and the band slipped out of the limelight and into the world of might have beens. Shame.[120]

Fuller wanted the song to be kept for the LP and Slater's argument that if the song wasn't recorded as the first single then there would be no LP, and no single either, failed to make Fuller change his mind. At least, this is how the group's management remembers things: it's only fair to point out that Dave Evans and Dave Fuller have different – and differing – memories of these events. As Dave Fuller says:

> ... all I can say is that we were there and that's not what I recall, nor is it what Rob Spensley remembers! We were very keen to have a release of the single, however not the version they put up ... Most matters were discussed behind closed doors without our involvement, as was the way in those days... and indeed Al Read and his partner Steve Webb had very different views as to the direction the band should take and so we also did demos for Paul Brett and his label. Finally, Dave Evans was a brilliant

Bristol folk

guitar player/maker and a huge inspiration to us all, but he was not a bass player and the version they wanted to release had him on bass.

James Warren, who had recently left Stackridge, joined Canton Trig and Dave Evans left soon afterwards. The band ended up as a duo of Dave Fuller and Rob Spensley, who, under the name Walkie Talkies, released a wonderful record called *Surveillance* in 1980 on the Rialto label, which was, coincidentally enough, the label on which James Warren now recorded as part of The Korgis. It was again *Miss Karen Much* that had led to the Rialto contract, as Dave Fuller explains:

> Rob Spensley and I recorded an orchestrated version of Miss Karen Mutch later in the 70s, produced by Larry Fallon (Paul Simon/Bob Dylan) which helped secure our deal with the Rialto label and publishing with Warner Brothers Worldwide. So the song never died! However I nearly did as I had a massive heart attack whilst recording Surveillance!

Canton Trig remains an almost forgotten footnote in the annals of Bristolian music, which is, as Al Read says, a shame: it is criminal that such good music should be lying near enough forgotten and surely the time is ripe to issue what little remains nearly forty years on. Luckily, for fans, if not for copyright holders, some of the work recorded for the BBC is starting to appear on the Internet. Fuller, meanwhile, continues to release excellent music.

Dave Evans left Bristol soon after leaving Canton Trig and his fortunes took a rise when Stefan Grossman signed him to his Kicking Mule label alongside such internationally-renowned players as Duck Baker and Jim McLennan. Being signed to Kicking Mule was an accolade in itself because it meant that you had proved yourself to be one of the best players around. The first Evans LP on the label in 1974, *Sad Pig Dance*, was completely instrumental and included a guitar tablature book that frightened off many a would-be guitarist. Evans, whilst still in Bristol, had appeared on the *Old Grey Whistle Test* to illustrate fingerstyle guitar technique by playing the wonderfully difficult *Stagefright* [121] and this track ended up on the new album. In the sleeve notes, Evans described the tune thus:

> I've just worked it out from the tablature sheets that this piece has 3,071 notes in it, working out at about 14 notes per second. Took its name from when I did it cold in front of a T.V. concert audience. I played it at about 10 bum notes per second!

Evans' Kicking Mule follow-up was called *Take a Bite Out of Life*, released in 1976, and featured him back in singer-songwriter mode. Apart from these two albums, Grossman used Evans on two showcase albums, *Contemporary Guitar Workshop*, which was recorded in 1977 and released in 1978 and *Irish Reels Jigs Hornpipes & Airs*, which was released in late 1979. However, Evans had already left the UK before these LPs were issued.

In 1977, Evans moved to Belgium where he met ceramist Patrick Piccarelle and became enthusiastic about potting again. When Piccarelle moved on, Evans went back to making and repairing all sorts of stringed instruments in Brussels. Evans renewed acquaintance with Piccarelle in 1996 and began making pottery with him. Evans also began making beer with

Patrick Broeckx – fiendish and highly-drinkable Belgian beer, some of it 8%. According to Evans, "This beer is not to be trusted - it's so easy to drink with its fresh hoppy taste - but before you know it, you're talking nonsense - and your legs belong to someone else."[122] He certainly looks happy on the website, though as Evans warns, "The website is at least 8 years out of date – just been too lazy to take it down."[123]

As for the records, the two Village Thing LPs, if you can find copies will set you back quite a lot of money. *The Words In Between* is likely to cost you about £50 and *Elephantasia* can set you back even more, mainly because it includes Steve Swindells, who later joined Pilot and Hawkwind's alter-ego band, Hawklords. Pilot and Hawkwind collectors have pushed the price up, but the record is still worth whatever you have to pay for it. To hear Evans' guitar work on Steve Tilston's *An Acoustic Confusion* will set you back about £50, or more if you find a copy on the first Village Thing label design. The four Kicking Mule LPs shouldn't cost more than £15 apiece – or perhaps £20 if they include their guitar tablature inserts. However, people have a tendency to hold on to Dave Evans records, so finding copies will not be that easy. No Canton Trig material was ever commercially available, though the Walkie Talkies' sole LP, *Surveillance*, on Rialto is well worth hunting out.

Frank Evans

> British jazz guitarist, Frank Evans, passed away on February 6th 2007 at the age of 76. A former member of Tubby Hayes Quartet, Frank performed and recorded most often as a solo guitarist. Since the mid-sixties, Frank generally shunned the London scene, preferring to operate from his home in Bristol.[124]

Frank Evans was a jazz guitarist who was also at home playing in blues and classical styles. He learned guitar by the usual method of trial and error and played jazz clubs and other venues around the world before ending up back in the UK with the Tubby Hayes Quartet. He formed his own trio and they appeared on an LP on Doug Dobell's 77 label in 1968. The LP was recorded live at Bristol University on 18 November 1966 and was called *Jazz Tête à Tête*. There are three groups on the LP: the first is Tubby Hayes and the Les Condon Quartet; the second is The Tony Coe Quintet; the third is the Frank Evans Trio, with Peter Ind on bass and Jackie Dougan on drums. The Trio's tracks are *Blues for Sunday* and *Polka Dots and Moonbeams*. The LP is extremely rare and stupidly expensive should you be lucky enough to locate a copy.

Evans' second LP, *Mark Twain Suite*, subtitled *A Jazz suite for Guitar and Strings*, again released on the 77 label, was recorded in Bristol during March, September and November 1969 and was a much more subdued affair than was the first. It featured Norman Cole and Jim Richardson on bass and Eddie Clayton and Tony Faulkner on drums. This is also very hard to find – when Mole Jazz at Kings Cross were asked a good few years ago if they would be able to find a copy, the response was, "Not a chance!"

In the meantime, Evans was becoming quite well-known on TV and radio, his music being used on various programmes.

Bristol folk

> He had appeared on about 250 shows for BBCTV and ITV as accompanist, soloist and musical director, and a regular contributor to BBC2 late night music programmes, either alone or with his small radio orchestra 'Nova' ... His film and TV scores amounted to twenty, the latest of which were three of a series of six called 'Leap in the Dark', and 'The Flowering of Britain' in the 'World About Us' series for BBCTV ... His own TV appearances included his own 'Frank Evans and Friends' with guests Marion Williams and Georgie Fame for ITV, and [he] was featured on the 'Michael Parkinson Show' ... in competition with Rod Hull's Emu![125]

In December 1971 Evans released his third LP, *Stretching Forth*, on local label, Saydisc, with Dave Olney on bass and Ian Hobbs on drums. This LP was not a particularly big seller and is very hard to find. Gef Lucena of Saydisc explains:

> I see from my ancient pressing cards that we pressed 595 copies in Dec 1971 and it never went to a reprint. I suspect some stocks went as deletions so it probably only sold a few hundred at normal price.[126]

In 1972 *In an English Manner*, credited to the Frank Evans Consort, which also consisted of bassist Graham Southcott and drummer Ian Hobbs, was issued. This LP harked back to *Mark Twain Suite* by including some dreamily-understated string passages, this time from the Barton String Quartet. *Summer Song* shimmers like a lazy, hazy, hot Summer's evening and might just be the best single piece of music that Saydisc released. Judging by the number of copies that crop up, the LP must have sold substantially more than its predecessor.

Not only had Evans retreated from the London music scene, but he now decided to do without a record deal, starting his own label, Blue Bag, which was for a while distributed by Pye. The label was run from Westbury-on-Trym with the fan club run from an address on Shirehampton Green. Evans recorded his first LP for the label on 9th November 1975 with Graham Southcott on bass. It was called *Noctuary*, and it topped the UK jazz charts when it was issued in early 1976.

> Frank set up his own label 'Blue Bag' to release his solo album 'Noctuary'... Although today countless musicians have set up their own label and are able to distribute their music digitally, this was an unusual move at the time. "I was fed up with being mucked about by record companies and that whole hassle of the music business. Someone in London said I'd be lucky to sell 500 altogether. But I sold 500 in the first two weeks." Frank said at the time. The album went on to top the UK jazz charts.[127]

In 1977 *Soiree* was issued, again with Graham Southcott plus Mike Hope on electric piano, Evans' son, Chris, on drums and Lester Thompson on flugel. These musicians only appeared on one side and the other side was recorded live and solo. This was followed up by *LA3* where Evans joined the Laurindo Almeida Trio, probably as a result of name-checking Almeida as an influence on *Soiree*. The final LP of the 1970s was the wonderfully punning *...for Little Girls*[128] with sleeve designed by The Shirehampton Art Factory. As Evans explained in the sleeve notes:

Bristol folk

> Throughout my guitar playing career I've been plagued with this pun, by using it as the album title, hopefully I will put an end to it once and for all. – If I hear it again I'm likely to damage my guitar on someone's head.

The sleeve notes go on to mention that the guitar he would have damaged on someone's head was an Ibanez electric guitar, strung with D'Addario half round strings, which he had used on a duo session with George Benson in 1978. Unfortunately, this particular name-check did not produce an LP with Benson, who was then an acclaimed jazz guitarist, but is now best remembered for his soft jazz-soul-pop crossover chart hits of the 1980s. How a Bristol-based guitarist could routinely play with the likes of George Benson and Laurindo Almeida can be explained by Evans being Vice President of the International Guitarists Association, a position that shows the respect in which he was held by fellow guitarists: one Bristol-based guitar-maker, Geoff Gale, said of Evans after working on one of his guitars, that he effortlessly played every chord and inversion possible from the bottom to the top to test the repaired guitar for unwanted buzzing and ringing and once he was satisfied proceeded to serenade Gale and his wife with flawless playing. Meanwhile, Evans, despite his global credentials, was content to play various residencies around Bristol, such as at the Hawthornes Hotel in Kingsdown and upstairs at Vicki's Club, best-known as a strip club in the 1970s and 1980s, and also at his local, The Forrester's Arms, in Westbury on Trym.

In the 1980s Evans released *Ballade* and *Great Jazz Standards* on his Blue Bag label, as well as an LP by pianist, Tony Mockford. He also played on a Saydisc LP by dulcimer player Jim Couza, an LP that raises Evans' folk credentials by including both Peter Kennedy, at this point living in Portishead, and Eileen Monger. Evans was musically active until his death in 2007.

> Frank enjoyed living in the little village of Westbury-on-Trym, near Bristol, as well as a glass of real English ale, in the company of numerous friends and with those who stopped by to play, to be taught and just to listen to his playing.[129]

If you want to try your luck at finding Frank Evans' 1960s and 1970s records, you will find the first two impossible. *Jazz Tête à Tête*, because it includes Tubby Hayes, is most likely going to be in excess of £200, if a copy turns up, whilst *Mark Twain Suite* is no less rare, but would probably be somewhere in the £50 to £100 range. The first Saydisc LP will set you back between about £15 and £25, whilst *In an English Manner* is fairly common and should cost between £10 and £15. *Noctuary* should cost between £8 and £12 but the other Blue Bag LPs are quite hard to find and should set you back about £15 to £20 each.

Flanagan's Folk Four

Andy Leggett came to Bristol in 1966 to work on the Concorde project at Filton. He moved into a top floor flat in Pembroke Road, Clifton, and found that the chap living in the flat across the hall was Adge Cutler, who was just putting together the Wurzels. Leggett has some nice anecdotes about finding Cutler locked out of his flat and so climbing out of his own window – on the top floor, remember – shuffling around the building to clamber into Cutler's window to open the door from the inside. Evidently this happened more than once!

Bristol folk

Leggett was soon playing on the local scene with Patrick Spearing[130] and got together with Mike Flanagan and Roger White at the Troubadour in early 1967 to form Flanagan's Folk Four. Flanagan was from Galway and Spearing was from Northern Ireland so they played a mix of Irish material, always popular in Bristol. The band briefly became a five piece when Richard Lee joined after overhearing the band rehearsing. Andy Leggett explains:

> One day we were rehearsing in Pat Spearing's front room - one of those huge flats facing onto the terrace of Royal York Crescent. A neighbour passing by liked what he heard, knocked on the door and asked if he could join us on fiddle. This was Richard Lee … At about that time Roger White was on the point of parting company, so in effect Richard replaced him.[131]

During this changeover stage the group was recorded by Derek Burgoygne over two nights at the Troubadour and both old and new line-ups were recorded, as was Roger White as a soloist. The subsequent LP was called *Troubadour Folk* and was limited to 99 copies, so as to preclude payment of Purchase Tax. Flanagan's Folk Four's tracks were *Hear the Wind Blow, Cooley's Reel & the Mason's Apron* and *The Star of the County Down*. The other artists on the LP were Mudge and Clutterbuck, Adrienne, "Big Brian" Webb and Graham Kilsby. Someone borrowed Andy Leggett's copy and never gave it back – own up, who's got it? Meanwhile, Leggett's memories of the recording go thus:

> On "Hear the wind blow" Roger White sings the verses, while Patrick Spearing and Mike Flanagan add harmony and bass lines. Roger, Pat and I were all on guitars, my contribution being the occasional obbligato bits … For Cooley's Reel and the Mason's Apron, Roger is out and Richard in. Patrick plays guitar, Richard fiddle, Mike thunders away on a bodhran, and I start off on a tin whistle and switch eventually to banjo … The "Star of the County Down" is sung by Mike Flanagan, again with Patrick on guitar and harmonising on the choruses. Richard is on fiddle and I think I'm playing one of those Indian bamboo flute things found in shops smelling of joss-sticks.[132]

The line-up with Richard Lee now decided to record an LP and this is by far the rarest Bristol folk record, though oddly not the most highly-valued. The LP was again recorded by Derek Burgoygne and only four copies were pressed, one for each of the band members. The recording took place in, as Andy Leggett says:

> … the echoing back room of my freezing top floor flat at 26 Cotham Grove. Only four copies were made as we were all skint. It's an acetate ("Gosport Sound Products") with no designed sleeve, of course, just a brown paper job.[133]

As already mentioned, thanks to the ethnic make-up of the group, they were happy to play all sorts of Irish music, of which Leggett says:

> … Henry Joy and the Valley of Knockanure are Republican songs which we wouldn't have dreamed of putting out later on once the Troubles had restarted. We felt we had some justification at the time, as Mike Flanagan was from [Galway], whereas Pat Spearing was from Fermanagh, so we performed music from both Northern and Southern Irish cultures quite happily.[134]

When the group broke up, Andy Leggett joined the Alligator Jug Thumpers, which sort of evolved into the Pigsty Hill Light Orchestra, before he left to play with a bewildering variety of local and National jazz bands, as well as arranging and writing material for Sweet Substitute. Mike Flanagan is now in Tasmania, whilst Patrick Spearing lives in Canada. Richard Lee remains local, and still practises as an architect in Bristol.

Values for the two LPs are very hard to determine. It is unlikely that any of the four Flanagan's Folk Four acetates will ever enter the collectors' market, so making up a value out of thin air seems a bit pointless, but the Pigsty Hill Light Orchestra connection would suggest that there would certainly be a market should a copy surface. There is just a little more possibility of a copy of the *Troubadour Folk* LP turning up, and because of the inclusion of Mudge and Clutterbuck, and Dave Mudge's later phantom Village Thing presence, this is likely to sell for somewhere higher than £100, though as this LP is all but unknown on the collectors' circuit, it is again hard to assign a value.

Folkal Point

This group recorded the highest-valued LP to come out of Bristol, though not much is known about them. From mid-1972, they had weekly residencies at the Adam and Eve pub in Clifton Wood, where they played on Tuesdays between 8.30 and 10.30, and at the Alma Tavern, near Clifton Down Station, where they played on Wednesdays, also between 8.30 and 10.30 – 10.30 being closing time for pubs in those days. The group consisted of Cherie Musialik on vocals, Martin Steed on lead guitar, Paul Cook on lead and rhythm, Stuart Amesbury on rhythm and Brian Murray on bass. Murray and Amesbury also sang. They played mainly in an acoustic vein but also ventured into an electric folk sound on occasion.

The group made a self-titled LP for the Midas label, which was an early offshoot of the Folk Heritage label. The cover drawing of the Clifton Suspension Bridge was done by local artist, Griffin, who seems to have always been secretive about his (or her?) first name. Plenty of pubs in the Bristol area sport prints by Griffin, which tends to indicate that their last refurbishment was either in the late 1970s or early 1980s, when these prints were very popular. Meanwhile, the LP was issued in 1972 and only 500 copies were pressed, and if that wasn't enough to create a future rarity, half of the LPs are reputed to have been destroyed in a flood. Sales of the LP were not great and many of the undamaged copies are rumoured to have remained unsold – somewhere in Clifton, someone may have a good few thousand pounds' worth of records sitting about in a dusty old box in the attic.

Still, there is more to making one of the record collecting scene's most sought-after folk records than there not being many copies around – though this helps – the record also has to be good. Not only is the Folkal Point LP good, but it is considered by many to be one of the best 'psych-folk' LPs around with reviews tending to eulogise the LP. The author's own views don't go quite that far – it is certainly a pleasant enough LP with the two opening tracks probably being the best of the bunch due to some very nice guitar interplay.

Bristol folk

> Bristol area outfit Folkal Point ... is an obvious delight, with elements likely to attract almost anyone with an ear for gentle rural 1970s sounds with psych overtones. Sweet female vocals ... from Cherie Musialik are gorgeous to a point where I have to cast a wide net to come up with comparisons; but if you can imagine a warm tone halfway between the girl-child charms of Vasthi (sic) Bunyan and the lush village-beauty sound of early Mandy Morton, then I guess we're in the right shire.[135]

The songs on the album included traditional fare, gospel and modern songs. In fact, pretty much the same fare played by many semi-pro folk bands around the country at that time.

In 1973 Folkal Point's only other vinyl outing was on the cheap compilation. *Sweet Sir Galahad* from the Midas LP was included on a compilation of Folk Heritage label artists, called *Folk Heritage*. This compilation has one other point of note – one of the other songs, by a group called Parke, is *Dancers of Stanton Drew*. The group was not local, but Stanton Drew is, being a small village about six miles south of Bristol and famous for its stone circles. These 'dancers' are reputed to be a wedding party that was petrified after dancing to the Devil's pipes past Saturday midnight and into the Sabbath – an old and widely-found legend, but none the worse for that. If you're in the area, the stones are worth a visit, but don't forget to put a couple of quid into the collection box – and don't worry the sheep.

As to values, it might be time to hold your breath. The Midas label LP, if in near-new condition, tends to sell for upwards of £500 with the last known near new copies selling on eBay in 2005 for £1,298 and in 2006 for £1,300. Even the compilation goes for somewhere between £8 and £35 depending on condition, thanks to including tracks by not only Folkal Point but also Gallery, whose Midas label LP is another one that sells for over £1,000.

Kelvin Henderson

Bristol-born Kelvin Henderson was initially influenced by the folk and blues of Woody Guthrie and Ramblin' Jack Elliott, followed by rock and roll, courtesy of Carl Perkins and the like. Henderson played in a duo for a while with Dave Gould on banjo and was also joined on occasion by Bob Stewart. In 1966, Henderson moved briefly to Ireland and played with The Cotton Mill Boys, who scored several big hits on the Irish charts and later seem to have plummeted to obscurity after appearing on Opportunity Knocks in the mid-1970s.

In 1967, back in Bristol, Henderson co-ran a folk club in Lawford Gate, called Folk Under Cover, and started a short-lived folk/country magazine with the same name, which ran for about three issues. He then decided to tour around Europe. The upshot of this was that he ended up in Sweden for two years and, whilst there, he put together a country band made up of local musicians. They made two LPs for Polydor, though Henderson moved back to Bristol before the second LP, *Songs for Travellin'*, was released, his return to the UK being documented in the June 1972 edition of Preview[136]. Neither LP was issued in the UK despite Polydor in London being sent the masters for consideration. Other labels showed interest in licensing the records, but nothing came of this and the two Swedish LPs seldom appear for sale now, though when they do they tend to be fairly cheap[137].

Bristol folk

Henderson called on Dave Gould again and added a lead guitarist and drummer. The subsequent band played locally as well as gigging further afield, becoming a popular live draw and winning respect amongst younger fans for playing not just the expected standards but a choice of newer material from up-and-coming country writers. In 1974 Henderson took part in the Jimmy Payne Show and released the *Kelvin Henderson Country Band* LP on the Westwood label. Reaction to the LP was mixed: firstly, the sound fidelity wasn't particularly good – a noted problem with several Westwood releases, which were generally recorded on a very tight budget; secondly, it presented too wide a range of styles for many country fans' tastes – country fans, along with progressive rock fans, tend to be conservative in taste and loath progress in their respective genres.

In 1975 *Slow Movin' Outlaw* was issued on the budget Windmill label, complete with sleeve notes from Bryan Chalker, editor of the *Country Music Review* magazine. Although on a budget label, the production was superior to that on the previous LP. The band on the LP comprised Henderson on vocals and acoustic guitar, Stewart Barnes on lead and other guitars, Dave Gould on bass, Pete Wisher on pedal steel and Al Saxon on keyboards. Backing vocals were by Jeannie Denver, another stalwart on the country scene, and Barnes left soon after this recording to join Denver's popular JD Band.

The band continued to play the circuit, including playing with American country stars, such as Slim Whitman and Vernon Oxford, and also played the Wembley Country Music Festival on two occasions. However, the club scene in the UK didn't exactly pay well for home-grown country bands and in 1976 Henderson took a break from the gig circuit and let the band break up. In 1977 he put together another band, again including Dave Gould, and made the popular *Black Magic Gun* LP on Checkmate, a specialist country music label. As Henderson said:

> I feel that in 1976 I was stagnant. The band was not really what I wanted and I never seemed to be able to progress. Now this is all changed. I have high hopes of the album and the band, now, is the best I think I've had.[138]

The line-up on the LP included Ian Lawrence – who had previously been with Shaking Stevens and the Sunsets – on dobro, Dave Sheriff on harmonica, Larry Newman on lead guitar, Kenny Green on drums, Drew Taylor on fiddle, Derek Thurlby on pedal steel and lead guitar, Gerry Hogan on pedal steel and Dave Knowles on tenor sax. On the road, the band was made up of Henderson, Gould, Thurlby and Green: Lawrence had been in Henderson's band for almost two years, and although on the LP had left by this time. Reviews of the LP were generally enthusiastic, as were reviews of the band themselves:

> They are an appealing team and acquit themselves well on low-key numbers, whilst really excelling on kick-out-the-jams boogie-ing music. They have been hailed by many fellow musicians and now the Country public at large is beginning to appreciate their simplistic energy and cheerful approach to the art of propagating good Country music.[139]

In the autumn of 1977, Henderson made a pilgrimage to Nashville to meet old acquaintances, such as Jimmy Payne, pick up musical tips and hear new songs direct from the songwriters. His reputation and ability was such that he was asked to play on several radio shows whilst over there. In late 1977 the band was one of those chosen to play at the Merseyside's 2nd Annual Country Music Awards Show. They were judged to be the best live act at the show, despite some reservations that their material strayed too far on the Waylon Jennings and Willie Nelson side.

Henderson remained an evangelist for modern country music and continued to make records, including the self-titled *Kelvin Henderson* LP on GMP in 1978 and the *Country Comes West* TV tie-in LP on Chopper in 1979. He was still performing until recently with what is believed to be the longest established professional country band in the UK, with Dave Gould still in the line-up. Nowadays, Henderson is perhaps better remembered for his *Country Comes West* TV series and as a presenter of BBC South and West's *My Style of Country* radio show. To bring the story up to date, Henderson was inducted into the British Country Music Hall Of Fame in 2008 for his contribution to the furtherance of British Country music.

You *shouldn't* have to pay more than £10 for any of the LPs, except for the Westwood one, which can be anything up to £25. That said, the GMP and Chopper LPs are both difficult to find, as are the Swedish Polydor LPs, and it is possible that you *may* have to pay more. Generally on the few occasions that they surface they sell for around the £10 mark, but more recent copies have been seen with asking prices of up to £30. Whether they will sell for this is another matter. The 1979 Chevron reissue of *Slow Moving Outlaw* should be around £5.

Hunt and Turner

> Touring the folk-clubs and Universities of Britain with a heady mixture of rag-time, self-penned lovesongs and good-time, 70s acoustic ballads, Hunt and Turner became one of the most popular duos of their era.[140]

John Turner had been in Mike Storm and the Comets before joining the Downsiders. When the Troubadour opened, in 1966, Turner's bass seemed to have its own place against the wall behind whoever happened to be playing and, like many of the regulars, he would often join other acts. Turner moved into the flat above the club and was later put in charge by the Troubadour's new owner, after the club's founder, Ray Willmott, had returned to Australia. The Downsiders did not make any records in their own right, but did play on Dave (Mudge) and Tim (Clutterbuck)'s *Sheep* EP on Saydisc, for which they received a sleeve credit. Turner then joined the Pigsty Hill Light Orchestra, though his next recording credit was for "base fiddle" on an LP by Pat Small's group, the West County Three.

In December 1969, Turner, along with Ian Anderson, started to put together the Village Thing agency and record label. One of the reasons for starting their own record label was because Turner had been concerned about the recording future of the Pigsty Hill Light Orchestra. The group was offered a contract with Argo but three out of the four members decided that their future lay with the new Village Thing label, and consequently the group recorded the new label's first LP. Not content with running a club, co-running an agency and record company and playing in a touring group, Turner found time to play on the next four Village Thing LPs, these being by Sun Also Rises, Ian A. Anderson, Wizz Jones and Steve Tilston.

In mid-1970, however, Turner left and formed a duo with celebrated local guitarist, Ian Hunt, who was also on the Village Thing agency's books. Turner said of his leaving:

> … as much as I loved the good-time humour we did, I wasn't really into the jazz we played. I preferred a more contemporary style which sounded out of place with typical Pigsty material, so when the chance arose, I left to play with Ian.[141]

Hunt, who was signed to the Village Thing agency was no stranger to playing on Village Thing LPs. On the Pigsty Hill Light Orchestra's LP he played on a John Turner composition, which predicted the future somewhat. Later in the year, after playing a pop festival at Pilton[142] in September, he played on Ian A. Anderson's *Royal York Crescent*. After hooking up with John Turner, Hunt later played on Fred Wedlock's *The Folker* LP, where he did a very good imitation of Stefan Grossman on Wedlock's 'instructional' *Lurn Theeself Fawk*. Wedlock credited him with "flashy guitar" – in fact, Grossman's style was a great influence on Hunt, as it was on many other guitarists. Hunt, by now sporting a natty moustache, also played on Ian A. Anderson's *A Vulture Is Not a Bird You Can Trust*, which was recorded at Rockfield Studios in deepest Monmouthshire.

Both Hunt and Turner wrote songs and continued to be in demand for playing on other people's records in between their own gigs on the university circuit and the folk club scene. Turner played barefoot in best Sandie Shaw style - in an interview with *Preview* magazine[143] he claimed that this was because he had no shoes! As well as playing around the country, the duo was one of the resident acts at the White on Black Folk Club at the Arts Centre on King's Square, Bristol, where they alternated with White on Black, Adrienne and others.

Originally, the duo had intended to record an LP during December 1971 and early 1972 for a March release, as reported in the December 1971 issue of *Dogpress*. However, this schedule slipped and, as was noted in the Melody Maker: "Hunt and Turner's album, scheduled for May, has been put back to September as the duo are finding it hard to fit recording sessions into their schedule of gigs."[144] Squidd members, John Merritt and Rodney Matthews, played electric bass and percussion respectively on the sessions and when *Magic Landscape* was finally issued it got universally excellent reviews and reached number 6 in the *Melody Maker* folk charts. The duo continued playing on other people's records in-between their own gigging schedule and even the fact that they broke up in early 1973 didn't stop them both performing on Rod Neep's *Heading for the Sun* that same year and on the follow-up, *I Give You the Morning*, in 1974.

Turner continued to session on Village Thing LPs, including playing on the label's final LP, *Murf*, by Noel Murphy, and now became more closely involved with Saydisc, producing and playing on many of that label's records. These were as diverse as those by popular folk group, White on Black, and that of close-harmony group, Five In a Bar, where he also played guitar. The Five in a Bar LP included one of Turner's compositions, *Lady of Fortune*, after which the album was named. Turner had another string to his bow, having joined BBC Bristol with whom he presented popular shows on both radio and TV. He retired in 2007.

Back with Ian Hunt, Rod Neep's *I Give You the Morning* LP had comprised covers of Tom Paxton songs and Paxton, who had recently moved to the UK, was so enamoured of Ian Hunt's guitar playing on this LP that Hunt was invited to both tour and record with him. Hunt continued to play in both Bristol and London and almost played on an Al Stewart tour. Stewart came to Bristol to see if he could put together a backing band, having previously used the Bristol-based Canton Trig on two tours. A band was duly formed, made up of Ian Hunt on guitar, Graham Smith, who had been in Canton Trig, on bass and Tony Bird, currently with Kind Hearts and English, on drums. They rehearsed furiously and played one gig with Stewart at the Stonehouse. The whole thing was deemed a success, but somehow it all fell though and Stewart toured with a different band. Ian Hunt next went on to achieve 'exposure' in the Joan Collins film, *The Stud*. During the film, Hunt walks past in the background and, according to the Bristol set, with his well-documented height and good looks, manages to steal the scene.

Although he did not record commercially again during the 1970s, Hunt recorded for library albums issued by De Wolfe. These were not available to the public, but it is likely that you have heard Hunt's playing on radio and TV as several adverts used his music. He's still making extremely good albums, which evince J. J. Cale and Lowell George influences in amongst the more obvious Delta blues influences, though the only way to buy them is to go and see him play. Sadly, for Bristol-based folk fans, he is no longer in Bristol and gigs in the West Country are few and far between, though he did play both Troubadour Reunion concerts. At the second reunion he smilingly refused to play the Hunt & Turner-era *Silver Lady* and instead played echo-plexed electric guitar very loudly. A near perfect copy of the Village Thing LP will set you back around £40.

Erik Ilott

Bristol-born Ilott served with both the Merchant and Royal Navies and saw active service on destroyers, cruisers and battleships during the Second World War. He was a member of the Bristol Shiplover's Society, which had been formed in 1931 and had also included Stanley Slade[145] of Pill, from an earlier generation of Bristol shanty men, amongst its number. Ilott accompanied himself on banjo, autoharp, concertina and bones[146] and began to write songs about his experiences at sea to complement his more traditional fare.

Ilott was a natural singer with an innate feel for the songs he sang and each performance of a song tended to be different:

> A professional musician said that Erik must never learn musical theory … Many folk song collectors have altered songs to make them "right" in terms of conventional music theory … Erik's songs are good just the way that he sings them.[147]

Bristol folk

Ilott was one of the last of a dying breed, a singer unfettered by the conventions of musical theory, who knew innately how the songs should be sung. He began to sing professionally and performed around the folk clubs, such as at the Folk Tradition Club, billing himself simply as *Erik Ilott, Shanty Man* or *The Bristol Shantyman* and gaining a reputation as an authentic and charismatic performer.

> The first time I played my bones in public for years was down at the [Folk Tradition] club at the *Old Duke*. I didn't know anyone was interested. It was only Stan Hugill who got me down.[148]

In the early 1970s, Ilott was commissioned to record a tape of Bristol-related sea shanties for the launch celebrations of the new Royal Navy Type 82 destroyer, H.M.S. Bristol[149]. The songs were shanties and forbitters collected from members of the Bristol Shiplover's Society over the years, including some from Stanley Slade. The tape was so popular that Ilott was often asked to make the tape available, which led in 1973 to the recording of an LP on Ilott's own Folk'sle label. The LP was called, suitably enough, *Shipshape & Bristol Fashion* with the subtitle *Sea Songs*. On the record Ilott was supported by Ray Andrews, now considered to have been one of the finest of the English style banjo finger pickers. Andrews had been known as *Bristol's Boy Banjoist* when he first started playing publicly in the 1930s and, although a land lubber, his father had been a seaman on the Elder Dempster Line: Andrews' affinity with playing sea shanties is perhaps as a result to his having learned banjo from his father. The other musicians on the LP were Roger Digby on mandolin and tin whistle, Alan Tod on fiddle, Gerald Hayles on percussion and Philip Hayles on guitar. All bar Andrews joined in with the choruses too.

Ilott played with Ray Andrews into the 1980s. In 1974 the pair competed at the Llangollen Festival, evidently coming second to Portugal having played a selection of George Formby and Gilbert and Sullivan tunes amongst more traditional material. In the late 1970s, Ilott recorded Andrews for a cassette issue, *Banjo Maestro*, again released on Folk'sle. Ilott was then recorded for a compilation LP called *The Shanty Men* which was released on Joe Stead's Greenwich Village label in 1978. Ilott appeared alongside singers such as Alex Campbell and John Tems singing *Whisky Johnny* and *Put Your Shoulder Next to Mine*.

There was also one oddity that included Ilott – a two-sided 7" flexidisc called *Sounds of the Sea*, issued in a booklet sleeve by Ribena sometime in the 1970s. It is narrated by Michael Aspel with sound effects from the BBC, Edwin Mickleburgh's collection and the Saydisc Electronic Workshop, amongst others, with shanties sung by Ilott. Gef Lucena explains:

> … Saydisc did the recording of Michael Aspel which was at The Meeting House, Frenchay and added the other bits in studio – I think the Saydisc Electronic Workshop amounted to our engineer David Wilkins adding manipulated 'white noise' from a radio tuner to simulate the seven seas![150]

Ilott became involved with various Morris Dancing teams during the 1980s, becoming an honorary member of the Bristol Morris Men and the Earlsdon Morris Men from Coventry.

For the last few months of his life, in 1986, Ilott lived in Bishop Road in the Bishopston area of Bristol: when he died his funeral took place at the Spiritualist church in Cairns Road. After Ilott's death the two Morris teams kept his memory alive with the *National Erik Ilott Day* and *Memorial Tour*, where they danced and spent a lot of time in pubs.

Shipshape & Bristol Fashion is no longer as common around Bristol as it used to be and, complete with booklet, could set you back anything up to £30. *The Shanty Men* compilation LP should cost around £10. The *Sounds of the Sea* flexidisc shouldn't cost more than £5.

Independent Folk/Cul-de-Sac

Independent Folk was formed at Bristol Grammar School in autumn 1976 and comprised five teachers and two sixth form students. To begin with they played at school events, but once the student faction was old enough to play on licensed premises they began to play folk clubs, though using the name Cul-de-Sac on these dates. The group's repertoire was an intelligent mix of traditional material and modern songs by the likes of Richard Thompson (the less well-known *Albion Sunrise*, written by Thompson for the Albion Country Band), Gordon Lightfoot (*Early Morning Rain*), Leon Rosselson (*Across the Hills*) and Sydney Carter (*Lord of the Dance*), plus crowd-pleasing singalongs like *Liverpool Lou* and more introspective songs such as *Peat Bog Soldiers*, which was written by Rudi Goguel in a concentration camp in the 1930s.

The group was made up of Mike Speake on double bass, guitar and whistle, Jon Wride on guitar, Peter Drewett on violin, Dorinda Offord on recorder and percussion, Jon Edwards on guitar and banjo, Graham Fellows on whistles, hammered dulcimer and spoons and Graham Anderson on concertina and tabor. All bar Drewett and Wride sang. In 1977 they made their only LP, *Independent Folk*, and income from sales of the LP supported the fund raising activities of The Friends of Bristol Grammar School. The LP was recorded at Mushroom Studios in West Mall, and was released on the Great Western Records label – both the studios and the record label were part of Dema Directions Ltd. The LP was pressed by Lyntone, a company more often associated with manufacture of flexidiscs.

The two students, Jon Wride and Peter Drewett, left in 1977 and Jonathan Edwards also left at the same time. The group continued but no more recordings were forthcoming. As to value, the LP is currently unknown on the collectors' scene, but a copy has been rumoured to have changed hands recently for around £30, though in the West Country you are just as likely to find the odd copy in a charity shop for a quid or two. This one is a future rarity and if you are lucky enough to find a copy, keep it for a while and see if the investment turns out to be a good one … and if not, you can still play it because, despite the cheesy photo on the front, which was probably done to please the School Governors, it is a decent enough LP by working musicians – you can sense a certain hesitancy in some of the playing, especially from the younger members, but that doesn't necessarily spoil things.

Al Jones

Al Jones moved to Bristol in 1966 when his job with Pye Electronics brought him to Filton. Almost on arrival, his landlady pointed him toward a local folk club and Jones immediately involved himself in the Bristol folk scene. He linked up with Ian Anderson and harmonica player, Elliot Jackson, going out under the name of Anderson, Jones, Jackson. When the Troubadour opened in 1966, Anderson, Jones, Jackson was the first group to play there, becoming a regular fixture with a residency. When the Folk Blues Bristol and West club, started by Anderson in 1967, moved from the Troubadour to the Old Duke in King Street, the group maintained a residency there and also supported national artists.

Meanwhile, back in December 1966, the trio made an EP for Saydisc, with the recording taking place at the Quaker Meeting House in Frenchay. The session included Noel (King George V) Sheldon, another Folk Blues Bristol and West resident, who still plays around the Bristol area occasionally. With their first record under their belts, the trio played further afield, appearing at Les Cousins folk club in London. In early 1967, Jones played on two tracks on Graham Kilsby's *In a Folk Mood* EP – these were *Chastity Belt*, which was recorded live at the Troubadour, and *Man of Constant Sorrow*. Around this time Jones replaced Barry Back in the Alligator Jug Thumpers for a tour of Devon, but no-one seems to remember for sure quite when this was. Of this period, Ian Anderson explains:

> We recorded the Anderson, Jones, Jackson EP in December '66, got voted Bristol's most popular group in the Troubadour Poll in spring '67, then Al started heading off regularly to London at the invitation of John Renbourn. But not before … we'd been offered an album by early Fleetwood Mac [and] Chicken Shack producer Mike Vernon at Decca – one of those mirage deals that never actually came off.[151]

In 1967, Jones moved to London and his friendship with John Renbourn led to rumours that he was to join Pentangle. After exposure on the London scene, including a certain amount of tutting from blues purists when Jones played his Buddy Holly medley, he was signed, on the suggestion of Ian Anderson, by Sandy Roberton's September Productions, who got him a one-off deal with Parlophone, then the home of the Beatles[152]. Anderson says:

> Sandy Roberton had asked me about other artists I'd recommend for him to produce, so I'd naturally introduced him to Al Jones who got an unsatisfactory Parlophone album out of it. One or the other of us introduced Sandy to Keith Christmas and Keith in turn introduced him to Shelagh MacDonald. So there was quite a chain of events from my signing that helped put the Bristol scene on the discographical map in the early '70s.[153]

The recording sessions for the Parlophone LP took place between 5th and 13th March 1969 at Sound Techniques Studios in London and included Percy Jones from The Liverpool Scene, Harold McNair and Gordon Huntley, the latter of whom went on to enjoy a number one hit single with Matthews Southern Comfort. March was a fairly productive month for Jones and a gig at Les Cousins was recorded on the 17th. Two more tracks were recorded in April 1969 at the same studio as the album and these were put out on a 1970 RCA Victor compilation album, *49 Greek Street*[154]. The Parlophone album was slow in appearing and was finally advertised in the music press during September but, when released, it didn't sell well and it has a very silly price tag on the few occasions that it surfaces.

It seems odd in hindsight that as Jones was so involved in the blues scene that his Parlophone LP, *Alun Ashworth Jones*, should be considered an almost perfect example of what is now referred to as 'acid-folk' or 'psych-folk', though Jones later told the Melody Maker that he didn't think the LP was a true reflection of his style[155]. Jones did not have a happy time with Parlophone and he soon returned to Bristol with just a brief return to London, along with John Turner, to back Ian Anderson on a session for the World Service Rhythm and Blues programme in September 1969. Toward the end of 1969, both Jones and Anderson toured Belgium briefly along with Dave Kelly and on his return Jones stated to the music press that he nowadays enjoyed playing with the Pigsty Hill Light Orchestra: "Whenever I can, I get the Pigsty Hill Light Orchestra to back me on rock numbers, as they are right in the idiom of rock and roll."[156] The mind boggles.

Nothing was forthcoming with the live tracks recorded early in 1969 and all plans to record another album were thwarted for the next couple of years. For example, in December 1970 there was news that Jones was recording an album with local singer and guitarist Adrienne Webber. As Webber said, "A company representative heard us singing together and decided to use us both for the LP."[157] All the songs on the LP were to be Jones' compositions including *Earthworks* and *Lady Lee*. However, nothing came of this and neither of these songs were ever recorded. There was, however, some TV exposure the same month, when Jones and Webber appeared on a local TV programme, *Folk in the West*, along with the Pigsty Hill Light Orchestra, Fred Wedlock and Devon-based trio, The Westwind. Jones next came to the attention of Bill Leader, who had recorded many classic LPs for Transatlantic. He had recently set up his own Leader and Trailer folk labels and recordings with Jones were made in 1971 at Leader's home in Camden. Again these were not released and the tapes were given to Jones: these tracks plus the live tracks from 1969 were finally released as bonus tracks on the reissue CD of *Alun Ashworth Jones*.

The November 1971 issue of *Dogpress* reported that Jones and family had moved to Cornwall and that he was concentrating on non-musical pastimes. In 1972, however, things began to look up on the recording front. *Searching the Desert*, one of Jones' early blues recordings from the British Blues Boom-era, was included on the Village Thing compilation, *Matchbox Days*. This attracted good reviews and Ian Anderson went about persuading Jones to come back to Bristol to record another album. He did and *Jonesville* was duly released in 1973, complete with a Rodney Matthews sleeve design. The LP was produced by Anderson and included Pete Moody, on bass, Dave Gillis on electric piano and organ, Graham Smith on harmonica and jazz drummer, Tony Fennel. The last local recording Jones made was with Bristol folk trio, White on Black, playing along with the Pigsty Hill Light Orchestra's Jon 'Wash' Hays and Decanter's Ritchie Gould. The White on Black LP was recorded in 1973 and issued in 1974. He then appeared on the first Hot Vultures LP with Ian Anderson and Maggie Holland in 1975, and that was it until the 1990s.

Jones was settled in Cornwall, where he developed a range of pickups for acoustic guitars, using the experience he had gained with the Pye Electronics group in the 1960s. In the 1990s Jones found himself back writing songs and playing local gigs in Cornwall. In 2002 he played at the first Troubadour Reunion and he appeared on the CD of that concert playing both solo and as part of the for-one-night-only reformation of Anderson, Jones, Jackson. In 2008 came the news that Al Jones had died at 62. The following was written by Ian Anderson on hearing of Jones' death.

> ... Al decided to head in the opposite direction to the music business and moved to Cornwall, where he briefly became a coastguard ... He was also developing the Ashworth range of instrument pickups which became his main business, and later, with guitar maker Nigel Thornbory, the extraordinary little rubber-stringed Ashbory basses, much sought after by session musicians and still made under licence by Fender ... All his early works ... were released as the double CD *All My Friends Are Back Again* by Castle just last year. Hearing it all again really brought it home what an original guitarist and supremely clever songwriter he was ...[158]

Any Al Jones records that you are lucky enough to find are going to cost you quite a lot. The Anderson, Jones, Jackson EP was a strictly limited edition and copies do not surface often: it is likely to cost you somewhere around £60. The Graham Kilsby EP was also a limited edition of 99 copies and Jones' inclusion is likely to mean that any copy of this that surfaces should sell for £30 or more. Things don't get much better with the Parlophone LP and it will cost you something close to £200. Even the Village Thing LP could set you back about £50. The White on Black LP seems to have peaked at around £70 ten or so years ago when Jones' inclusion became widely-known in folk collecting circles, but it has now settled down to a more sedate £25 or so, since collectors realised how many copies there are about. The *49 Greek Street* compilation on RCA Victor is difficult to find and a near mint copy of this could cost anything up to £30.

Graham Kilsby

Graham Kilsby started singing in the Church Choir at St. Albans in Westbury Park and later sang for a short while at Bristol Cathedral. In 1955 he began broadcasting on *Children's Hour* and progressed to solo broadcasting in *Chapel on The Hill*. From 1960 to 1965 Kilsby worked as a photographer with the Evening Post and Western Daily Press, during which time he started to sing around Bristol and Bath's folk clubs. As Kilsby says:

> The folk scene when I started was singing at the various Bristol Folk Clubs, mostly at the Bathurst in Cumberland Basin in the 60's, even singing at the Poetry and Folk Club there, but a few of us often went over to Bath and the Hat and Feather Pub which had a folk club.[159]

In 1965, he was one of the local artists featured on Saydisc's first LP, *Bristol Folks*, on which he performed *Dona, Dona, Dona*, a translation of the Yiddish song, and *Farewell*, which comprised Bob Dylan's words to the tune of *The Leaving of Liverpool*. This LP was a limited edition of 99 copies to preclude payment of Purchase Tax, which kicked in on

Bristol folk

pressing runs of 100 and over, and is very rare indeed. In 1966 the Troubadour opened in Clifton Village, and this became a magnet for the area's folk singers. Of the Troubadour, Kilsby said, "All of us sort of met up at The Troub … They were great times, and an amazing time for creating music."[160]

In 1967 Kilsby appeared on another Bristol folk LP, this one recorded over two evenings at the Troubadour and called *Troubadour Folk*. Kilsby's songs were *Suzanne* and *The Old Man of the Sea*, a tribute to Francis Chichester, who had recently sailed around the world in *Gypsy Moth*. Again, the LP was a limited edition of 99 copies, issued on the local Kernow label. Kilsby also performed *The Old Man of the Sea* on HTV News, accompanied by Al Jones and, along with Jones on twelve string guitar and John Turner on stand up bass, Kilsby later performed on the BBC TV folk show *In a Folk Mood*. This gave its name to Kilsby's first record, an EP issued by Saydisc, and again a limited press of 99 copies. Three of the tracks, *She's Like the Swallow*, *Man of Constant Sorrow* and *Keep the Willow*, were recorded at Frenchay, and *Chastity Belt* was recorded live at the Troubadour, as the sleeve notes attest:

> … he is a very popular entertainer … as can be heard from CHASTITY BELT: a neo-Elizabethan song recorded live at the Bristol Troubadour Club. Graham's several voices are joined by Alun Jones-12 string guitar, Patrick Small-guitar and vocal, Fred Wedlock-bicycle horn and frenzied applause …

She's Like the Swallow was an American ballad from a collection by Maud Karpeles and *Keep the Willow* had words by Bristol writer, Berry McDonald, to Kilsby's music. Al Jones played twelve string guitar on *Man of Constant Sorrow*, which included traditional words with the tune revised by Fred Wedlock.

According to the Western Daily Press, at some point in 1967 Kilsby was to record for EMI under the name Buddy Graham, but it is unlikely that any records were released – certainly nothing under the assumed name of Buddy Graham is known about on the collector's scene: as Ian Anderson says:

> … the Western Daily Press had a weekly folk column from maybe April to the end of 1967 under different titles - Folk Spot/The Flowerpot (!)/Folk Routes - and it first reported that he'd made a single of a Dave Mudge song for EMI, to be released under the name Buddy Graham, then later that it had been shelved and he was about to record "Suzanne" (presumably the Leonard Cohen song) and "Bristol Fashion" with Al Jones on guitar. I have no recall on whether that was ever released.[161]

Kilsby also kept up his old hobby of photography – his photos were used on the first two Crofters EPs. The last known Kilsby photo credit was on Ian A. Anderson's first Village Thing LP, *Royal York Crescent*.

> Doing the various photographs for the various albums was a result of being a photographer for the Evening Post and Western Daily Press from 1960 until 65. So all the gang got pictures free, so to speak.[162]

Bristol folk

Kilsby played other styles and, mostly through agents Arthur Parkman or Peter Burman, had regular gigs in clubs in the Welsh valleys. Kilsby remembers that some of the purists did not take kindly to someone playing music other than folk.

> I was the "non folky" one who started getting gigs outside of the folk world … I remember coming back to the Troubadour from doing cabaret at Ashton Court Country Club and everyone looking at me very strangely when I got up to sing. It was not the thing to do. You were either folk or not folk, you didn't sing in both places.[163]

Back in a folk style, Kilsby did some concerts at The Little Theatre, as opening act for The Settlers, who are probably best remembered for *The Lightning Tree*, the theme to the TV series, *Follyfoot*. Under the name Tony Graham, Kilsby played on Adge Cutler's 1968 *Wurzelrama* road-show along with, the Dave Collett Trio, Fred Wedlock, the Alligator Jug Thumpers and Chas McDevitt & Shirley Douglas. McDevitt asked Kilsby to record with him in London: Kilsby enjoyed the experience and caught the 'session bug'. Of the time around the early 1970s, Kilsby explains:

> I ended up getting married in 1972 (for a short time) to Julie Harrison, hostess of Alan Taylor's "Mr & Mrs". Worked at The Webbington Country Club for five years, working as compere, singer, and manager at the club, working with just about all the big names of the time. Also managed and compered … at Ashton Court Country Club for a while.

In 1973, Kilsby was signed by EMI as a writer and singer with the Hollies' producer, Ron Richards, who worked closely with George Martin. However, nothing came of this period, as Kilsby said, "Did a bunch of recordings with the orchestra at Abbey Road including Billy Joel stuff … EMI was sold, I lost my contract and the stuff was shelved."[164] In 1980, Kilsby moved to Nashville, where he wrote and recorded for Scott Turner, head of Liberty Records in California and Nashville. With Turner he finished Buddy Holly's *Am I Ever Gonna Find It?*, which was discovered in a school exercise book in a guitar case in 1981. In 1982 he went to Gilley's in Pasadena and of this time, Kilsby says:

> Wrote the Gilley's theme song as well as writing for Mickey Gilley, Johnny Lee, Brenda Lee, and Gilley's cousin Jerry Lee Lewis with the song "Rocking Down at Gilley's Tonight". Wrote the song with John Marascalco who wrote "Good Golly Miss Molly" and "Rip It Up".[165]

After getting fed up with the associated hassles inherent in being a part of the music scene - such as trying to get paid monies owed - Kilsby moved to St. Thomas in the US Virgin Islands where he acted as anchorman on *The Morning Show* for the CBS affiliate, WVWI Radio. One of the more dramatic moments came when he was sunk on his boat by *Hurricane Hugo*. He returned to Nashville in 1997 and continues to write, sing and produce, concentrating mainly on spiritual and Christian music. He renewed connections with Bristol in 2003 when involved in a project with the Bristol Heritage Collection in Tennessee, to renovate a Bristol Bolingbroke fighter-bomber, which he donated to the Bristol Aero Collection in Filton in 2007.

As regards values, all the records on which Graham Kilsby appears are problematical because they are so rare that they are unknown on the collecting circuit. *Bristol Folks* and *Troubadour Folks*, should a copy of either come to light, could easily achieve over £100. The EP, again, is likely to sell for at least £30 based on the inclusion of Al Jones.

Kind Hearts and English

Kind Hearts and English comprised songwriter and guitarist, John Tippet, and singing drummer, Tony Bird, who, in the late 1960s, had played in a band called Dawn along with Paul Birchill and Jim (later James) Warren, where they mixed original material with Byrds and Dylan covers. The January 1970 edition of Dogpress reported that Dawn was recording for an LP and that Keith Tippett had played on some of the tracks, though Tony Bird has no recollection of this. Perhaps Dogpress was short of news that month.

Early Kind Hearts rehearsals took place at the Dug Out club. Plastic Dog's Steve Webb spent some time with the group, after Squidd had split, and Paul Anstey played bass on live dates. In late 1975 local guitarist, Huw Gower, also got involved following the break-up of Magic Muscle. DJM's Phil Sampson liked the resulting demos and the band got a deal, which involved a large advance that has still not been paid off – Gower's then current band, The Dragons, was also signed by Sampson, though they only got a deal for a one-off single.

The first LP, *A Wish for a Season*, was made up of Tippet's compositions and apart from Gower, other musicians involved in the recording were Elton Dean on saxello, Brian Godding on guitar and Joe Burt on bass. The title track of the LP was dedicated to "Keith and Julie Tippetts"[166] and Keith played piano on the title track. There was also a certain amount of the Tippetts' influence in evidence amongst the other players: Dean was from London's free-jazz scene and had previously played with Keith Tippett's Band; Godding was currently with jazz rock band, Mirage, and just happened to be Julie Tippetts' brother-in-law. Burt was ex-Troggs and was nothing to do with the Tippetts, though he was currently in The Dragons with Huw Gower, which explains his presence on this particular piece of DJM product. Many of the songs were given orchestral settings by Keith Roberts and it was very obvious that money was being spent on this album.

Call Me Darling was issued as the first single, followed by *Kareen (Thank You for the Way You Are)*, backed with *A Wish for a Season*. The latter single was played regularly on BBC Radio with the b-side often used as Radio 2's closedown music. A promotional EP was put out with both tracks from the second single and *Call Me Darling* when the LP was issued on 5th November 1976.

The duo returned to Bristol to put together a band to promote the LP and pre-release white label copies were passed to prospective band members. Paul Birchill joined the band on guitar and Kevyn Jones joined on bass. Birchill had been in Mike Tobin's band, The Obsessions, in 1968 prior to joining Dawn in 1969. Jones, meanwhile, had been in the thick of things during Bristol's blues boom in 1968, playing with the short-lived Biafra Jug Band, followed by the slightly longer-lasting Pink Coffee Blues Band.

Whilst back in Bristol, Tony Bird was involved in one interesting musical episode. Al Stewart, following his success a couple of years earlier touring with Canton Trig, returned to Bristol to see if he could do the same again with more Bristol-based musicians. So it was that with furious rehearsal a band made up of Ian Hunt on guitar, Graham Smith on bass and Tony Bird on drums backed Al Stewart at a packed gig at the Stonehouse. The gig was deemed a success all round, but somehow when Stewart went on tour, it was with a completely different band.

Meanwhile, DJM looked to be on to a winner with Kind Hearts and English and the second LP, *Beachcomber*, was recorded and released indecently quickly in retrospect and although a decent LP, was not as strong as the first. Sales of *Beachcomber* were not as encouraging as those of the first LP and so it was that the third LP of a three-LPs-in-three-years deal never got recorded. Perhaps odd to note is that a breakdown of Tony Bird's royalty statements shows that Kind Hearts sold more records in California than they did in the UK. Certainly, the feel on side two of *Beachcomber*, especially, was similar to that of laid-back West Coast bands of the time.

The group broke up, though not before recording the soundtrack to a 'soft porn' film for which they ended up being paid nothing, and Tony Bird went on to well-respected Bristol bands, Looney Tunes, which unfortunately was never signed[167], and post-punk-power-pop band, The Fans, which was signed and whose singles are now highly collectable. John Tippet turned up again in the mid-1980s, playing well-received duo gigs with guitarist and singer, Samantha Howard, before moving away from the live scene. Tony Bird plays occasionally with The Carrot Crunchers, who don't otherwise get a mention because they are famously from Gloucestershire and not Bristol.

As regards values, the first LP could cost you anything up to £20, though copies surface occasionally around Bristol for around £10. *Beachcomber* is harder to find, though it shouldn't cost you more than £10 when you find a copy. The singles are surprisingly hard to find and will probably cost you anything up to £5 each. The real rarity is the promotional EP, which was issued in a picture sleeve. Expect to pay up to £10 for the EP, though don't expect to see it often.

Siobhan Lyons

Siobhan Lyons was a member of the Bristol Old Vic Theatre School and is remembered by Gef Lucena, of Saydisc, to have had a good voice. This is borne out by the fact that Lyons' one and only appearance on record was in the form of a 1966 EP on Saydisc, named *Patriot Games* after the title track. On the EP, Lyons was accompanied by John C. Edwards, who played Spanish guitar. The EP, SD 116, was a limited edition pressing of 99 copies, to preclude Purchase Tax, and was issued in a generic Saydisc picture sleeve with artist credits and track listing printed on the front. The other tracks included were *She Moved Through The Fair*, *Every Night* and *Slean Libh*. Apart from this one EP, Lyons remains a mystery - information please!

Shelagh McDonald

Shelagh McDonald became famous, not so much for her music, but for her sudden and long-term disappearance in 1972. More people know about her disappearance than have heard her music, which is a shame because she had a voice in the mould of Sandy Denny, only better, and through being signed to September Productions had access to some of the most receptive musicians around. The LPs she recorded for B&C, *Album*, and *Stargazer*, are amongst the most highly-sought after folk records on the collectors market.

McDonald first moved from Scotland to London, where she played the clubs and made some primitive recordings for the BBC *Dungeon Folk* LP, issued in January 1969. She received so little interest at this point that she gave up singing and worked in a bookshop instead. A little later, McDonald decided that this rest away from music scene had been beneficial and she moved back onto the folk scene, saying:

> The rest did me good … For a start, it taught me one thing, that I have got to sing. Like lots of others, it was something I started because it seemed rather nice, but I didn't have any real dedication to it. As a result, I got nowhere.[168]

McDonald decided to move to Bristol because of the reputation of its folk scene and was soon playing at the Troubadour, signing up with the newly-formed Village Thing agency. One review of a two day event at the Troubadour highlighted McDonald's set, which was no mean feat when the 'competition' was provided by John Martyn, Al Jones, Steve Tilston, Al Stewart, Ian Hunt, Keith Christmas, Ian Anderson, Dave Evans and Strange Fruit. Jerry Gilbert of Sounds wrote:

> … one of the best receptions of the evening went to Shelagh McDonald who has also moved to Bristol and the main feature of her set was "Silk and Leather" which spotlights her own fine guitar technique.[169]

McDonald continued to play solo at folk clubs throughout mid-1970, but no record deal was forthcoming, despite several promises. This changed when Keith Christmas invited her to play a few of her songs at one of his gigs. Sandy Roberton, who had already signed Christmas, was there and pretty much signed McDonald on the spot. Initially, McDonald wasn't convinced that anything would come of this and said:

> Keith Christmas took me to a concert with him and I did a few songs. Sandy Robertson (sic) was at the gig but I thought it was just another false promise when he mentioned recording.[170]

True to his word, Roberton organised joint recording sessions for Christmas and McDonald, from which both released LPs. The sessions included various musicians from Mighty Baby and Sandy Denny's backing band, Fotheringay. Others at the sessions were labelmate Andy Roberts, who was currently with a non-gelling band called Everyone, and London-based Bristolian jazz pianist, Keith Tippett.

Bristol folk

McDonald's LP was called *Album*, issued on B&C on 6th November, 1970. Instead of concentrating on her own compositions, she included two songs by Christmas and one each by Roberts and Gerry Rafferty. Versions of Christmas' song, *Waiting for the Wind to Rise*, appeared on both his own and McDonald's LPs and folk journalist, Karl Dallas, stated that, despite the song being written by Christmas, "… Shelagh's version gets closer to the essence of the song than Keith's."[171] The reason for including covers of other people's songs was, according to McDonald, "I could have put some more of my own songs on the album but I feel that when people are paying over £2 for an album you shouldn't put any weak stuff out."[172] This was perhaps overly modest because her second LP, comprising her own compositions, is considered to be her best.

In early 1971 McDonald decided to go, "… into semi-retirement for six months to write songs …"[173] though this didn't prevent her from appearing at the Troubadour on Friday 18th June. Before starting work on her next LP, McDonald moved to London, where she was reported to have signed with the successful Chrysalis agency – which explains why her name no longer appeared on Village Thing agency adverts after June. Sessions for *Stargazer* included a very strong line-up of Keith Christmas and Pat Donaldson, who had both played on the first LP, Richard Thompson and Dave Mattacks from Fairport Convention, Danny Thompson from Pentangle, and B&C artist, Ray Warleigh. Warleigh had also played on the sessions for the first album but had only appeared on Keith Christmas' album. Reactions to *Stargazer* were uniformly positive – except for a review in *Dogpress*, where only side 2 of the album had been provided by B&C for no adequately-explained reason[174] – and folk stardom was waiting in the wings, if only sales would match critical acclaim.

Even with two LPs under her belt, eulogies and photos in the music press and a BBC session under her belt[175], you could still see McDonald at the Crown and Anchor Hotel Folk Club in Stonehouse in January 1972 or at Cardiff's UCC & UWIST Combined Folk Club in the February for 25p a go. McDonald recorded several songs for a third LP but in April 1972 she disappeared suddenly and completely from the music scene after a damaging drug experience. Rather than giving a wrong impression about this, it should be pointed out that McDonald has been documented as someone who hadn't previously been into drugs, the event blamed partly on the appalling living conditions in which she had wound up in London, stuck on a rough estate and surrounded by undesirables. Keith Christmas said:

> … it wasn't really her – she was too nice for that. But she went and did an acid tab, had a bad one, and wound up in hospital – which I can only imagine is the worst bloody place to be while tripping. Her parents came down from Scotland and carted her off – never to be heard from or seen again …[176]

She stayed with her parents for a while but then drifted off to the extent that none of her old friends or family knew of her whereabouts, though there were many rumours, some of which were surprisingly accurate in retrospect and many purely fanciful. In those days, if there wasn't an act to promote a record release, then the records got deleted after the first pressing run, though the lack of a second press might also have been related to the record company's current financial problems. Roberton put one each of the songs recorded for the third album on the two *Club Folk* samplers, just to keep the interest up in case McDonald should return. It wasn't until the digital age that CDs of the two LPs were finally issued and a new generation started to fall in love with both the music and the romantic image of an artist who had disappeared or, perhaps, had died young and unnoticed. Her name started to be mentioned in much the same terms as those of Syd Barrett and Nick Drake.

Shelagh McDonald reappeared out of the blue in November 2005 and her reappearance was reported, complete with photos old and new, in the Scottish Daily Mail:

> Now it's very strange to hear my albums are enjoying a revival - I don't even have a copy of my original, and haven't heard it since the 1970's. I was amazed to find out people were still talking about me after all this time. I've just come forward now to let everyone know I'm safe and well.[177]

She had, as had been rumoured, been living a nomadic life around the Scottish Islands and elsewhere. A journalist put her back in touch with Keith Christmas, who, despite a 33 year gap, recognised her voice on the phone immediately. After over thirty years of mystery, it may be interesting to see what happens next, especially as McDonald said:

> The happier I have become over the years, the more my voice has improved. I am writing songs and I enjoy music again. I don't know if I would have been so popular had I not had the experience I did and disappeared. Perhaps my music would have just burned out.[178]

Dungeon Folk sells for around £60 based on McDonald's presence, though a few years ago it could be picked up for less than £10. The two B&C LPs sell for close to £200 each. The two *Club Folk* samplers with songs from the never finished third album tend to be between £10 and £15 each. There were two more compilations with McDonald tracks on: these were *Clogs*, which sells for about the same amount as the above samplers if it includes the insert and the original 99p sticker, and the *Rave On* sampler on the Mooncrest label, which also sells for around £10 to £15 if original. Original copies have a matt sleeve with artist photos on the rear. These are missing from the gloss sleeved 1976 and 1983 repressings, which both sell for around £6.

Mudge & Clutterbuck

Dave Mudge and Tim Clutterbuck met at the Troubadour in January 1967, prior to which Clutterbuck had played in a jug band, of which Ian Anderson says:

> It was The Backwater Jook Band from Weston-super-Mare which I was in too. Tim and I were at school together there ... I have a very poor acetate of [them] from the soundtrack of a TV appearance, but nothing was ever released.[179]

In November 1967, they were recorded at the Troubadour by Derek Burgoygne for the limited press *Troubadour Folk* LP, which was released on Burgoygne's Kernow label. Mudge and Clutterbuck's songs were *Whistling Kettle Blues* and *How Long, Baby, How*

Bristol folk

Long? and the LP also included songs by Flanagan's Folk Four, Adrienne Webber, "Big Brian" Webb, Graham Kilsby and Roger White: only 99 copies were pressed.

As "Dave + Tim" they recorded the *Sheep* EP for Saydisc in October 1968, on which they were backed by the Downsiders, and the pair sold the record at gigs. Mudge did most of the songwriting, specialising in 'chorus songs' that the crowd could easily learn and sing along to, whilst Clutterbuck specialised in arranging the songs. In May 1970 the music press reported that Al Stewart had persuaded them to move to London, though the news was a bit late because they had moved the previous summer and had enjoyed a residency at the Ferryboat Folk Club in Westbourne Park since December. Things were looking up – Julie Felix had recorded Mudge's *The Young Ones Move* and Clutterbuck was reported to have recorded a specially-commissioned song about Sir Francis Chichester for Westward TV. They recorded demos of a selection of Mudge's songs and record company interest was reputed to be intense[180].

Despite their burgeoning popularity, getting a recording contract proved to be a major problem and they found themselves in a chicken and egg position on the gig front, where many folk clubs wouldn't book artists unless they had an LP out, and the duo, like many others, needed to play the folk clubs to get the exposure to get signed in the first place. The promise of a deal with Warner Brothers came to nothing, though ironically, Nick Pickett, who regularly played with the duo, got a solo deal and an album titled *Silversleeves* on the label in 1972, supporting Curved Air and the Gary Moore Band on tour to promote it[181].

The duo signed with Joe Boyd's Witchseason Agency and looked to Island for a deal. The agency, with its Warlock publishing section, and its less well-known Werewolf management section, currently handled Nick Drake, Fairport Convention, John and Beverley Martyn, Sandy Denny, Brotherhood of Breath, the Incredible String Band and so on, most of whom were signed to Island. Ian Anderson remembers:

> … the Troubadour newsletter reported with great glee in early 1970 that Mudge & Clutterbuck were to record for Island, but like many other of their rumours it never happened. Dave was famously untogether.[182]

In late 1970 there was a rumour that the duo had now turned down two recording contracts and that they were awaiting another offer, though nothing was forthcoming.

From this point on almost every time the duo was featured in one of the music papers it was with some new tale of woe or impecunity, and usually both. For example, they had appeared with Al Stewart and the Third Ear Band at the Queen Elizabeth Hall on London's South Bank: the concert was very high-profile, with Al Stewart being backed by an orchestra. Mudge and Clutterbuck played *Memory Book* and *Lowly Lowly Lo* to an enthusiastic reception, but the expected surge of bookings failed to happen. It wasn't a problem of people not wanting to book them, but one of people not being able to find them to book them. As Clutterbuck said:

Bristol folk

> It was a little bit disappointing not taking off after the Al Stewart concert but it was our own fault for not having any promotion. People didn't know how to book us and we couldn't afford to advertise. We can't even afford to spend £5 on posters and envelopes…"[183]

It was further noted that as late as November 1970 they had still only sold 400 copies of their Saydisc EP[184], thus ensuring a very high future value, but not exactly helping their current financial situation.

The duo began making inroads in various Midlands folk clubs thanks to the promotional efforts of Colin Scot, a larger-than-life American who was popular on the folk scene. Gigs around this time often featured Nick Pickett on violin and mandolin and Fiona Stuart on vocals. In late 1970 the duo was surprised when they played a new Dave Mudge song, *Ragmus*, at a folk club in Doncaster. The audience joined in on the *first* chorus despite the duo not having previously sung the song there. Another member of the Bristol set had played it at the club a few days before, which introduces another facet – others on the folk scene, such as Derek Brimstone, included Mudge and Clutterbuck's songs in their own sets.

However, the simple economics of life on the folk club scene were taking their toll and both Mudge and Clutterbuck had to take part-time jobs to pay their debts. They also opened the *Safari Tent* folk club under a restaurant in Westbourne Park Road, with Colin Scot as the first booking. They couldn't charge large fees for their own gigs because they would have priced themselves out of the market, but they were unable to live as touring musicians on the money that their music was bringing in. Indeed, their popularity around the country didn't ultimately help, because they found themselves playing up one end of the country one night and down the other end the next and simply getting enough petrol money to get between gigs became a problem. For example, in mid-January 1971, their itinerary included playing King's Lynn, St. Albans, Leytonstone, Rose (in Cornwall), Penzance and Shrewsbury – in that order. As Clutterbuck said, "Take next week. We've got Birkenhead, Bristol and Kent. We just can't afford it. We'll be lucky to break even."[185] The pair decided that the only way to survive was to get out of the folk clubs and onto the concert circuit and they started to change the act to work in this new environment.

Things began looking up on the record deal front in late 1971, though only for Dave Mudge, Mudge and Clutterbuck having finally given up as a duo and broken up. The November 1971 edition of *Dogpress* reported that, "Dave Mudge is back in the West Country getting a solo act together and at long last thinking of doing an album." The December edition of *Dogpress* added:

> Dave Mudge has signed to Village Thing Records and has been recording during November with Keith Christmas on guitar, Hunt & Turner and Andy Leggett."

However, the proposed LP, although being assigned the catalogue number VTS 10, was not issued and it was for many years debatable on the collectors' scene as to whether anything was actually recorded. Ian Anderson clarifies the situation:

> Long time Bristol-associated songwriter Dave Mudge had been working with my old schoolfriend Tim Clutterbuck as a successful duo, except they never seemed to be able to materialise the record deals they were offered. In 1971 we started work recording a solo album by Dave – like Dave Evans' debut we were recording in the Royal York Crescent flat which had good acoustics and thick walls. It was given a catalogue number, VTS10, and a title, Mudge. A few tracks got recorded and Rodney Matthews designed a cover for it, a yawning hippo (a play on Flanders & Swann, as in "Mudge, mudge, glorious mudge…") but recording ground to a halt due to Dave's famous untogetherness, not unconnected to a certain herbal intake. The hippo artwork eventually got used on a VT sampler album, Us – waste not, want not – though the number VTS10 never got re-assigned and so became a great enigma to collectors.[186]

Maggie Holland provides further insight into the probable reason why the recordings were abandoned, having serendipitously got just this far in transcribing her diaries.

> … the recording took place in the living room of our flat in 12A Royal York Crescent, so normal existence was suspended for the duration. Ian would have been recording it on Gef's Revox. There's an implication that there may have been some more tracks planned ("finished the acoustic tracks"). However, there's also some suggestion of DM's ill health including [a] rather startling remark about him having hepatitis, which I'd forgotten - maybe this had a bearing on it not getting completed?[187]

The LP was abandoned and things were quiet until April 1972 when, along with ex-Troubadour regular, Pete Airey, Mudge became a resident musician at the new Mushroom 'soft rock' club in Trowbridge. Nothing much else was heard until his name cropped up as co-composer of the title song on Al Stewart's LP, *Modern Times* in 1975, this being an adaptation of Mudge's composition *Lowly Lowly Lo* from the Mudge and Clutterbuck days. Tim Clutterbuck moved to the US and gave up music for a while: he was for several years unaware that Dave Mudge had died in 1998.

Nick Pickett stated at the 2004 Troubadour Reunion concert that he was looking for Dave Mudge recordings and compositions to put out on CD. Until – and if – this happens the Saydisc EP remains the only record issued solely by them and in its picture sleeve can sell for around £30. The *Troubadour Folk* LP on which they also appeared is a bit of a question mark. Only 99 copies were pressed, and its existence is unknown on the collectors' scene. Therefore assigning a value is difficult until such time as word gets out to the global folk collectors' scene. I would tentatively place a three figure price tag on the LP.

Rod Neep

Rod Neep was a Nottingham-based folk singer who played several times around the south west in the very early 1970s. Bristol band, Decanter, also played at some of the same clubs on occasion and Neep moved to Bristol specifically to be close to Decanter's singer and flautist, Sarah Bale, whom he later married. He lived initially at Patchway, where his arrival in Bristol was commemorated by an article by Peter Patson in the Western Daily Press, and later moved in to the same house as John Turner.

Bristol folk

Neep had already been approached by Alan Green of Folk Heritage to record an album and this was recorded at the Folk Heritage studios in Wales in June 1973 with John Turner and Ian Hunt plus Sarah Bale, Richie Gould and Andy Hammond from the recently defunct Decanter. The LP was provisionally titled *Untrodden Sands*, but when issued the title had been changed to *Heading for the Sun*. The LP comprised songs by Neep as well as covers.

Much the same team that played on the first LP reassembled in 1974 to record an LP of Tom Paxton songs, called *I Give You the Morning*. Again recorded by Alan Green, it was issued on a subsidiary of Folk Heritage. Neep doesn't even have a copy of this LP, though odd to note is that tracks are available for download as ringtones! The recording sessions were evidently fun, as Neep explains:

> The gang of us had a real hoot of a time in mid Wales for a whole week ... and worked from early morning until late. Alan Green provided several crates of red wine and that added to the general atmosphere. The whole session was full of jokes and fun, and in fact there are places in some songs where it shows. One such example was where Ian Hunt was singing a harmony to "Peace Will Come", which became "Pigs.... pig swill.... pig swill come" and "Sweet peas" instead of "Sweet peace". It came out as a great track, but I still smile knowingly every time I hear it. "I Give You The Morning" was my favourite album and still is. The music, and all of the musicians, just "clicked" together. A classic example of that was where Graham Turner (playing a harpsichord sound on his new keyboard), Sarah Bale (recorder) and I (guitar & vocals) were in separate rooms. They could both hear me but they couldn't hear each other, and yet both of them played an improvised baroque style arrangement that was so tight and similar that it was uncanny, especially at the end of the song.[188]

Neep remained a familiar sight on the local folk scene until he left Bristol for Cheltenham in 1979. To bring things a bit more up to date, in March 2000 Neep started the Archive CD Books project, the aim of which was:

> ... to make reproductions of old books, documents and maps available to genealogists and historians, and to co-operate with libraries, museums and archives in providing assistance to renovate old books in their collection, and to donate books to their collections, where they will be preserved for future generations.[189]

Neep retired in 2007 and now spends his time making and selling hand-crafted wooden pens as well as singing and playing – and even building the occasional stringed instrument.

The first LP crops up for sale infrequently and can sell for anywhere between £20 and £70. The second LP, however, seems to be unknown on the collectors' scene and any copy that appears will most likely sell for rather more than £20, though until a copy is offered for sale, your guess as to value is as good as mine.

Sally Oldfield

Sally Oldfield, sister of the subsequently more famous Mike and of the much less famous, though no less musically-prolific, Terry, had been at convent school in Reading with Marianne Faithfull, where, inspired by Joan Baez, she took up folk guitar. She gained a place at Bristol University and so moved to this city, where she soon became a regular fixture on the folk scene. Soon after moving to the city she received a 'life-affirming' moment whilst watching the sun setting over the Bristol Channel at Portishead, stating, in brother Mike's words that, "… her whole life ever since has been about that moment."[190] Unlikely as this may seem to those who remember Portishead in those days with its run-down docks overshadowed by a large power station, it might be worth remembering that it was the Bristol Channel that provided the inspiration for Turner's glorious sunsets, such as that in *The Fighting Temerere*. Meanwhile, Ian Anderson remembers Oldfield thus:

> She came to Bristol to study English & Philosophy, and made her first appearances at Bristol University Folk Club and then the Troubadour when that opened. By then she'd become influenced by people like Bert Jansch and Dorris Henderson - I remember a version of "Come All Ye Fair And Tender Ladies" in that style. As well as being a good guitarist and singer, she was also predictably popular among the male part of the audience for both being very pretty and wearing extremely short mini-skirts![191]

Anderson also remembers Oldfield's first paid gig as a folk singer, mainly because it was also his own first paid gig:

> Fred Wedlock invited three artists he'd spotted doing floor spots in local clubs to be a triple bill at a folk evening he was organising at a teacher training college in Redland: myself, Sally Oldfield and Keith Christmas. For all three of us, I believe it was our first ever paid, advertised solo gig! [192]

When the Troubadour opened in October 1966, Oldfield was a regular performer and she had a certain amount of prestige because of the Marianne Faithfull connection: Faithfull was currently big news with singles in the pop chart plus a lovely, un-commercial, folk album, *North Country Maid*, with arrangements by Jon Mark, not troubling the charts one jot. Faithfull invited Sally and brother Mike to see Mick Jagger recording at Olympic Studios in London and, later, arranged some studio time for them on which Jagger engineered: none of these recordings have surfaced[193]. Mike was around a fair bit and remembers his sister playing in one of Bristol's folk clubs, where he noticed that she didn't just strum her guitar as did many folkies, but included, "… lots of little submelodies and harmony lines."[194]

Whilst still at university, Oldfield performed as part of a duo, which perhaps gave her the idea of teaming up with younger brother, Mike. Of Oldfield's last days in Bristol, Ian Anderson says:

> For a while, she also worked in a duo doing mostly traditional material with a fellow student called Ian Bray - as "Sally & Ian" - but also began songwriting. The Western Daily Press reports her as doing local TV and cabaret too. John Renbourn spotted her

at some point and brought her and her brother Mike to the attention of Nat Joseph at Transatlantic Records, for whom they eventually made the "Sallyangie" album in 68 ... but that was after she'd left Bristol when she presumably graduated - which at a guess I'd say was mid 67 or could have been mid 68.[195]

Mid-1968 would seem to be a good guess, because it was then that she invited Mike, who had just left school and was at a loose end, to form a duo to play the folk club circiut. After playing both the UK and France[196], the duo did the rounds of record companies, during which they walked into the Transatlantic offices and played to Nat Joseph, who liked what he heard. Joseph gave them the name Sallyangie, the 'angie' part of which came from Mike's favourite Bert Jansch tune, which he had learned to play at a very early age – and he was still just 15 at this point. The Sallyangie's style was very similar to the 'baroque folk' of Jansch and John Renbourn and was understandably influenced by Pentangle.

In late 1968 the duo recorded the *Children of the Sun* LP, which included several songs originally honed in Bristol's folk clubs. Despite Mike getting a couple of short instrumental pieces on the album, he acted more as a support musician to his big sister's vocals and guitar. The LP was issued in November 1968 but was not a particularly big seller, despite the duo getting a radio session broadcast on John Peel's Night Ride show in early December. They later recorded, potentially toward another LP, but all that was forthcoming was a single, *Two Ships*, issued in September 1969, by which time the duo had split up. Transatlantic declined to pick up Sally as a solo artist, which is probably why the recent recordings remained otherwise unreleased. Sally had also auditioned for the BBC as a solo artist in the July, but had not passed the audition, the panel's verdict being that she was "not considered suitable" for use by the BBC[197]. The Transatlantic LP was reissued in 1978 after Sally's own belated chart success, though it didn't sell well and is hard to find. The initial press was issued in a laminated sleeve, which is harder to find than the later matt sleeve issue.

The Sallyangie broke up because of the usual big sister/little brother tensions, exacerbated by their being in such close proximity on the road - and Mike also objected to their performing in bright green, Mediaeval-style clothes at the Cambridge Folk Festival in 1969. He formed a four piece rock band, called Barefeet, with flautist brother Terry, but they soon broke up and Mike next joined Kevin Ayers and the Whole World, with whom he recorded two absolutely wonderful albums, *Shooting at the Moon* and *Whatevershebringswesing*. Oldfield borrowed a reel to reel recorder from Ayers and put together a self-recorded, multi-overdubbed twenty minute piece of music, which was subsequently rejected by every record label he took it to. Eighteen months later he was still trying to get a deal. Eventually, based on an early hearing of the demo, the new Virgin record label decided to sign Oldfield after he returned, still unsigned, to Virgin's Manor Studios with sister Sally for some recordings as a session musician in late 1972[198]. The rest, as they say, is history.

Meanwhile, Sally continued to perform solo and even continued to use the name Sallyangie, releasing a single on Philips under this name in December 1972. From this point on, Sally, in a reversal of roles, played second fiddle to her brother for several years. She sang backing vocals on *Tubular Bells*, issued in May 1973, and reprised this role on both *Hergest Ridge*

Bristol folk

in 1974 and *Ommadawn* in 1975. Also in 1975, Sally sang on sessions for Steve Hackett's first solo LP, *Voyage of the Acolyte*. Hackett was still a member of Genesis at this point, but had a body of material written that the parent band wouldn't use for one reason or another – perhaps because the material was so strong that Genesis as a band never bettered it. Sally sang on *Shadow of the Hierophant*, a glorious showcase of opposites comprising quiet, acoustic guitar and flute-accompanied verses – a perfect vehicle for Sally's voice – which were then juxtaposed with heavy Mellotron-soaked sections that would have fitted happily on King Crimson's *Court of the Crimson King*; in fact, the LP seems to be heavily influenced by a mix of early King Crimson and Erik Satie, a mix that works surprisingly well.

Back with brother Mike, Sally sang, along with Katy Hacker, on a film called *Reflections*, distributed in 1977. This film was directed by Lawrence Moore and was funded by the Arts Council, featuring otherwise unavailable music by Mike. Around this time, Sally is reputed to have joined a group called Baby Whale[199], which was a Cambridge-based band led by Nick Barraclough, who later became a Radio 2 presenter. Also in 1977, Sally sang on an LP by Finnish bassist, Pekka Pohjola, who had been in the now highly-regarded Finnish group, Wigwam. Pohjola had a solo deal with Virgin for UK issues and was recording at Mike Oldfield's Througham Studio. The UK release was titled *The Mathematician's Air Display* and the Finnish release on the Love label was titled *Keesojen Lehto*. This LP might only have remained a footnote if not for what happened on the record's reissue on several US and European labels in the early 1980s. These reissues relegated Pohjola to last place, if he was lucky, and instead the LP appeared titled variously as *Mike Oldfield, Sally Oldfield / Pekka Pohjola* and *Mike & Sally Oldfield / Pekka Pohjola*. Sally and Pohjola missed out altogether on a later edition that credited the LP as a Mike Oldfield release under the title, *The Consequences of Indecisions*.

In 1978 it was Sally's turn in the limelight once again and she was signed as a solo artist by Bronze records, which was currently home to Manfred Mann's Earth Band, Uriah Heep and Motorhead. The first album was called *Water Bearer*, but due to the ornate font used on the sleeve, many are still convinced that it was called "Water Beaver"! *Child of Allah* was resurrected and re-recorded for the album, though the track selected as a single this time was a non-album track called *Mirrors*, which became a surprise hit over the Christmas of 1978, reaching number 19 and remaining on chart for thirteen weeks.

Bronze added *Mirrors* to the second press and gave the LP a large promotional push, adding a sticker to the sleeve to point out that it now included the hit: they also sent out large numbers of promotional materials to record shops, whose subsequent multi-poster displays of Oldfield in a glowing white get-up brightened up many a record shop window in what was otherwise a fairly dark and depressingly-cold Christmas. The album still did not sell well enough to chart in the UK, though sales in other European countries were more than encouraging. Further singles and another LP, *Easy*, were issued during 1979, though these did not chart, leaving Oldfield as a 'one hit wonder'. She continued to make records on Bronze through the early 1980s and much of this material is now being reissued on CD.

The original Transatlantic records are very hard to find with the LP likely to set you back about £70 or more with the single somewhere between £20 and £40. Even the reissue LP could cost you between £20 and £35. The values attached to these early records are based on the involvement of Mike Oldfield and the Philips single, shorn of collector's interest in Mike, should cost around £10 to £20, though a few hopeful dealers are asking double this based on the rumour that Mike does appear on it. The Bronze label material is quite common, with the two LPs costing between £5 and £10 each (copies of *Water Bearer* with and without *Mirrors* are worth about the same). Mirrors was not issued in a picture sleeve in the UK and should cost around 50p. The other Bronze singles should cost somewhere between £3 and £5 with *The Sun In My Eyes* in its picture sleeve costing anything up to £8.

Dave Paskett

Prior to coming to Bristol, Dave Paskett studied art at Hornsey, Exeter and Liverpool Colleges of Art and won the Queens Award in 1965. He was part of the London folk scene in the late 1960s before moving to Bristol. Whilst based in Bristol, he played the usual folk clubs and also made the semi-finals of the Melody Maker National Rock/Folk Contest[200]. The finals for the soloists were held at Haverstock Town Hall, Hempstead, on 4th June 1972, with "solo" being about the only qualifier for counting as a folk artist, judging by some of the names. Paskett didn't win – a chap called Lloyd Watson did. You may well ask, "Who?"

Shortly afterwards Paskett joined the Pigsty Hill Light Orchestra and, apart from the musical side of things, he collaborated with Andy Leggett on a wonderfully 'juvenile' set of poems, published by Plastic Dog as *Pigtales*. *Pigtales* was illustrated and produced by Terry Brace and Rodney Matthews, the latter reprising his *Matthews Pigshit Elongated* 'font' as used on the *Piggery Jokery* sleeve. Paskett and Leggett further collaborated on a rewrite of the pantomime, *Treasure Island*, which was performed by The Pigsty Hill Light Orchestra and Stackridge during December 1972 at various venues around the country, including the Victoria Rooms, Bristol, on the 15th December. Rodney Matthews drew a lovely picture, caricaturing both bands, which was printed in the 8th December issue of the *Preview* arts and entertainments listings magazine.

Paskett stayed with the Pigs for about a year before reverting to solo performances, including performing as a one man band in folk clubs around the country. He gigged regularly around Bristol, often playing alongside Bristol group, Hamstrung Bones, and was one of the few artists to play, on 13th December 1975, at the Granary's short-lived New Grain Folk Club. Paskett wrote most of his own songs, such as *Boghole Botticelli* and *The Wicked Grocer*, though the song that most people seem to remember is *I Could Not Take My Eyes Off Her*. At this point, Paskett also had a Saturday spot on Radio Bristol and, for a while, was a spoof arts critic, going under the name of Reubin St Werburg.

Paskett released two LPs on his own Thinks! label, the first, issued in 1975, was called *I Still Dream About Your Smile*. Paskett sang and played guitar, whilst Chris Newman played guitar, bass, mandolin and rhythm box, Mike Evans played violins, Andy Hammond played bongos and Min Newman, sang harmony vocals. The second LP, issued in 1979, was called

Pasketry. On this he was joined by Dave Griffiths on double bass, mandolin and fiddle, and Shortwaveband's Phil Harrison and Stuart Gordon on sundry instruments. Paskett and Griffiths gigged to promote the LP and those who bought a copy got something that was to increase in value, other than the LP, that is – this was the cartoon that Paskett invariably included along with his signature. The reason why the cartoon has appreciated in value is because Paskett has become better known as an artist than as a musician in later years.

In the mid-1980s, after providing sleeve designs for Bath's Pump House Trio[201], Paskett moved to Hong Kong, where he found inspiration for his painting and made this his full-time career. He moved back to the UK in 1990 and has become regarded as one of Britain's leading watercolourists. He is now President of the Royal Watercolour Society, based at the Bankside Gallery, next to the Tate Modern. His paintings are in many private collections, including that of the late Queen Mother. He is currently a member of the Famous SOAS Rebetico Band and also plays bouzouki in a Klezmer setting. The two LPs tend to sell now for about £10 to £20 apiece, and those with cartoon alongside the autograph can sometimes go for £5 or £6 more, though only to those who know that Dave Paskett the musician is Dave Paskett the artist.

Lindsay Peck/Friary Folk Group

This lot recorded a concept album called *Reality from Dream* in 1975 in glorious mono. The LP was pressed by Saydisc and marketed privately by the group. Most included a wrap-around card sleeve, which illustrated the concept covered within, and these were housed in a PVC outer sleeve. The concept was basically that of the manipulations, trappings and drug and alcohol-induced downsides associated with stardom in the music industry, at least so it would seem from the sleeve design – the titles and lyrics don't really give too much away.

Meanwhile, the LP has assumed near legendary proportions in private label folk collecting circles mainly because of the first track, *Dawn*, a solo effort by Lindsay Peck. However, after the promise of the opening track, most of the LP is enthusiastic at best, mawkish and cringe-worthy at worst – all depending on your reaction to teenagers' voices not quite hitting the note, that is. Peck's remaining solo tracks stand out as by far the best. One is left with the feeling that they should have waited a few years before recording this, as there is definitely promise. This mixed quality doesn't stop the record from commanding a price tag of between £15 and £50, those complete with wraparound sleeve and PVC outer and some in plain white sleeves realising pretty much the same prices.

The Pigsty Hill Light Orchestra

The Pigsty Hill Light Orchestra was reputedly formed for Fred Wedlock's 1968 New Year's Party at the Troubadour and the group quickly gained a residency at the club. They took much of their inspiration from novelty jazz from the 1920s and 1930s playing in a similar vein to The Temperance Seven, The Alberts, the early Bonzos or Bob Kerr's Whoopee Band[202], with blues, jugband, ragtime and folk influences galore added to the mix.

Bristol folk

Barry Back and Andy Leggett had played with the Alligator Jug Thumpers[203], a band that was put together by Cliff Brown of the Okeh Rhythm Kings, when he mistakenly thought that Adge Cutler had asked him to form a backing band. Williams hadn't realized that the Wurzels had already been put together and to make up Adge Cutler offered the band a place on his *Scrumpy and Western* shows. Dave Creech had been with the Pioneer Jazzmen and the Elastic Band, and had run the first folk club in Bristol, at Lawford Gate, whilst John Turner had been in the Downsiders.

The Pigs reprised some of the Alligator Jug Thumpers' material, such as *Sweet Miss Emmaline*, and continued that band's tradition of playing household utensils and instruments made out of odd bits and pieces, including the Ballcockaphone and Egg Cupaphone. The Alligator Jug Thumpers had used such instruments as the Karma-Sutraphone, the Thunderbox and the Stud-Box: if you really need to know more about these instruments, see *Recollections of Jazz in Bristol: My Kind of Town*[204]. They played an instrument called the Somerset death pipes at the 1969 Cambridge Folk Festival and gained nine bookings from this appearance. Based on this success, they turned professional, though it was noted that Andy Leggett, who had been a French translator on the Concorde project, "...[took] out an insurance policy in the form of offering his services as a freelance translator."[205]

By December 1969, John Turner was running the Troubadour and was also putting together the Village Thing record label and agency, so plans were made for the first Pigs LP to be released on this label. To add a certain amount of complexity, an offer was made by Argo, via Decca's Kevin Daly, but this was vetoed when three members to one decided to run with Village Thing. The subsequent LP was titled *Pigsty Hill Light Orchestra Presents!* – or *PHLOP!* for short – and was released in September 1970. Apart from the jazz and traditional covers and original compositions by John Turner (*Company Policy*) and Barry Back (*On Sunday*), there were also a couple of contemporary covers in the shape of Ralph McTell's *Sleepy Time Blues* and Dave Cousins' *Nothing Else Will Do Babe*, though these were done in a Piggies style. Julie Bridson sang on the Dave Cousins song and Ian Hunt played guitar on *Company Policy*, whilst Ian Anderson, according to the sleeve notes, snored and rattled tea cups. The back of the sleeve shows the band posed amongst some of the instruments of the Mickleburgh collection, which, sadly for Bristol, was later sold off and dispersed, though part was bought by Bristol Museum.

The Piggies were becoming a popular live attraction, thanks to positive reviews of their LP and live performances in the national music press. Despite a rigorous national gig schedule various members played on other Village Thing records. Both Turner and Leggett played on the second Village Thing release by Cardiff folk duo, Sun Also Rises, and Leggett also painted the sleeve, for which he got a free copy of the record – eventually quite a good deal as the LP now sells for up to £100. The whole band played on Fred Wedlock's first LP, *The Folker*, which must have been a bit of a squeeze because the LP was recorded in Ian Anderson and Maggie Holland's flat in Royal York Crescent. This takes us a bit too far forward, however.

Bristol folk

Back in mid-1970, John Turner left and teamed up with Ian Hunt. As Hunt and Turner they performed in the UK and abroad and made the lovely *Magic Landscape* LP. Turner was replaced by occasional member, Bill Cole, from Ken Colyer's band, who played Sousaphone as well as bass. The group began to record a second LP but the August edition of *Dogpress* reported that the group had, "… scrapped the tapes done a few months ago … to record live at the Room at the Top, Redruth, in August." The LP was recorded live over the end of August and the start of September 1971 by Ian Anderson during a week's residency at the club. Trivia fans may be interested to know that the LP included a joke that Stan Arnold also put on record a few years later - the one about the crematorium.

Piggery Jokery was issued in December 1971 to mixed reviews: it was felt that the lack of visual element often made the listener feel left out, wondering what the laughter was about. One local review was extremely positive, the only negative comment being that Rodney Matthews' name was misspelled in the sleeve credits[206]: Ian Anderson, in a letter published in the February 1972 edition of Pre-View, pointed out that Rodney Matthews, as sleeve designer, was actually responsible for the misspelling of his own name. Matthews' had designed his own font for the sleeve, which he called *Matthews Pigshit Elongated*. On the back of the sleeve both Andy Leggett and Barry Back are seen proudly sporting the ultimate in early 1970s Bristol musicians' accoutrements – Plastic Dog t-shirts: these are now extremely rare with Andy Leggett's probably being the only original still in captivity.

In early 1972, just after the release of the second LP, Barry Back left and was replaced by Jon "Wash" Hays.

> …the group seems to have a built-in answer to the need for new vitality in their act – line-up changes. Last year they lost John Turner, who left to play double bass with Ian Hunt. Now Barry Back, guitarist and frontman, has departed to return full-time to his job as a sound recordist.[207]

Dave Paskett, a recent semi-finalist in the Melody Maker's National Rock/Folk Contest, joined during 1972 and he and Leggett collaborated on a booklet called *Pigtales*, illustrated and produced by Rodney Matthews and Terry Brace from Plastic Dog. The poems within were, depending on your point of view, either very funny or of questionable taste. Just to give you a clue as the quality of the poems, there was one about the snot garden up your nose, complete with a Rodney Matthews pig picking its snout, and also one about using the back end of an elephant to give you a spectacular parting in your hair, complete with a Matthews picture of … well, you can probably guess. A reprinting of these poems and illustrations is long overdue.

Leggett and Paskett collaborated on a rewrite of the pantomime, *Treasure Island*, which was performed around the UK by The Pigsty Hill Light Orchestra and Stackridge in December 1972. The Pigs also performed in White on Black's Bristol Arts Centre Folkie Pantomime on 29th and 30th December, along with White on Black, Decanter and Fred Wedlock, finishing off the year the following day with a gig at the Granary with Strange Fruit and various Plastic Dog musicians.

Bristol folk

The next couple of years saw quite a few people come and go, including Robert Greenfield, Dave Peabody, Chris Newman and ex-Wurzel, Henry Davies, from Henry's Bootblacks. Pinning down exact line-ups is difficult, but on a tour with Stackridge, where the Pigsty Hill Light Orchestra got to play in both Paris and at the Theatre Royal, Drury Lane, the line-up was Creech, Leggett, Hays, Paskett, Greenfield and Peabody. Shortly after this, Dave Peabody remembers[208], Chris Newman also joined, and Newman's memories are as follows:

> I joined Pigsty Hill Light Orchestra in August 1972. My first gig with them was at a folk club in Pelshall (near Brownhills). I replaced Andy Leggett and joined the band that then consisted of Dave Creech, Jon (Wash) Hayes and Henry Davies. It was [a] very busy band at the time, and we spent a lot of time in a terrible old (even then) dark green Transit (XGO 509G - how's that for trivia?) travelling around the UK and a few European countries too. While I was with them we played a lot in Belgium, Germany (for the UK military), Switzerland and France … Henry left sometime in 1973 and was replaced by a set of bass pedals that I used to play along with the guitar. The band became a three piece until I left (to join White on Black) in 1975. I can't for the life of me remember the name of my replacement …[209]

Andy Leggett left the Pigs to play, seemingly, in every jazz band that ever existed[210] as well as in Bob Stewart's touring theatrical company. A few highlights include his playing jug on sessions at Virgin's Manor Studios in 1974 for 'art rock' band Slapp Happy. This session came about because the band wanted a jug player and Leggett was evidently the only person in the Musician's Union directory with 'jug' still listed next to his name. He then, amongst other commitments, became musical director for three piece girl group, Sweet Substitute, who recorded some excellent LPs for Decca, Transatlantic and Black Lion. They even released a Christmas single, *A Musical Christmas Card*, written by Leggett, which picked up considerable airplay in the lead up to the festive season in question, but was then released by Decca in February – real life always beats comedy.

The next LP was called *The Pigsty Hill Light Orchestra*. It was issued in 1976 with a line-up of Creech, Hays and Greenfield, with Chris Newman, although no longer a member of the band, producing as well as adding bass and guitar. This LP, which sported the aforementioned Rodney Matthews pig picking its nose on the rear of the sleeve, was a private issue and it seemed to rely heavily on Shel Silverstein songs. Soon after the LP was issued, Ritchie Gould joined on bass and the line-up settled for a while as Creech, Gould, Greenfield and Hays – at least, they lasted long enough to have publicity photos made for their new agency, Dick James Music, but then rather ruined the effect by switching to the Pat Vincent Agency in Westbury-on-Trym: this meant that they had to glue bits of paper with the new agency details over the old address on their otherwise nicely glossy photos.

Dave Creech was the only original member to last out to the end in 1979. The band was reformed in 1988 around Barry Back and included Dave Creech, Andy Leggett, Jon Hays and Bill Cole. Later on Pat Small joined as did Dave Griffiths and Jim Reynolds, but in 1992, Barry Back died and the band lost the heart to carry on, though they fulfilled remaining bookings. They reconvened once more for the Troubadour reunion concert in 2002, consisting of Creech, Hays, Small, Roger White and Paul Godden. Andy Leggett was committed to gigs in Germany with Rod Mason's Hot Five and so was unable to get back to the UK to play on the night.

The two Village Thing LPs appear most often and these will usually set you back no more than £15 each. The privately issued LP from 1976 is quite rare; consider yourself lucky if you find one for less than £20. In 1992 a compilation cassette called *Musical History* was released, which included tracks from the three 1970s LPs. This last, along with the reformation cassette, *Back on the Road Again*, from 1991, is almost impossible to find.

Pat Purchase

Pat Purchase was a big-voiced blues and gospel singer and is included in the book despite the fact that she did not release any records in the UK during the 1960s or 1970s. She did, however, record in Australia during the mid-1960s with records released in both Australia and the US. Purchase finally released a private CD in 1998 of recordings made between 1960 and 1978, most of which were recorded in Bristol.

Purchase started out as a rock and roll fan. She sang a Connie Francis song at a party in 1959 and was approached by jazz musician, Gerry Bath, who told her that she had the voice to sing jazz if she wanted. Not long afterwards she was singing for the Milenburg Jazz Band, followed soon by singing in the split-off group, The Pearce Cadwallader Stompers. Purchase had a predilection for songs by big-voiced female blues singers, such as Bessie Smith, Gertrude 'Ma' Rainey and Rosetta Tharpe. Luckily, she had the voice to do these great singers justice and a style of her own so that she did not come across as a mere copyist.

In 1962, Purchase married trumpeter Nigel Hunt, and they emigrated to Australia on the now famous £10 tickets (known in Australia as the *Ten Pound Poms* scheme). Once there Purchase joined the Yarra Yarra New Orleans Jazz Band with whom she recorded several records between 1963 and 1965, the first being an EP appropriately named *Introducing Pat Purchase*, which included *Weeping Willow Blues*, *Schonnenberg*, *Gatemouth* and *Lullaby*. The Yarra Yarra Band remains highly-regarded amongst jazz aficionados in Australia and elsewhere. In 1966 Purchase and Hunt returned to Bristol, where Purchase sang with her husband's Imperial Jazz Band, as well as with the Avon Cities and the Blue Notes. Between 1973 and 1977 she sang with the Bayou Blue Five, which featured Gerry Bath on piano, Norman Thatcher on trumpet, Dave Stone on clarinet, Gerry Gittings on drums and Sean Bolan on sousaphone. With this line-up they recorded a BBC Radio Bristol session in 1973.

In 1978 Purchase set up her own business and decided to stop performing – but only after she'd had a go at forming a gospel group, something she had always wanted to do. She enlisted jazz singer, Kate McNab, and folk singer, Min Newman: Newman had played the Bristol folk clubs in the early 1970s as a third of Pussy and, later, as half of Angie and Min. Purchase called her new band Shine. The group was backed on gigs by The Dave Collett Trio and soon recorded a session for BBC Radio Bristol as well as appearing on the local HTV TV station. The group only lasted a short while, however: Newman left to have a baby and later left the UK altogether for New Zealand – though not before singing a trio piece with herself and herself on, then husband, Chris Newman's second LP – and McNab joined Sweet Substitute. Purchase now concentrated on her business.

Purchase still sings occasionally – she was involved in Leon Hunt and Josh Clark's production of *To Kill a Mocking Bird*, which ran at the New Vic Theatre in Stoke-on-Trent in late 2004. On the soundtrack CD, she can be heard singing *Precious Lord* and she still sounds as if she means every word.

The records that Purchase made in Australia are hard to find, with only one of the EPs having turned up for sale recently and this selling for somewhere around £20 in fairly poor condition. The 1998 retrospective CD was called *Blues & Gospel* and was re-mastered by David Lord of Crescent Studios/Terra Incognita. Putting a price on this is difficult as there are probably only a couple of hundred copies, these being privately issued, but also there is not yet any sort of collectors' market for it because it is unknown on the collectors' scene. It is the sort of thing you are likely to either find in a local charity shop for 50p or never see at all. As regards the CD, the quality of some of the recordings is suitably crackly with distortion on the high frequency parts, which makes them sound just like the real thing – and thinking about it, at this juncture some of these recordings are now older than were the 78s that Purchase was emulating back in those days. Basically, many of the recordings are taken from the only remaining sources, be these acetate or whatever, and in whatever condition, with the best brought out of them by David Lord.

Pat Small

Pat Small began by playing rock 'n' roll and country, influenced by Buddy Holly and Chet Atkins. By the early 1960s, he had discovered folk music and became a regular player and singer at the Bristol Ballads and Blues and Poetry and Folk Clubs. As a member of these clubs, Small was recorded for the 1965 Saydisc LP, *Bristol Folks*, on which he sang *Man of Constant Sorrow* and *Flora, Lily of the West*. The former was a modern song with its tune revised by Fred Wedlock and the latter was the well-known American variant of what had originally been a West Country song. On the cusp of 1966/67 Small played on Graham Kilsby's *In a Folk Mood* EP. Kilsby, who had also appeared on *Bristol Folks*, included the 'infamous' *Chastity Belt* on this EP, and this track was recorded live at the Troubadour with Small, Al Jones and Fred Wedlock responsible to varying degrees.

Small became part of a trio called The West Country Three and on 6th November 1968, they played on Radio 2's *My Kind of Folk* along with Jackie, who was best known for her TV show tie-in song *White Horses*. In 1969 the trio made a tribute LP for Pye's budget offshoot, Marble Arch, called *The West Country Three Sing the Hits of Peter, Paul & Mary*. Odd to note is that the West Country Three remained anonymous throughout the sleeve notes and only John Turner, guesting on "base fiddle", got a name check.

After the group broke up, Small, billed in listings as "Pat" or "Patrick" in a cheerfully hit-or-miss fashion, became a regular fixture on the West Country folk circuit, and an average few months in 1971 saw him playing at the Blue Boar in Frome, the Toby Folk Club in

West Pennard, the Bristol Hotel in Clevedon, the Village Pump Folk Club, Trowbridge, the Crown and Anchor Hotel in Stonehouse, and so on. Small continued playing and writing songs and his song *Bramble Cottage* was singled out for praise in a review when recorded by White on Black on their eponymous Saydisc LP. Small also made his own record in 1976, a single, recorded at Mushroom Studios on West Mall, Clifton, comprising *A Man of Bristol* with *Sand in My Shoes* as the b-side. Henry Davies played stand-up bass on the a-side, whilst of the b-side Chris Newman said:

> I … played electric guitar on 'Sand in my shoes'. Also on the latter song were backing vocalists Malcolm Perret, Suzi Knowler and Min Newman (my ex-wife). I think (though may very well be wrong) that the drummer was Tony [Fennell]…[211]

Man of Bristol is very rare, to the extent that the only two copies discovered during research for this book were those in the collections of Henry Davies and Chris Newman.

To go back a bit, Small had been approached by Andy Leggett in 1968 to join a notional group but hadn't been convinced about Leggett's idea of a jug-based jazz band. The group, when put together, was called the Pigsty Hill Light Orchestra. Small wasn't going to escape, however, though he got away with it for nearly 25 years – he finally joined the reformed Pigs in the early 1990s and joined them again at the first Troubadour reunion concert in 2002. He was billed to play the second Troubadour reunion concert in 2004 but did not appear on the night.

The West Country Three LP can generally be found for around £10 or less. The *A Man of Bristol* single could easily be worth around £10.

Stackridge

Stackridge was certainly an odd band with early songs seeming to be set in some other reality, where Syd Barrett-type whimsy and carpet slippers ruled. The group was formed from the remnants of the blues-based Griptight Thynn and the West Coast-flavoured Dawn, both of whom played regularly at Bristol's Dug Out and Granary clubs. Griptight Thynn broke up in July 1969 and Andy Davies and James 'Crun' Walters from this band started rehearsals for a new group in Royal York Crescent, Clifton, and at Davies' parents' house in Yatton. Early rehearsals included drummer, Tony Fennel[212] and keyboard player, Bob Thompson, though neither stayed long. In late summer Billy Bent joined on drums, so rumour has it, from a band that had toured the UK pretending to be The Zombies and Jim Warren joined in November from Dawn. Mike Evans, who had played in the Westlanders and Moonshiners folk groups, was the next to join and Mutter Slater joined in January 1970.

The new group was initially called Stackridge Lemon and their first gig was at the Granary on 19th February 1970, supporting Graham Bond's Initiation. The 'Lemon' got dropped a couple of gigs later and the band's first appearance with the shortened name was at the Granary on 2nd July, where they supported James Litherland's Brotherhood, a band formed by the ex-Colosseum guitarist. They continued to play locally and, along with several other

Bristol folk

local acts, were booked to play an event billed as a "Pop Folk & Blues festival" at Worthy Farm, Pilton, an event that later became better-known as the Glastonbury Festival. The festival took place on 19th and 20th September 1970 and Stackridge opened the festival, thus becoming the first band to play Glastonbury, something the reformed band has used to its promotional advantage. They also closed the festival after headliners, The Kinks, pulled out. The Stackridge website helpfully informs all that the first note played was a 'B' and that the final note a day later was an 'A'.

Stackridge played their first Granary Club headliner on 20th December 1970 and by 29th March 1971 they were pulling in £30 for headlining there. The band had started to play further afield and they were signed by MCA on 1st January after a well-received gig at Bristol's Victoria Rooms. The first single, *Dora the Female Explorer* was issued on 21st May and the LP, *Stackridge*, was belatedly issued on 13th August. The promotional gig at the Granary saw their fee rise to £40 – after all, they had an LP out now. A local review of the LP gave a little background to one of the songs, *32 West Mall*, describing it as:

> ... a day or two in the life of starving Stackridge, recalling ... the time they were evicted from their flat in West Mall, Clifton, for forgetting about things like rent.[213]

A review in the July 1971 Dogpress by Chris West concluded:

> It's a very interesting album indeed, a kaleidoscope of contrasting styles and ideas, subtle permutations of light and shade, with a prevailing atmosphere of wistfulness, a longing for a fantastic world which exists in the labyrinthine depths of Stackridges (sic) mind – and it's bloody good.

The band had supported Wishbone Ash on a national tour to promote the album, but despite the national exposure sales were relatively poor, with the LP selling around 4,000 copies on release. The reason for the poor sales was that the LP had been delayed because of a problem with the sleeve design and, ludicrously, it was not issued until after the promotional tour had finished. Much easier to find is John Lennon's *Imagine* – during the recording of the Stackridge LP the call went out that Lennon wanted several acoustic guitarists for his current sessions. Andy Davis found himself roped in and of these sessions he says:

> The Imagine sessions ran on into the weekend but I had to pull out because I had some gigs to do in the north and I couldn't let the band down. That weekend Ringo Starr sat in on Drums and George Harrison played lead guitar. And so it was that I turned down the chance to play with 3 of the Beatles in order to play with Stackridge at Cleethorpes Winter Gardens.[214]

Publicity-wise, the band gained favourable national press coverage by becoming the first UK band to tour Ireland since the troubles had restarted there. They also appeared on a local BBC TV programme called *Stackridge, Squidd & Co*[215], which was recorded in June at the BBC's Whiteladies Road studios and broadcast in July. Crun, meanwhile, had left because, despite Stackridge's growing popularity, bricklaying paid more for a young father, though he returned in time for the band to record their second LP, *Friendliness* in August 1972. In

Bristol folk

fact, Crun was amongst the missing on two occasions, as Stackridge manager, Mike Tobin says, "Paul Anstey filled in for Crun when he was off sick. James Warren played bass when Crun left to lay bricks!"[216] Davis had moved over from guitar to piano and Mellotron by this time and the Mellotron began to give their music a more well-defined, decidedly pastoral English sound. The stage act by now involved Mutter Slater engaging in yokel dances – which Peter Gabriel of Genesis borrowed for his performance of *I Know What I Like* – and props such as dustbin lids for banging and rhubarb stalks for thrashing started to appear, all of which became much-anticipated parts of their show ... to the extent that fans turned up at gigs with their own rhubarb stalks and dustbin lids to join in with *Let There Be Lids*.

With a second album behind them and a growing national reputation, the Granary had to fork out £100 for their hometown album promotion gig on 5th August 1972. Having been booked for the Granary by the agency side of Plastic Dog, the graphics side of Plastic Dog put together a memorable programme for the *Friendliness* tour. In December 1972, Stackridge toured with the Pigsty Hill Light Orchestra, performing the pantomime *Treasure Island* – or at least, a derivative of it, written by Andy Leggett and Dave Paskett from the Pigs – playing Bristol's Victoria Rooms on December 15th[217]. The panto was very well received by the music press and the lucky third album was on the horizon.

The Man in the Bowler Hat was famously produced by George Martin and included the wonderful *God Speed the Plough*, which, although the band was now treading a fine line between producing Beatlesque pop, 1930s-style novelty songs and distinctly English progressive rock, sounded like the sort of thing that Vaughan Williams might have come up with had there been rock bands around in the 1920s. However, this period really draws a line after which the band became largely estranged from Bristol with the band maintaining an office in London, from which their fan club, the *Rhubarb Thrashing Society*, was run. Before the LP was issued Mutter Slater left to work in a garage, though he rejoined later, and Billy Sparkle[218] was sacked from the band, ending up as George Martin's driver.

Crun, James Warren and Mike Evans became conspicuous by their absence over the next few months and a band that sounded more like *Peaches en Regalia*-era Frank Zappa – on a couple of tracks, anyway – appeared playing some very complex jazz-rock in 1975 on their next LP, *Extravaganza*. Mutter's Somerset accent and Davies' Mellotron on *The Volunteer* was as close as the album got to the earlier Stackridge, though the traces were still there. This LP was issued by the group's new record company, Rocket, which also arranged in 1976 for Stackridge to appear at a prestigious all-day gig at Wembley, headlined by the Beach Boys.

More of a Stackridge feel was reintroduced for their final LP, *Mr. Mick*, perhaps with the return of Crun. However, the record company mucked about with the track listing of the LP causing relations to sour. The LP was supposed to be a concept album with Mutter Slater's spoken word passages linking the whole, but the record company wanted to include a cover of the Beatles *Hold Me Tight* that the band had recorded as a single, so moved the remaining tracks around and even dropped some from the album to make way. The album was finally released as originally intended on CD by Dap Records in 2000 and is currently available on the Angel Air label, along with other Stackridge albums, old and new[219]. The band broke up in 1976 with their final gig at Yeovil Town Hall, which was either ironic or fitting, because Yeovil was Mutter Slater's home town.

James Warren joined Canton Trig for a while and in the late 1970s was reunited with Andy Davies, where they maintained an up-down relationship in chart-hitting pop band, The Korgis. After the Korgis, Davies went on to play with, amongst others, Kevin Brown, the Three Caballeros, Tears for Fears and, more recently, Goldfrapp. Mike Evans played with Fred Wedlock during the 1970s and later joined the Pump Room Trio in Bath, with whom he made a couple of very pleasant Palm Court Trio-influenced LPs on Bath City Council's imaginatively-named City of Bath label. Stackridge reformed in 1999 and, after a short spell as Stackridge Lemon, who released a limited edition CD, and with a few line-up changes the band now includes most of the old crew – Warren, Davies, Crun and Mutter.

Stackridge records are becoming quite pricey. An original, perfect condition copy of the first LP can cost anything up to £50 with copies on the two short-lived 1972/1973 label designs going for around £15 on a good day. An original *Friendliness* will set you back anything up to £25 and you can double that if it has the tour booklet with it – but beware that facsimile, single-sheet copies of the booklet were given away at the first Granary reunion in 1999, at which the then recently-reformed Stackridge played – supported by Mutter Slater, who wasn't in the band at that point, but was mostly playing R&B with his band, Dixie Chicken, along the south coast. The rest of their LPs and later pressings of the first two LPs on the rainbow label design shouldn't cost you more than £10 or so and most of their singles tend to sell for around £6 to £10. The exceptions are the first single, *Dora the Female Explorer/Everyman*, which could cost you £20 or so, and *Slark/Purple Spaceships Over Yatton*, which might set you back £15 for a perfect copy. The single version of *Slark* is not the same as that on the LP, and *Purple Spaceships Over Yatton* has a far superior sound on the single to that on the *Do the Stanley* compilation from 1976. There is also a US-only LP that was heavily imported into the UK, which includes tracks from both *The Man in the Bowler Hat* and *Extravaganza*. The LP was called *Pinafore Days*, named after a shop in Bath, and copies sell for around £12 if the sleeve is intact: most have import cuts and should cost less than £10.

Bob Stewart

Bob Stewart was barely out of school when he first began playing at the Bristol Ballads and Blues and the Troubadour clubs. He played with Kelvin Henderson and Fred Wedlock and quickly became highly proficient on several instruments, including a psaltery-like Swedish table harp with over seventy strings, which he adapted to his own specification. This ability to achieve proficiency on something with over 70 strings may be because of his mother's family's tradition of playing the Welsh Triple-Harp[220]. As a regular performer at both the 'traditional' and less traditional clubs, Stewart sang and played with many singers, such as Graham Kilsby and Paul Evans, and Ian Anderson remembers that, "In the Troubadour era he had a good duo with a singer called Albert Lightfoot."[221]

Bristol folk

Stewart's first released recordings were for Keith Christmas: he played psaltery on *Fable of the Wings* in 1970[222] followed by cittern on *Pigmy* in 1971. Also in 1971, Stewart backed Stan Hugill and various members of the Folk Tradition Club on recordings that were originally intended as background music for an exhibition on marine archaeology at Bristol Museum between April and July, and which was subsequently issued on LP as *Men of the Sea*. In his own right, Stewart was picked up on by Argo house producer, Kevin Daly, who had already produced records by others on the folk and country scenes, such as the Yetties, Trevor Crozier and Bob Skinner. He also played on sessions for Graham Kilsby, of which Stewart says, "I … played psaltery and guitar on some recordings by Graham Kilsby…but I cannot remember the content or a reference number for the disc …"[223] It is likely that no record was released as Kilsby, though recording prolifically in the late 1960s and during the 1970s, seemed to end up with his recordings shelved by EMI.

The first fruits of Stewart's association with Argo were seen in his arranging most of the instrumentation on Cyril Tawney's *I Will Give My Love* LP, issued in 1973. Stewart also co-produced a couple of cassette-only issues in collaboration with W. G. Gray. One comprised Gray and a group of ritualists enacting his Rollright Ritual on one side and magical songs by Stewart on the other. This was issued by the Helios Occult Cassette Club, an offshoot of the Helios publishing company. Stewart explains:

> There was an Argo album with Cyril Tawney, of the folk songs collected by Sabine Baring Gould: on this I played 73 stringed psaltery and did most of the arranging, but not Cyril's guitar which was his own … And a cassette recording (recently digitally remastered for CD) of "Magical Songs of Britain" from 1973. This comprised mainly my own songs, and some traditional magical ballads from Scotland.[224]

Back at Argo, Stewart recorded the theme and incidental music for the Demetriou production of *The Hobbit*, which effectively underpinned Nicol Williamson's famously dramatic narration. This four LP boxed set is hard to find in original condition, though the work is still available on CD and for download. In 1974, Stewart appeared on *One Night as I Lay on My Bed* from Shirley Collins' extremely rare *Adieu to Old England* LP on Topic. Stewart played psaltery and Shirley's sister, Dolly, played her gloriously breathy flute-organ.

In 1974 – despite an erroneous 1975 publishing date – Stewart's first LP, *The Unique Sound of the Psaltery*, was issued. Alistair Anderson of the High Level Ranters played concertina and, to add to the odd soundscape created by the psaltery, the LP also included synthesiser. The LP was in a series of releases showcasing out-of-the-ordinary instruments or instrumental styles and appeared along with Roger Nicholson's *The Gentle Sound of the Dulcimer* and LPs showcasing sitar and flamenco guitar, if memory serves.

Prior to the release of the Argo LP, Stewart had co-founded the Avon Touring Theatre, which included a young Tony Robinson. Andy Leggett, who had recently left the Pigsty Hill Light Orchestra, joined in a musical, rather than theatrical, capacity. Leggett later wrote and arranged for female vocal harmony trio, Sweet Substitute, and is grateful for his association with Stewart: as he says, "… eventually it was this contact through Bob Stewart that led to

Bristol folk

Kevin Daly offering a Decca contract to Sweet Substitute."[225] The Avon Touring Theatre presented several major productions, for which Stewart wrote much of the music, and this facet of his career eventually led to Stewart's writing music for radio, film and television, including a credit in Jim Henson's film, *The Dark Crystal*.

In 1976, now a resident of Bath, Stewart recorded an LP for the Bath-based Crescent label, which was run by David Lord. The LP, recorded at Bath University Arts Barn, was called *The Wraggle Taggle Gypsies O*. Apart from Stewart, who played guitar, banjo, cittern and psaltery, the LP included performances from Stewart Gordon on fiddle and Phil Harrison on guitar and harmonium – Gordon and Harrison went out under the name Shortwaveband, as which they later recorded *The Shortwaveband's Greatest Hats*[226] for Crescent. John Molineux played fiddle and mandolin, Stewart's wife, Laraine, and Albert Lightfoot sang backing vocals. The LP comprised songs collected by Cecil Sharp from southern England – mostly from Somerset – and also songs collected by Sharp from the Appalachians – where his dislike for instrumental accompaniment to folk song supposedly caused certain long-lasting misconceptions:

> According to [A. L.] Lloyd, legend has it that when Cecil Sharp was collecting in the Southern Appalachians during World War 1 … the people sent messages on ahead of him warning their friends to hide away their banjos and guitars, for Sharp's aversion to accompanied folksong became clear … As a result, Sharp's treasured belief that the English – and Anglo-American – folksong tradition was largely an unaccompanied one was undisturbed, thanks to the tact of the folk.[227]

In late 1976, Stewart recorded an LP with the Furey brothers, Finbur and George, called *Tomorrow We Part*. Finbar Furey played Uilleann pipes, whistles and bodhran, Bob Stewart played psaltery, cittern and guitar, George Furey played guitar, cittern and bodhran and Stuart Gordon played fiddle. The Crescent label, as a small independent, had limited distribution, and most copies of Crescent label LPs were sold by the artists at gigs. Consequently, although the Argo LP was a relatively small seller, the Crescent LPs are even harder to find.

In 1978, Stewart recorded an LP for the Broadside label, called *Up Like the Swallow*, which, as Stewart explains, "… [comprised] my own songs, traditional songs and original and traditional Celtic instrumentals, with Jackie Daley on melodeon and Jimmy Crowley on cittern, Greg Smith on fiddle."[228] In 1979, *Tomorrow We Part* was reissued on the Broadside label in a different sleeve, of which Stewart says,

> Tomorrow we Part was recorded by David Lord and Brian Preston at Bath University Hall, and was first issued on the Crescent Label, with an original artwork cover … The Broadside edition arose when Crescent stopped producing LPs, so it is somewhat later than the first edition. The Broadside cover art also came later.[229]

The LP was reissued again in the 1980s, though with Stewart relegated to second billing behind the Fureys. The reasoning behind this was probably to cash in on the Fureys' recent popularity in the UK, which was thanks to a successful TV-advertised LP.

Meanwhile, Stewart had gained a growing reputation for his research into and knowledge of Celtic mythology and moved into teaching and writing as well as advising for film and radio productions. This reputation led to his writing and producing a cassette-only issue for Van Morrison, which was based on the Irish epic, *Cuchullain*. Bob Stewart is now better known as Robert John Stewart and has many publications to his name, many of which have remained in print for an enviable amount of time, undergoing various translations along the way. He is still active in music, as well as teaching, writing and presenting workshops in the UK and the US.

Stewart's 1970s LPs are quite rare, though the Argo LP can be found for between £12 and £20. The Crescent label LPs are harder to find and could cost between £15 and £30. The box set of *The Hobbit* seems to sell for around £40 online, though it has been spotted in earthbound shops priced at a more useful £10. The Broadside LP, credited to "Bob Stewart and Finbur Furey", sells for between £10 and £15, though the 1980s reissue credited to "The Furey's and Bob Stewart" should sell for about £8. As for the Helios cassettes (only the one mentioned included songs by Stewart), it is hard to assign values: these are collectable for more reasons than the music aspect alone and they very infrequently surface for sale.

Strange Fruit

Strange Fruit comprised Keith Warmington on harmonica and jug and Pete Keeley on guitar. Despite both coming from Cornwall they met in France and toured around the UK and the occasional bit of mainland Europe before settling in Bristol around 1970, migrating back to Cornwall during summers. Apart from playing the folk clubs, the duo was booked to open for rock bands at Bristol's Granary Club. Being a two piece, they could fit onto the tiny Granary stage in front of the main act's gear. The reason that they were booked so often to open rock gigs was that the combination of Keeley's guitar and Warmington's harp playing was guaranteed to whip up an audience nicely so that they were ready for the main act – in fact, they could be a hard act to follow.

During April or May 1971 Strange Fruit, along with Fred Wedlock, were recorded for a Westward TV show, and in June they were supposed to record a single for Village Thing, but the recording fell through because, according to the June *Dogpress*, they had, "… lost the drummer!" The recording couldn't have been delayed for long because adverts for the single, *Cut Across Shorty*, which was issued in glorious mono, appeared in the July edition: the single would have set you back the huge sum of 47½p. In the meantime Warmington played on several Village Thing LPs: Steve Tilston's *An Acoustic Confusion*; *The Words In Between* by Dave Evans; Ian A. Anderson's *A Vulture Is Not a Bird You Can Trust*; and Dave Evans' *Elephantasia*.

In December 1971, Strange Fruit were involved in a 'free transfer deal' which moved them from the Village Thing books to those of Plastic Dog, not that it made much difference as the same edition of Dogpress later went on to say, "The Village Thing Agency work is now going to be handled entirely by Plastic Dog staff." Under this arrangement Strange Fruit continued gigging until the end of June 1972, including an informal band version, which played Sunday afternoon sessions at the Stonehouse, with Charlie Hart on drums. The duo then broke up, though Keeley's intention was to carry on as a solo performer. Warmington, meanwhile, began looking for a teaching job because being a musician alone was a precarious way to make a living.

> Bristol based duo Strange Fruit are splitting at the end of the month. Harmonica virtuoso Keith Warmington is reported to be looking for a teaching job, and ... guitarist Peter Keeley will be going solo basing his material on his own songs.[230]

> A sad announcement: Strange Fruit, the popular Contemporary/Goodtime duo who have graced the Bristol scene for a year or so are about to split. Keith Warmington, the fine harp blower and jug virtuoso intends to subside into a more "normal" way of life – Pete Keeley – poker-faced guitarist, with a driving style modelled on Broonzy, may continue working under the same name if a suitable working partner comes to light. However, their farewell gig in this form is at Redland College on June 29th.[231]

The post-Warmington Strange Fruit played until mid-1974 and then broke up for good, with the last known advert appearing in the Melody Maker for 6th April 1974. Warmington concentrated on his job as a French teacher but carried on playing, mostly locally, ending up in the new decade with Steve Payne's Paynekillers, the Parole Brothers and Alamo Leal's Blues Legacy amongst others. He began freelancing for the BBC in 1983 – the same year that he released the one and only vinyl record under his own name, a single titled *Evening Song* on the local Right Track label – and is still to be heard on air. He also still plays live occasionally, mostly with Stuart Gordon, Rick Payne and Kit Morgan.

The lone Strange Fruit single is quite rare and can cost anywhere between £8 and £20 depending on luck. Although outside the bounds of this book, Keith Warmington's solo single is no less rare, but currently has no value on the collectors' scene – except when sold on eBay with the Strange Fruit/Village Thing connection made clear: on these few occasions it sells for around £5.

Steve Tilston

Steve Tilston was born in Liverpool in 1950. He began singing and playing around Loughborough in 1967, where he lived in the same house as Dave Evans, a potter and guitar-maker, who also ran the local folk club. Tilston, who was already writing songs, encouraged Evans to write as well and they began playing together locally. By the late 1960s, Tilston had begun to make a bit of a splash on the London folk scene, playing Les Cousins regularly. However, by this time he had made his base in Bristol after being introduced to the city's folk scene by Ralph McTell. As Tilston said of this time, "... it was virtually commuting between the Cousins in London and the Troubadour in Bristol ..."[232]

Tilston was quickly signed to Village Thing and he began recording his first album during February and March 1971 at Gef Lucena's house in Inglestone Common. Dave Evans had also turned up in Bristol to play on the sessions and they were joined by Keith Warmington from Bristol-based duo, Strange Fruit, and John Turner. The LP was titled *An Acoustic*

Bristol folk

Summer Edition
FOLK UNDER COVER No.3
2/-
Presented by the UNDERCOVER Folk Club & the BALLADS & BLUES

TROUBADOUR NEWS

FOLK WEST
TRADITIONAL CONTEMPORARY FOLK SONG, BLUES, BEYOND

7.45 pm WEDNESDAYS
SINGERS WELCOME !

Guests for July and August
ROBIN DRANSFIELD GRAHAM KILSBY
FRED WEDLOCK The CROFTERS
WEST COUNTRY 3 MIKE COOPER
TIM HART & MADDIE PRIOR

BRISTOL HOTEL
Locking Road
Weston-Super-Mare

Bristols first & formost F.C
ballads & blues

Leading Local Singers
Top Guests Every Week

Re-Opens SAT 9th Sept
EVERY SAT 7.45pm—11pm
The BATHURST HOTEL Prince ST

THE TROUBADOUR FOLK CLUB

Every Wed. Fri & Sat in Summer
Wed to Sun Inclusive in Winter

8pm to 12pm

TOP RESIDENTS PLUS NATIONAL
& INTERNATIONAL GUESTS

Waterloo St. Clifton Bristol

FOLK BLUES
BRISTOL & WEST

First Sunday of Every Month
OLD DUKE
King Street Bristol 1

RESIDENTS INCLUDE
IAN ANDERSON MIKE COOPER AL JONES
ELLIOT JACKSON JOHN FAIRBANK

Enquiries concerning club or residents Tel Bristol 30016

FOLK BLUES
SUN. JULY 2 at
The Old Duke, King st.
JO-ANN KELLY
Anderson
Jones   8·00 pm
Jackson
and Others

Bristol folk

FOLK BLUES BRISTOL & WEST

residents
ian ANDERSON
alun JONES
elliot JACKSON
MAC
king george VI
and others

FIRST SUNDAY EACH MONTH
TROUBADOUR waterloo st clifton.

sunday march 5th 8·00-11·00
MIKE COOPER
(steel 'national' guitar)
JERRY KINGETT

The UNDERCOVER FOLK CLUB
every Sun 8pm-11pm
ADM 3s

The Celler
10 Lawford st
Old Market

The Folk Tradition
BRISTOLS ONLY STRICTLY TRADITIONAL CLUB

EVERY MON 8pm-11.45pm

ADM GUESTS 3/6
MEMERS 2/6
STUDENTS & NURES 1/6

BRISTOLS LEADING TRADITIONAL SINGERS
Including:
BIG BRIAN, ALBERT & JOHN
MIKE FLANIGAN
PETE MACNAB

'the old duke' King st

Bristol folk

YOU KNOW WHERE! HERE'S WHEN

Saturday March 25th.	HARVEY ANDREWS & CHRIS ROHMANN
Friday March 31st.	THE CROFTERS.
Saturday April 1st.	TIM HART & MADDY PRIOR.
Sunday April 2nd.	ALL BLUES NIGHT - DAVE KELLY.
Friday April 7th.	PATRICK BENHAM.
Saturday April 8th.	THE WEST COUNTRY THREE.
Friday April 14th.	NORMAN BEATON.
Saturday April 15th.	NEW MODERN IDIOT GRUNT BAND.
Thursday April 20th.	JOHN RENBOURN.
Friday April 21st.	JOHN RENBOURN.
Saturday April 22nd.	JACK & MARGARET KING.
Friday April 28th.	DORRIS HENDERSON.

COMING SOON.
ALEX CAMPBELL. JEREMY TAYLOR. JOHN FOREMAN. AL STEWART. MAC & MICK.

OUR OWN REGULAR SINGERS INCLUDE:-
ROGER WHITE SALLY OLDFIELD IAN BRAY
BIG BRIAN FRED WEDLOCK ALUN JONES ADRIENNE
BOB STEWART IAN ANDERSON DAVE MUDGE
ANDY LEGGETT PATRICK SPEERING MIKE FLANAGAN
THE TARRIERS SALLY & SARA SUE & WEITSKE
KEITH CHRISTMAS RICHARD PRINCE DOUG BOWEN

JUNE at the Bristol Troubadour
5 Waterloo Street, Clifton

Fri Jun 4th	Strange Fruit
Sat Jun 5th	Brenda Wootton & John The Fish
Wed Jun 9th	Adrienne
Fri Jun 11th	Steve Tilson
Sat Jun 12th	Derek Brimstone
Wed Jun 16th	Pat Tedbury
Fri Jun 18th	Shelagh McDonald
Sat Jun 19th	Nic Jones
Wed Jun 23rd	Pete Airey
Fri Jun 25th	Sun Also Rises
Sat Jun 26th	Tir na nOg

WEDNESDAYS 8-12pm 20p
FRIDAYS 8-12.30pm 25p
SATURDAYS 8pm-1am 30p

30+ YEARS ON [shhhh] TROUBADOUR 2ND REUNION CONCERT
SATURDAY MARCH 6TH
REDGRAVE THEATRE 6pm
PERCIVAL RD CLIFTON BRISTOL

Many of the original residents are appearing including:
**IAN HUNT • KEITH CHRISTMAS
AL JONES • FRED WEDLOCK
IAN ANDERSON • MIKE & MITCH
PAT SMALL • BEGGARS OPERA
MIKE EVANS • MAGGIE HOLLAND
ADRIENNE • STEVE TILSTON
PLUS MANY MORE**

£10

TICKETS ARE AVAILABLE FROM:
MR SWANTONS [BARBER SHOP], TEL: 0117 973 6157
SPANISH GUITAR CENTRE, TEL: 0117 942 0479
MIKE WEST, TEL: 0117 968 3964

The Village Thing
Side A
VTS 2 STEREO
SUN ALSO RISES
1. Until I Do
2. Wizard Shop
3. Part of the Room
4. Green Lane
all copyright Village Thing Music
© 1970
MADE IN ENGLAND

Bristol folk

The Village Thing

Pigsty Hill Light Orch.
Ian A. Anderson
Keith Christmas
Mike Cooper
Ian Hunt & John Turner
Strange Fruit
Sun Also Rises
Steve Tilston
Shelagh McDonald

77 Park Street,
Bristol 1.
Tel. (0272) 25360

Two noted Gentlemen
have taken residence in the Village

VTS 3 — 'IAN A. ANDERSON' (Royal York Crescent)
VTS 4 — 'THE LEGENDARY ME' Wizz Jones

RELEASED NOV. 13, 1970
'The Village Thing' Records

SAMPLE OUR WARES;
VTS X 1000 'The Great White Dap'
Four tracks by Wizz Jones, Sun Also Rises, Ian A Anderson, and Pigsty Hill Light Orchestra
7inch 33⅓ rpm stereo maxi-single for 9/6

The Village Thing

Autumn Bumflet 1971

Pigsty Hill Light Orch.   Ian A. Anderson

Bristol folk

PLASTIC DOGPRESS No. 28: April 1971

Special souvenir issue to commemorate the coalition of Plastic Dog and Village Thing. Forward against the forces of Evil!

Jerry Brace; Graphics — 77 Park Street, Bristol bs1 5pf
Telephone 26821

You just wouldn't believe some of the astounding things that we can produce for you: everything from a sleeve design for your next million-selling LP or a poster to advertise your orgy, to a groovy badge to wear on your lapel or a personal business card to tell people how important you are.

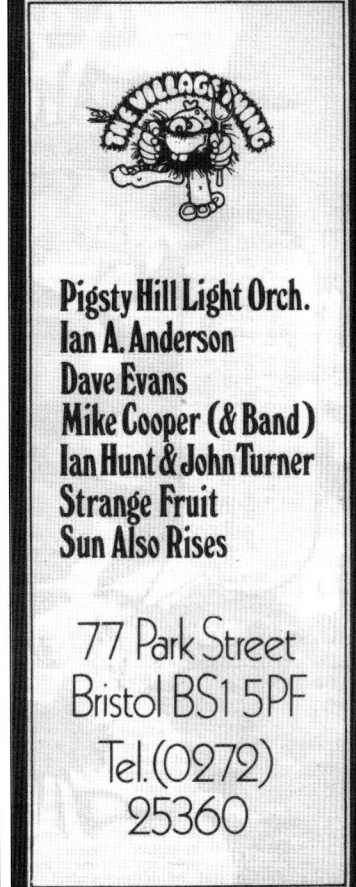

THE VILLAGE THING

Pigsty Hill Light Orch.
Ian A. Anderson
Dave Evans
Mike Cooper (& Band)
Ian Hunt & John Turner
Strange Fruit
Sun Also Rises

77 Park Street
Bristol BS1 5PF
Tel. (0272) 25360

Bristol folk

SPECIAL NOTICE
BRISTOL FOLK CRUISE SAT 13th OCTOBER ON THE M.V. BALMORAL
A fantastic opportunity to enjoy a voyage to Lundy Island. Singing, Drinking, Listening and mixing with a least 80 Folk Singers and Artists.
Bristol Shantyman, Graham Davis, Mike and Jaquey Gabriel, Rod Neep, Colin Scot, Pat Small, Talisman, Paul Weaving and Chad, Burgundy, Diz Disley, Ian Hunt, Pigsty Hill Light Orchestra, Heavy Shamrock, Dave Southall, John Turner, White on Black and absolutely everyone on the folk scene.
Will sail from Avonmouth (North Pier) at 8.30am., have two and half hours on Lundy Island and arrive back at Avonmouth at aprox. 10.30pm.

According to studies of the sea during the last 50yrs., this is usually a calm time of the year.
Lundy is a beautiful unpolluted island, no cars and large bird sanctuary for those interested in feathers?! but there is a Pub. There are two bars on board, light snacks are obtainable from the snack bar at all times.
Tickets are £3.50 but only £3 if purchased before September 1st. Early applications for tickets are essential as only 350 are available.

Bristol folk

99

Bristol folk

Bristol folk

101

Bristol folk

Bristol folk

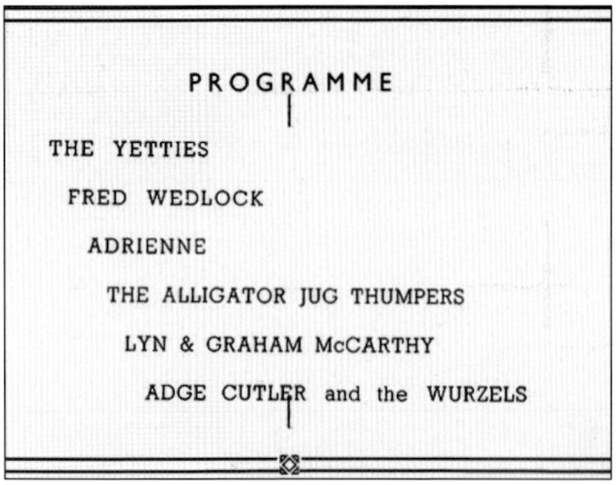

Bristol folk

PROGRAMME

THE YETTIES

FRED WEDLOCK

ADRIENNE

THE ALLIGATOR JUG THUMPERS

LYN & GRAHAM McCARTHY

ADGE CUTLER and the WURZELS

programme

DAVE COLLET TRIO

FRED WEDLOCK

TONY GRAHAM

ALLIGATOR JUG THUMPERS

interval

CHAS McDEVITT and SHIRLEY DOUGLAS

ADGE CUTLER and the WURZELS

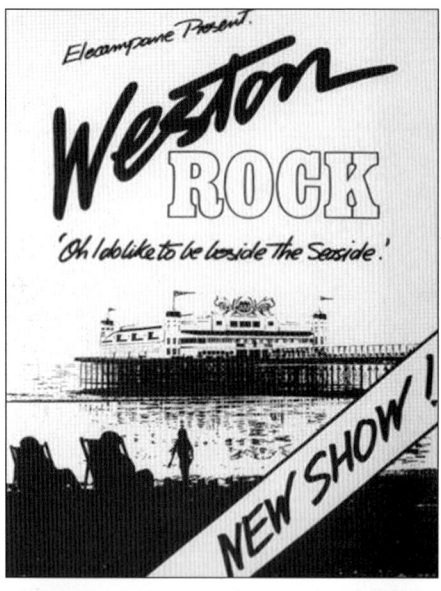

Elcampane Present

Weston ROCK

'Oh I do like to be beside the Seaside.'

NEW SHOW!

ELECAMPANE

The Greatest Little Show from Earth

We continue our tradition of outstanding debut records

Dave Evans – The Words In Between

Village Thing VTS 6

Trade distribution: Transatlantic/EMI

Village Thing Records, 77 Park Street, Bristol 1.

104

Bristol folk

Bristol folk

Bristol folk

KELVIN HENDERSON
t.v., radio, recording artiste

HUNT & TURNER

HARTFORDS; 77 Park St. & 1b Union St.

Bristol folk

Bristol folk

Bristol folk

Rod Neep: Starting all over again.

Rod takes it from the top...

110

Bristol folk

111

Bristol folk

Bristol folk

113

Bristol folk

STRANGE FRUIT

Their first single : "SHAKE THAT THING" / "Cut Across Shorty"
On Village Thing Records VTSX 1001
Price 47½p from your Transatlantic
stockist or Strange Fruit in person.

> Steve Tilston is probably the most important figure to emerge on the contemporary London folk scene since Bert Jansch.
> JERRY GILBERT
> "SOUNDS" May 1st 1971

STEVE TILSTON / An Acoustic Confusion

Village Thing Records VTS 5
TRADE DISTRIBUTION - TRANSATLANTIC

Village Thing Records, 77 Park Street, Bristol 1.
Recommended retail price £1.99

114

Bristol folk

Bristol folk

Village Thing Records present their first folk album:

Fred Wedlock
The Folker

Village Thing VTS 7

Trade distribution: Transatlantic/EMI

THE VILLAGE DOG'S PLASTIC THING;
The monthly section for acoustic music and all who sail in her.

FRED WEDLOCK -v- EMI RECORDS

Our great apologies for the delay of Freds album but it has been completely out of our hands. Some twit at EMI decided that certain jocular references to Prince Phillip were offensive (nobody was more surprised than Fred that anybody should take him seriously) and they refused to distribute it. Unfortunately they spent over a month after deciding this before telling us and by the time we knew it was too late to stop the press advertising. On top of that the sleeve printers then decided to cock their side up as well ! A "censored" tape was rushed to London and hopefully by the time you read this the album ought to be somewhere near the shops. Sorry !

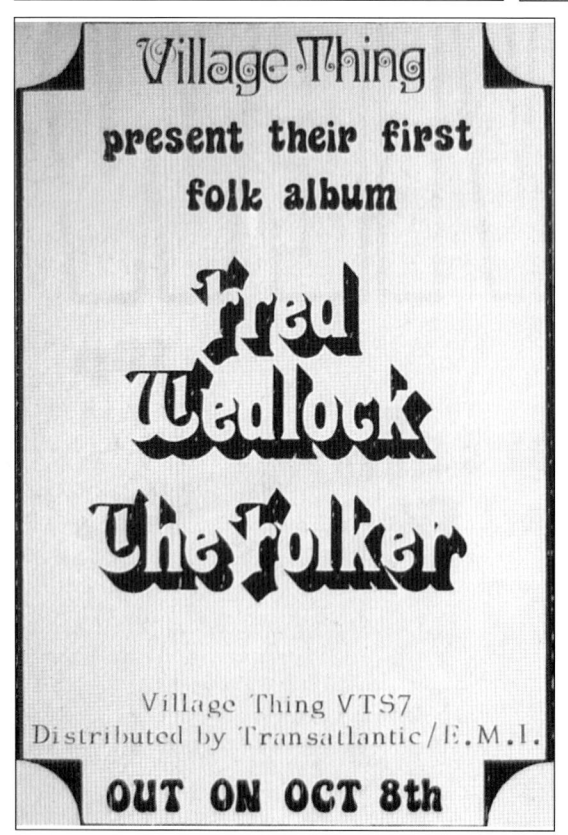

Village Thing present their first folk album

Fred Wedlock
The Folker

Village Thing VTS7
Distributed by Transatlantic/E.M.I.

OUT ON OCT 8th

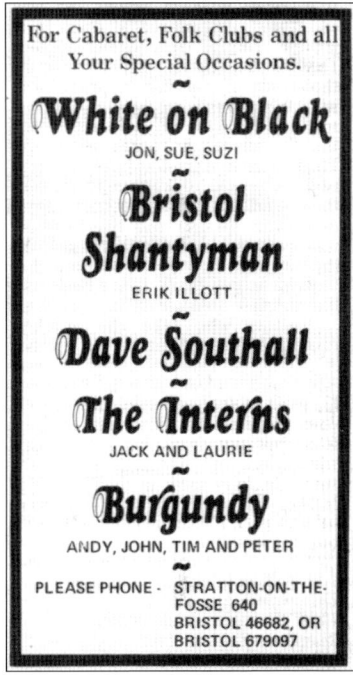

Bristol folk

For Cabaret, Folk Clubs and all Your Special Occasions.

White on Black
JON, SUE, SUZI

Bristol Shantyman
ERIK ILLOTT

Dave Southall

The Interns
JACK AND LAURIE

Burgundy
ANDY, JOHN, TIM AND PETER

PLEASE PHONE - STRATTON-ON-THE-FOSSE 640
BRISTOL 46682, OR
BRISTOL 679097

Bristol folk

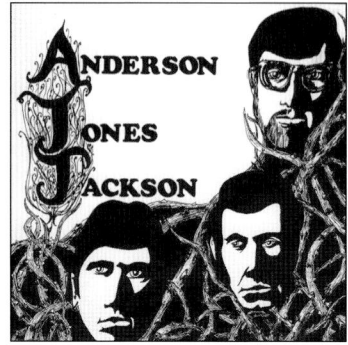

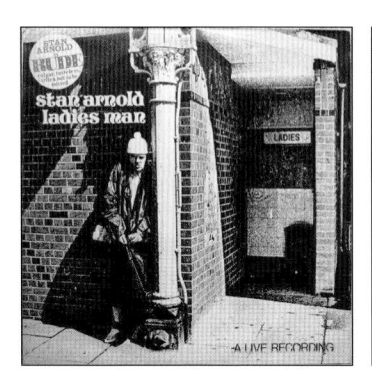

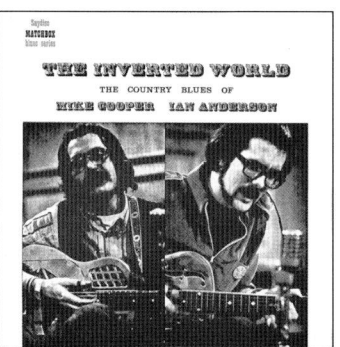

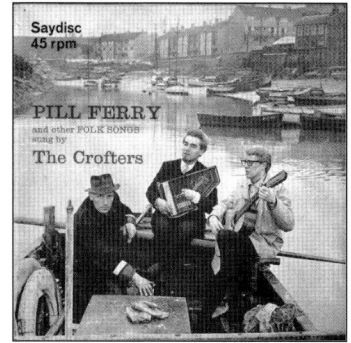

Bristol folk

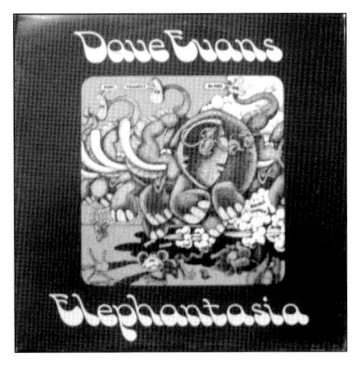

Bristol folk

Bristol folk

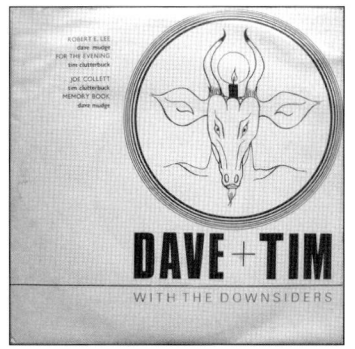

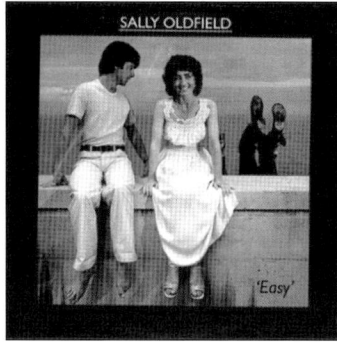

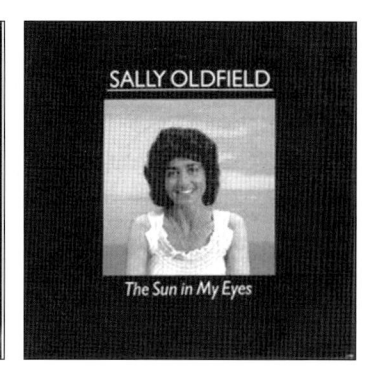

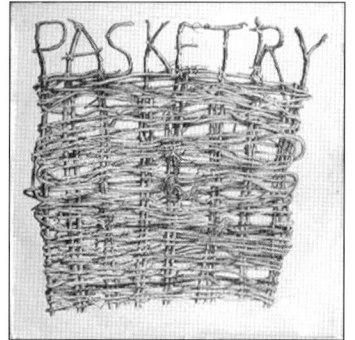

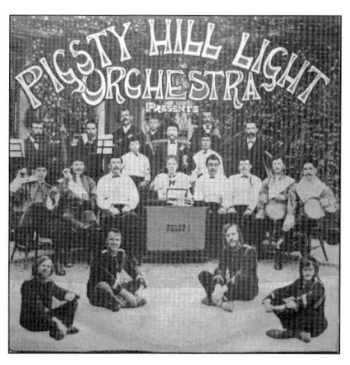

Bristol folk

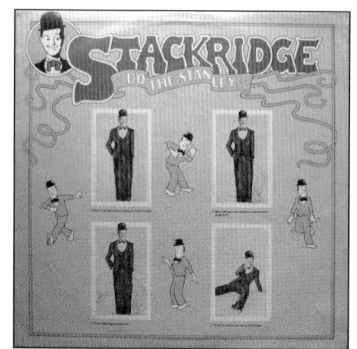

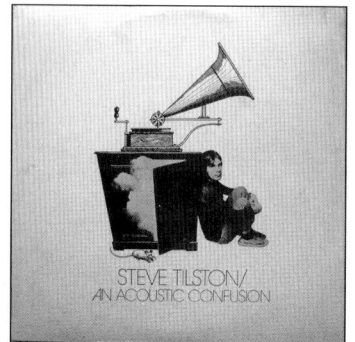

Bristol folk

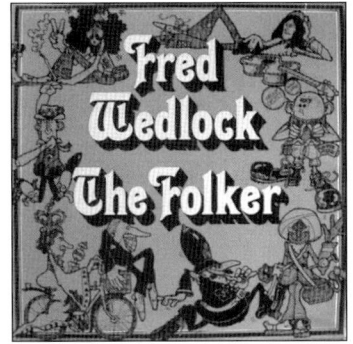

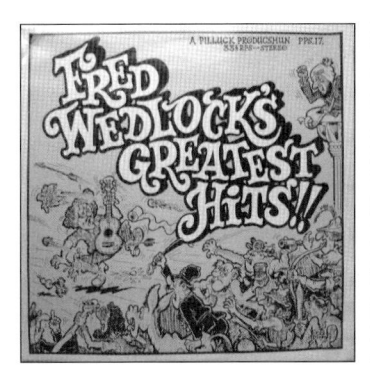

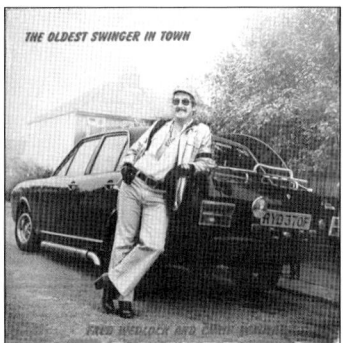

Bristol folk

124

Bristol folk

Saydisc hope to release a record of the Crofters singing all local songs. This will feature more Adge Cutler material - such titles as "Casn't Kill Couch" and "The Great Nailsea Cider Bet". If you would like us to advise you when this future issue becomes available please fill in the form below and send it to us.

··

(Crofters/Cutler record)

Name ....

Address ....

....

....

Saydisc Specialized Recordings Ltd.,
The Meeting House, Frenchay, Bristol.
Tel: 65-2000

"PILL FERRY and OTHER FOLK SONGS" (SD 113)

Our first E.P. by THE CROFTERS is still available and contains Adge Cutler's famous - "Pill, Pill, I Love Thee Still" - the humorous song of the Avon's ancient Ferry from Shirehampton, Bristol, to the village of Pill in Somerset.

SAYDISC specialized recordings - SD - I

FRED WEDLOCK - Volume one

Fred, born in Bristol 23 years ago was educated in Bristol, Swansea and London. His eclectic education gave him a degree in politics, philosophy and psychology.

Fred started playing uke in the Army cadets, then banjo in a Jazz band, aspiring to folk singing and ten string guitar playing a few years ago.

A NOTE ON THE SONGS:

i) Silbury Hill is a song from the heart (of Wiltshire). It was collected by Chas Upton's brother. "Old Nick" is the devil, the rest is self explanatory.

ii) Si Mi Quieres Escribir - a song from the Spanish Civil war. "If you want to write to me, write to me oh the Gandesa front". A protest song from an unknown someone qualified to protest more than the cult of beatnik guessers.

iii) Franklin: An expedition set out in the 1880's to the arctic to find the North West passage. They all died.

iv) Hey Nelly Nelly: Shel Silverstein and Jim Friedman recently wrote this song, perhaps to mark (not celebrate) the centenary of a civil war.

Bristol folk

Confusion and was mostly well-received by the music press – it even got a highly-positive review in the July 1 edition of the Daily Mail. Jerry Gilbert, a respected folk music journalist and frequent visitor to the Troubadour, commented in the sleeve notes on the rapport between Tilston and Evans.

One item of note is that white label test pressings included two extra songs that were subsequently left off the LP: Tilston says, "… I think they're 'What Would You Be' & 'She Sits Wondering', but not 100% sure as I've not heard a copy."[233] Just to keep collectors on their toes, there are also white label copies with the track listing as on the issued version. One fan of the LP was Rod Stewart, who was rumoured to have bought a whole box of the LP to give as presents to friends. Stewart was interested in covering one of Tilston's songs on his next LP, but as things turned out no meeting between the two to discuss this possibility was forthcoming, so Tilston had to wait a while longer for greater fortune.

In 1971, Village Thing negotiated a distribution deal with specialist folk music record label and distribution company, Transatlantic. On the back of this, Tilston signed to Transatlantic and he recorded the LP, *Collection*, which was released in 1972. The sleeve design showed Tilston in various hip costumes, something that was adversely commented upon by the music press, though they admitted to liking the music within. Tilston believed that this LP was a vast improvement on his first LP, and in an interview in the Melody Maker[234] almost brushed off his first LP as sounding more like a demo – though the first LP was subsequently issued by Transatlantic in Australia, so they were obviously happy with it.

To promote the album, Tilston went on a mini-tour with Transatlantic label rock band, Stray, and he was also booked to play the Cambridge Folk Festival later in the year. The music press was almost unanimously impressed with the LP, one anonymous review in the Melody Maker stating, "The lyrical gymnastics and fanciful metaphors of Tilston's first album (Village Thing) have largely been replaced by a more direct approach."[235]

Despite the good reviews, the LP was not as big a seller as his record company had hoped, and Transatlantic further promoted Tilston by including him on various samplers. Most common are two on the budget Contour label, *A Stereo Introduction to the Exciting World of Transatlantic* and *The Best of British Folk*, both issued in 1972. These were among five or six LPs of Transatlantic product that were licensed to the budget label so as to reach an even wider market through Contour's saturation of 'job racks' in supermarkets and garages: these two LPs were priced so as to promote impulse and speculative buying from those who might not otherwise frequent record shops. The hardest to find sampler was a free promotional 7" EP given away for Valentine's Day, 1973. It included songs by Unicorn, John James and Pete Berryman, Gerry Rafferty, The Johnstones and Stray as well as Tilston's *Falling*.

A briefly-bearded Tilston recorded a BBC *In Concert* programme in May 1973, on which he was backed by Canton Trig. In the same year, Transatlantic's *Guitar Workshop* showcase included the otherwise unreleased *Rock Salmon Suite* and the sleeve notes stated that a second LP was "in the pipeline". However, no new LP was issued until 1976, when Tilston, fed up with Transatlantic for various reasons, recorded *Songs from the Dress Rehearsal* on his own Cornucopia label. The sleeve notes stated that Bristol was the city that Tilston loved best, and the LP does not let the city down. John Renbourn played as did the rhythm section of John G. Perry, ex-Caravan, on bass and Mike Giles, ex-King Crimson, on drums. Perry and Giles were making a career at this point out of backing various guitarists of a folky or progressive persuasion, including ex-Genesis guitarist, Anthony Phillips. In 1979, more tracks were recorded by Stefan Grossman, but these were not released and finally appeared as bonus tracks on the CD issue of *Songs from the Dress Rehearsal*.

In the 1980s, Tilston recorded the LP *In for a Penny* on the local TW label. Despite the inclusion of musicians such as ex-Camel keyboard player, Pete Bardens, a label-mate back in the Transatlantic days, and local stalwarts, such as Keith Warmington, and despite it being a more than competent rock album, it was never going to set the world alight – with poor distribution not helping. It had one of the worst LP sleeve designs ever, and the sleeve seemed to flake and peel as soon as you looked at it, which also didn't help, and even in Bristol it was quickly remaindered. By the mid-1980s, Tilston could still pack out folk clubs, playing fairly regularly at folk nights at The Bell, in Jamaica Street, but he was in danger of becoming another parochial name, rather than a national one. However, in the late 1980s, Tilston started to release records on the Run River label, a company of which he was a director, and in the end it was his song writing that told, as others, including Fairport Convention, began to cover his songs leading to a deserved wider audience. Since the late 1980s Tilston has made a multitude of albums, which are again making a bit of a splash, which is pretty much as it should be.

Finding a copy of the Village Thing LP is likely to be very hard and when you do it is likely to cost you around £50, or possibly up to £100 if you manage to find an original press on the first label design in a matt instead of a laminated sleeve. Either white label test pressing should cost near to £100 or even more. The Transatlantic LP is the easiest to find and should set you back no more than £20 or so in near perfect condition. *Songs from the Dress Rehearsal* is occasionally seen around Bristol, but the price has been going up steadily, and although you might be lucky enough to find one locally for £20 or so, eBay prices have been hitting the £40 mark of late. Even though *In for a Penny* is a 1980s release, it is worth noting that those who did pick a copy up for £1.99 or less when it was remaindered got a bit of a bargain – copies have been seen selling on eBay for up to £20 recently. The two Contour LPs should be no more than £8 each, though you may need to pay a little more for the first with its Transatlantic advertising insert. The EP is not yet well-known on the collecting scene: between £5 and £8 should get you a copy now, but be prepared for this to rise in the near future as more collectors get to know about it.

Adrienne Webber

Adrienne (or Aj) Webber was an early and regular performer on the Bristol folk scene, working in 1966 and 1967 with Adge Cutler and the Wurzels, and appearing in Adge's Scrumpy and Western shows along with Fred Wedlock and the Alligator Jug Thumpers. She was recorded at the Troubadour in 1967 - the subsequent *Troubadour Folk* LP was issued

Bristol folk

on the private Kernow label as a limited edition of 99 copies, and included tracks by Flanagan's Folk Four, Mudge and Clutterbuck, "Big Brian" Webb, Graham Kilsby and Roger White. Webber's songs on the LP were *The Ballad of Amy MacPherson* and *Sleep in My Bed Once Again*.

In 1970, Webber spent four months with her sister in New Jersey and, whilst in the US, played across the country, reputedly travelling more than 26,000 miles in the process. She was supposed to play at several prison camps but illness intervened, though she still hoped to give a Christmas concert for the prisoners in Pentonville Prison in the UK on her return. Whether she did get to play Pentonville is unknown, but what she did do when she got back was to record a series of six children's shows for Radio Bristol and also made known, in an interview with a local paper, that she wanted a purple Rolls Royce![236]

In late 1970 came the news that Webber and Al Jones were going to record an LP of Jones' songs[237]. However, no LP was forthcoming, though there was subsequent TV exposure for the pair when they appeared on the local *Folk in the West* HTV programme along with the Pigsty Hill Light Orchestra, Fred Wedlock and Devonian group, The Westwind, at Christmas 1970. In July 1971 Webber sang on sessions for Dave Evans' first LP, *The Words In Between*, and both Webber and Evans supported the Rev. Gary Davis at a Village Thing-promoted Victoria Rooms concert. Shortly after Evans' LP was released, Webber could be found playing in a trio with Evans and guitarist, Pete Airey.

Webber moved up from the folk clubs and began to gain a wider reputation, helped by a Sounds write-up late in 1973, which began, "Aj Webber is neither to be confused with dustbin Dylanologist A.J. Webberman nor with British bumpkin Adge Cutler, although like Adge she comes from the West country."[238] Like others from the Bristol scene, she began supporting up-and-coming and major acts on their UK tours, including supporting Greenslade at Friars and the Lyceum amongst other venues during July 1974. Greenslade didn't quite make the big time, but a wider exposure was provided when she opened concerts for the Blue Jays[239] during November and December 1975. The tour included Bristol University's Anson Rooms on 27 November and finished up at the Royal Albert Hall. Blue Jays was a Moody Blues spin-off comprising Justin Hayward and John Lodge: the Moody Blues was a major group at this point with a near fanatical fanbase, so this really was excellent exposure. Webber even supported Kraftwerk at one point and one can only imagine what fans of electro-Krautrock made of having a West Country folk singer on the bill.

The increased exposure from playing the concert circuit helped Webber to secure a record deal with Anchor. She went into the studio with some high-profile session musicians, such as keyboard player and arranger, Tony Hymas, who was currently working with Jack Bruce. Mike d'Abo's *Power of Prayer* was issued as a single in early 1976 to promote the LP, which was called simply *Aj Webber*. Webber continued to gig and was chosen to support the Wurzels at the Ashton Court Country Club where they recorded parts of their *I'll Never Get a Scrumpy Here* LP. Webber's second LP, *Of This Land*, was issued in the early 1980s with arrangements by Robert Kirby, who had earlier worked with Keith Christmas, Shelagh McDonald and, more famously, Nick Drake. Although this LP was not as well received as the first, it is infinitely more sought-after by folk collectors and has been spotted priced at anything up to £250 on websites that specialise in obscure and rare private folk records. Whether it sells for that is another matter.

Webber played both Troubadour reunion concerts, the first of which included an extremely chaotic and amusing performance – a certain amount of raucous laughter can be heard on the performance of Bob Dylan's *Don't Think Twice* on the *Waterloo Street Revisited* CD. The second was not quite so chaotic, but again involved stopping several times so that she could peer at the lyrics. A highly entertaining performance was rounded off with Jeremy Taylor's song about the Police Constable in Barnstaple. Of the reunions, Ian Anderson says:

> The night of one of those Troubadour Reunions a few years back a whole gang of us went off for a curry somewhere up Gloucester Rd afterwards and she was a complete star, very funny - her ability to drop in and out of local accent had us in stitches - I still laugh about a saying she said she learned at school … (adopts Bristol accent) "Africal's a Malarial Areal".[240]

The Anchor single shouldn't set you back more than about £5 with the album cropping up fairly often on eBay for less than £10 – sealed American copies seem to be more plentiful than UK copies and shouldn't cost any more than £8 or so.

Fred Wedlock

> … when I started singing in Folk Clubs about ten years ago we were all busy banning the bomb and discovering Dylan. I used to do a lot of serious songs but I always got more reaction from comic numbers so gradually I began to specialise. Now I tend to be classed as "an entertainer" – I'm never sure whether I should be pleased or offended about that![241]

Fred Wedlock started singing when he was two, as a therapy for asthma, and got so good at it that he later sang in St. Mary Redcliffe Church Choir. However, to jump ahead a bit, it was when he was doing a post-graduate course in London in 1963 that he played his first floor spot, in a folk club at the Station Hotel in Sidcup. The guest that evening was Nigel Denver, a Midlands based Scot, and Wedlock was spellbound by the combination of traditional songs and satire added to Denver's power and technique, and in that moment found his own musical direction.

Two years later he went back to London, teaching in the East End by day and learning the folksinger's trade by night. He returned to Bristol and by the mid-1960s was doing floor spots in the Bristol Ballads and Blues Club and the Bristol Poetry and Folk Club, both at the Old Duke. When the Troubadour opened in 1966 he started to work there, both playing and acting as compere, and it was in this latter capacity that Adge Cutler used him during his *Scrumpy and Western* shows in 1967.

However, to now rewind a couple of years, Fred Wedlock was considered a bit of a local folk hero and so got to release the first record on the new Saydisc label in May 1965. The

Bristol folk

record was a 7" EP titled, appropriately enough, *Volume One* and was recorded by Gef Lucena at the Poetry and Folk Club at The Bathurst. There was no catalogue number assigned and the EP is sometimes referred to under the title of *Silbury Hill* – misspelled as "Sibury" on the sleeve, trivia fans – which was the first track one side 1. Only 99 copies were pressed, to avoid having to pay Purchase Tax, and it was issued in a generic Saydisc sleeve with artist and song credits stuck on. No catalogue number was assigned to the record. A Roneo insert was included, which included the following potted history:

> Fred, born in Bristol 23 years ago was educated in Bristol, Swansea and London. His eclectic education gave him a degree in politics, philosophy and psychology ... Fred started playing uke in the Army cadets, then banjo in a Jazz band, aspiring to folk singing and ten string guitar playing a few years ago.

In 1966 Wedlock released a second EP on Saydisc, this time with accompaniment from fellow Ballads and Blues and Poetry and Folk Club regulars, Bev and Richard Dewar, on guitar and fiddle respectively. The record was named after, and included a cover of, Adge Cutler's *Virtute et Industrial* before Cutler got around to recording his own version. Although the EP was a limited edition and sold out very quickly, the title track was reissued on the cheap and cheerful *Sounds of Bristol* 7" in 1973[242]. In early 1967, Wedlock appeared on the *In a Folk Mood* EP by Graham Kilsby – or at least he was credited with "bicycle horn and frenzied applause"[243] on *Chastity Belt*, which was recorded live at the Troubadour.

Wedlock, meanwhile, was making a career of teaching, with gigs taking second place in the making a living stakes. It was October 1971 before he released his next record and, although there were still some serious songs, the humorous side was in the ascendant. *The Folker* was recorded in July 1971 by Ian Anderson in his bedroom in true Bill Leader style and included performances by the whole of the Pigsty Hill Light Orchestra, Ian Hunt – who masqueraded as Stefan Grossman on *Lurn Theeself Fawk* – and Stackridge's Mike Evans. There was, however, a problem that caused the release to be delayed: the ladies that worked at EMI's pressing plant objected to a line on the LP about the Queen being Prince Philip in drag, to the tune of the *National Anthem*. These eagle-eared ladies must have suspected something, because the track wasn't even credited on the sleeve[244]. To get the record pressed, this short track had to be removed and only a few white label test pressings exist of the original version of the LP: these are very rare. Interesting to note is that the LP was advertised as being the first *folk* LP on Village Thing.

It was decided to record the next LP live and so, the Troubadour having closed in 1971, *Frollicks* was recorded by Gef Lucena and David Wilkins at the Stonehouse. Wedlock was joined by Barry Back, Ritchie Gould, Ian Hunt and Martin Runnacles. Wedlock's Village Thing LPs were extremely successful and a Melody Maker article on Wedlock had the following to say about them:

> ... his two albums, "The Folker" and "Frollicks" have easily outsold all other records on the Village Thing label. In fact when it was released "Frollicks" outsold the Rolling Stones in Bristol.[245]

Bristol folk

The Village Thing label folded in 1974 but Wedlock's first two LPs remained on catalogue until the early 1980s through the auspices of Saydisc: these later copies were on a yellow label design. The folding of Village Thing coincided with Wedlock's decision to leave teaching to go fully professional, starting in September 1974 – as Colin Irwin wrote for the Melody Maker, "... he has previously resisted the temptation to leave his job and devote all his time to playing but has now changed his mind,"[246] Wedlock giving the reason as, "The situation now is that I can earn a decent living three nights a week and my wife would see more of me than if I was a teacher."[247] Rather than sign with one of the several interested record companies, Wedlock began his own record company, called Pillock Productions – or Pilluck Producshuns, or any of several other spellings.

In August 1974[248] Wedlock said that he wanted to record the next LP live though not in Bristol, where he felt that his material was too well known. So in 1975 *Fred Wedlock's Homemade Gramophone Record* was recorded at Birmingham Polytechnic, the Strode Theatre in Street and also back home at the Stonehouse. Original copies included an amusing insert, which apologised for a 'technical hitch'. Mike Evans, a regular on Wedlock's gigs, played violin on several tracks and was the butt of several jokes, generally about the inhabitants of Clifton Village. The next release on Pillock was *Greatest Hits*, despite the fact that at this point there hadn't yet been one. This was followed up in 1978 by *Out of Wedlock* on EMI's One-Up imprint, on which Mike Evans and Chris Newman both played.

Wedlock and Newman next recorded a jointly-credited LP, which was released on Pilok – with yet another spelling – in 1979. Dave Cousins, from the Strawbs, heard the LP in his guise as a radio DJ and suggested that *The Oldest Swinger in Town* should be released as a single. The single was pressed up on the hurriedly-invented Coast label, which was created by Wedlock's manager, Kevin Wyatt-Lown, as a limited press of 1,000, and was either sold at gigs or sent around the trade to get further bookings. One of the trade copies got into the hands of Noel Edmonds' producer, who suggested to Edmonds that it had the makings of a hit. Edmonds played it twice in the same show and by the next week had got hold of the news that Wedlock wasn't signed. The immediate upshot was that Rocket picked up the option and the Pilok LP was re-jigged with a different track listing – unfortunately losing *Tits and Bums* along the way – and released in a brand, new sleeve design. The single was reissued at the end of 1980 by Rocket – it entered the UK charts in January 1981, reaching number 6 and getting Wedlock a spot on Top of the Pops (available on YouTube). Rocket put out one more LP before the furore died down, but all this has taken us into the 1980s.

Wedlock, by now was making the transition from folk musician to TV personality and became very well-known on local TV in the 1980s and throughout the 1990s. He also appeared in stage productions, one of which, *Up the Feeder and Down the Mouth*, was staged on the docks and featured a real moving ship, working cranes and a steam train amongst the cast. Musically, Fred Wedlock does lots of private events and concerts but still plays folk clubs and festivals with undiminished enthusiasm – and is still extremely and refreshingly un-PC, as his rendition of *Swing Low, Sweet Charlie Dimmock*, complete with rather interesting hand gestures, at the second Troubadour reunion in 2004 showed.

The first two Saydisc EPs are extremely rare and are likely to set you back £30 or so each if you are lucky enough to find copies – perhaps even more with original sleeves and inserts. The Village Thing LPs shouldn't set you back more than £10, though the first press of *The Folker* on the original Village Thing label design is starting to sneak up as people discover that the LP was issued on the first label design as well. Later copies of these two LPs on the later yellow label design might cost up to £15 as these are much harder to find than originals. Also, if you are lucky enough to find a white label test pressing of *The Folker*, check it to see if it includes the offending line about the Queen being Prince Philip in drag: if it does, you might be looking at £40 to £50. An original Pilok label copy of *The Oldest Swinger in Town* LP could cost anything up to £10 on eBay, and the original single could cost anything up to £5, though you are equally likely to find them both for 50p at local carboots. The Rocket issues of these records, apart from being outside of the bounds of this book as 1980s releases, are near worthless because they sold in truckloads – though remember that the LP is not quite the same as the Pilok original, so if you're a completist you'll need to buy both.

White on Black

White on Black was formed in Hartcliffe by Sue Franklin, Jon Knowler and Suzi Lawrence. Jon Knowler was a teacher at Hartcliffe School, and both Sue and Suzi were pupils when they first met. They formed a group, initially to play at school concerts and charity events, and covered popular folk, pop and country in a very easy-listening fashion. They also played compositions by musicians on the local scene, such as Andy Leggett's *Morning* and Pat Small's *Bramble Cottage*. To begin with they wore stage gear that matched their name with swirly black patterns on a white backing – as promotional photos show, these outfits were very much of their time.

They were kept busy on the folk club and cabaret circuits where their uncomplicated approach, confident vocal harmonies and a clever choice of material that specifically suited them made them a lot of fans over the next few years. Andy Leggett remembers that the group started their first folk club, "… in a pub on the Wells Road at Whitchurch (The Little Thatch?)"[249], after which they went on, with manager, Pam Tobin, to start the popular White on Black Folk Club at the Arts Centre on King's Square. By 1972 they shared a residency at the club along with Hunt and Turner, Decanter, Adrienne and Angie and Min, though their popularity on the folk scene caused regular absences, which were commented upon in a local listings paper:

> White on Black, still touring above the arctic circle, (Middlesborough was it?) wish to apologise for not appearing at their club as often as they would like: in the meantime nonetheless the faithful squad of residents headed by Hunt & Turner and Adrienne are doing the honours.[250]

Members of the White on Black club were able to benefit further from their membership because of a reciprocal deal with the Toby Folk Club at the Red Lion in West Pennard, Somerset. Members also benefitted from the *Bristol Arts Centre Folkie Pantomime*, which

Bristol folk

took place on 29th and 30th December 1972 with the Pigsty Hill Light Orchestra, Decanter and Fred Wedlock adding to the fun.

The group went into the studio to record a single and recorded four tracks, so as to have a choice of material, including two songs written by local songwriters, Con Moore and Pat Small. A newspaper article[251] made much of the fact that there were many Bristol connections associated with the recording: the musical director was avant-garde composer and jazz musician Neil Ardley, who had been a Chemistry student at Bristol University, and Mike Jones, the engineer, had been a pupil at Colston Boys School. With no other evidence than an anonymous newspaper clipping available, whether the single was ever released remains a mystery. Certainly no copies seem to have filtered out into the collectors' scene – the White On Black that issued at least one single on Philips in the mid-1970s was a different group.

In 1973 the group made an LP for Saydisc, and this was issued in early 1974. Apart from Pat Small's *Bramble Cottage*, the songs were covers of popular songs by the likes of Joni Mitchell, Lindisfarne, The Beatles and Simon and Garfunkel. The music press was kind to the White on Black LP, sometimes with implied criticism for aiming squarely at the less-discerning end of the folk audience, but praising the LP for being a good example of genre, *Bramble Cottage* picked out for especial praise.

> … they shouldn't be criticised for aiming at a less specialised audience and in fact show a great deal of promise here. Singers Sue Franklin and Suzi Lawrence shine in parts and the whole performance is one of enthusiasm and vitality … "Bramble Cottage" is provably (sic) the best track.[252]

All three members of the group played guitar and Franklin also played cello and recorder, whilst Lawrence played flute. They were supported on the LP by John Turner on acoustic bass, Al Jones on guitar, Richard Gould from Decanter on electric bass and John 'Wash' Hays from the Pigsty Hill Light Orchestra on percussion. Perhaps the most surprising person to appear on the LP was Al Jones, who at this point had all but left playing behind him – certainly Jones' inclusion is the main reason for this LP to be valued so highly in collecting circles. Copies have sold for anywhere up to £70, though after peaking a few years ago you should be able to pick a copy up on eBay for around £25. The LP was sold at gigs and the trio happily signed copies – it is certainly hard to find non-autographed copies of the LP and some Japanese collectors have been known to pay more for a non-autographed copy. Although the group never made another record, they did get a "Special thanks" on the sleeve for the Avon Cities Jazz Band's *Silver Collection* LP in 1974.

In 1975, Chris Newman left the Pigsty Hill Light Orchestra and joined White on Black and in December of that year they played, along with the Pigsty Hill Light Orchestra, at Fred Wedlock's Christmas Concert at the Colston Hall. Jon Knowler acted as compere for the evening wearing a giant frog costume. He evidently did a very creditable imitation of Kermit the frog as well as presenting an updated version of the *12 Days of Christmas*, where the recipient of the gifts ended up instructing their solicitor to stop the persecution of being sent such bloody stupid presents as eight maids a-milking. I mean, thinking logically, where *would* you keep them?

Meanwhile, Jon Knowler married Suzi Lawrence and in 1976 Suzi Knowler, as she now was, sang backing vocals along with Chris Newman's wife, Min, on the sessions for Pat Small's *Man of Bristol* single and later played flute on Chris Newman's first LP. Sue Franklin formed a new group, called Sun, with Tim Brine and Andy Hammond, both of whom had been in Decanter. Sun played regularly at Reg Mann's Folk at the Flyer club at the Bristol Flyer pub and recorded a cassette album at Raspberry Studios in Chipping Sodbury before Sue and Tim, now married, went out as a duo, making a CD titled *Distances*, produced at the Bristol Old Vic Theatre School by the late John Waterhouse of Christchurch Studios. Jon Knowler later joined Bristol shanty group, The Harry Browns, who were named after the familiar, old ship that used to ply the river Avon in the 1970s. Knowler's joining the Harry Browns perhaps shows the interconnectedness of all things – in the mid-1970s, White on Black were represented by the same Stratton on the Fosse-based agent as was Erik Ilott, the Bristol Shantyman, and here thirty years later Knowler was singing much of Ilott's repertoire, such as the Bristol shanty, *Aboard the Kangaroo*. Sue and Tim are still singing, now in a group with their daughter and son-in-law.

The Wurzels

The Wurzels were put together by Adge Cutler in 1966 and became a popular act on the club and cabaret circuit. By 1974, the line-up was Cutler, Tommy Banner, Tony Bayliss and Pete Budd. They appeared in a TV series, *The Great Western Musical Thunderbox*, where Cutler waved his wurzel stick in time-honoured manner. The bookings remained plentiful, even if EMI had dropped the band in 1971, and the future looked bright. However, on 5th May 1974, Cutler was killed in a car crash on his way home from a week-long series of gigs in Hereford.

Cutler had been the undisputed star of the group, being the band's focal point and song writer and it would have been easy to call it a day in 1974. However, the band and their manager, John Miles, decided that the best way to pay tribute to Cutler was to carry on. The onus for becoming front man was placed firmly on Pete Budd because he was the only one with a Somerset accent. The band kept many old favourites in their set, but it was obvious that without Cutler things would not be the same, so they made the sensible decision to adapt the act, moving toward a more pop-oriented sound. There was a bit of sprucing up of the image as well and the soft hats went.

In July 1975 the first post-Cutler LP, *The Wurzels are Scrumptious!*, was recorded half in the studio and half at the Ruda Holiday Park, in Croyde Bay, Devon. It was issued with a sleeve photo that made the band look like the Bachelors – except that the Bachelors are usually holding comforting coffee mugs rather than pint mugs of cider. Much like Pink Floyd's first post-Syd Barrett LP, the ex-leader was still much in evidence with the band using several of Cutler's previously unrecorded songs – *Look At 'Ee, Lookin' At I*, *The Market Gardener*, which related back to Cutler's time as a market gardener in Nailsea, and

Bristol folk

I'm the Captain of a Dredger. All of these co-credited Henry Davis, who had acted as Cutler's musical director. The band also re-recorded old favourites *Twice Daily*, *The Shepton Mallet Matador* and *Drink Up Thy Zider* and Trevor Crozier's *Don't Tell I, Tell 'Ee*. The band wrote some new material in *A Drinking Man's Life* and *Cheddar Cheese*, but it was their adaptation of *Speedy Gonzales* that showed the shape of hits to come. Bristol drummer, Tony Fennel played on some tracks as did EMI session drummers, Dougie Wright – who had previously played on *Carry On Cutler!* – and Andy White, who is best-known for replacing an untried Ringo Starr on the first takes of the Beatles' *Love Me Do* single in 1962. *I'm the Captain of a Dredger* was planned as a single, but was not released, though incredibly rare test pressings exist. All in all, the first Wurzels LP was a bit of a pot boiler: it didn't do too badly, but it didn't trouble the charts either.

This all changed with the next LP. The material for *The Combine Harvester* LP was recorded at the Yew Tree Club at Langford, just off Mendip, in the newly-formed County of Avon. The LP release was preceded by a single, *The Combine Harvester*, which was based on Melanie's recent hit, *Brand New Key*, with new lyrics written by Bredan Grace, an Irishman, who had had a minor hit with the song himself. The single received a great deal of airplay and entered the UK charts on 15th May 1976. It hit number 1, staying on the charts for 13 weeks. The single is also documented as having topped the Canadian charts after the group toured Canada, though this would appear, on checking of the Canadian charts, to be an urban myth – or, in the context of the Wurzels, should that be a 'rural myth'?

The LP was issued in July and spent 20 weeks on the UK album charts, reaching number 15. The LP included some singalongs, such as Alex Glasgow's music hall-esque *Keep Yer 'And On Yer 'Alfpenny*, plus another previously unrecorded Adge Cutler song, the very gentle and pretty *Down In Nempnett Thrubwell* and there was also a throwback to *The Bristol Song* in Pete Budd's *Somerset Born and Bred*, which reprised the former song's light calypso feel. The band was featured on many local and national television shows and made the obligatory appearances on Top of the Pops.

Two further singles were released in 1976. The first was in the mould of their recent hit and was an adaptation of The George Baker Selection's *Una Poloma Blanca*, renamed *I Am a Cider Drinker*. This was issued in September and stayed on the charts for 9 weeks, getting to number 3. This was followed-up in November with *Morning Glory*. Worryingly, *Morning Glory* was not a national hit, though it sold well locally, especially as the song was picked up on by fans of Bristol City, which led to a rewording, re-titling and reissue of the song.

The band recorded the *Golden Delicious* LP in the studio and released it in April 1977. The winning formula was followed with more self-penned songs about Somerset, agriculture and cider, complemented by singalongs, though perhaps the real gem was a cover of John Christie's *Cabot Song*. The LP spent 5 weeks in the UK charts and got to number 32. Next up was the single, *Farmer Bill's Cowman*, based on *I Was Kaiser Bill's Batman*. This entered the UK charts on 25th June 1977 and got to number 35, remaining on chart for 5 weeks. The follow-up single, *Give Me England!*, was released in September 1977 and *One For the Bristol City* – an adaptation of *Morning Glory* – was issued later in the year, though neither

Bristol folk

single reached the charts. *One For the Bristol City* was issued in a picture sleeve and these copies are exceptionally hard to find, even in Bristol.

The next album, *Give Me England*, was another studio recording, some recorded at Rockfield, a studio more used to progressive rock bands, such as Van der Graaf Generator and Man. It was released in December 1977, just in time for the Christmas market, and the formula was almost the same, although there seemed to be some fudging of the focus with songs based on general nostalgia added to the more usual West Country themes for no adequately explored reason – perhaps because Somerset was popularly believed to be well behind the times. John Christie's *Willie Freise-Greene* was the low-key standout track.

Despite their waning chart success, the band remained a popular live act and parts of their next LP, *I'll Never Get a Scrumpy Here*, were recorded live at Ashton Court Country Club in front of an enthusiastic audience that included invited members of the Wurzels Fan Club. On this gig, they were supported by Aj Webber, who had worked with Adge Cutler's original Wurzels on the Scrumpy and Western shows back in 1967. The first releases from these recordings were two singles: *The Tractor Song* – an adaptation of *The Pushbike Song* – was issued in May 1978 and promotional copies of *I'll Never Get a Scrumpy Here* were sent out in August, though no normal copies were pressed. In between these two singles, EMI reissued the *Don't Tell I, Tell 'Ee* compilation in a different sleeve and with three extra tracks added from the *Cutler Of the West* LP. Oddly, this last is one of the hardest LPs to find.

In November 1978, the *I'll Never Get a Scrumpy Here* LP was released and this time around the standout track was Tommy Banner's instrumental *Somerset Jigolo*, a set of jigs played on accordion. There's just one thing that needs to be mentioned about the LP sleeve: if you look closely at the photo on the back you may notice that, far from being taken in France, it looks suspiciously as though it was taken just outside the Victoria Rooms at the bottom end of Whiteladies Road, with what is now Habitat just out of shot.

As new product was no longer selling as well as it had a couple of years previously EMI began to release further back catalogue. The *I Am a Cider Drinker* compilation was issued in June 1979 and this was followed obscenely quickly by *The Wurzels Greatest Hits* in November. The former included some otherwise single-only tracks whilst the latter included the previously unreleased disco version of *Drink Up Thy Zider*.

The early to mid-1980s saw little let down in the band's live schedule but EMI, with dwindling sales, again quietly dropped the band. Bob Barrett continued to work with them, producing their first post-EMI LP on their own label. The late 1980s and much of the 1990s saw fewer recordings and a gradual reduction in live work. However, in the new Millennium EMI saw fit to reissue much of the Wurzel's back catalogue on CD. Soon afterwards the group gained new management in the form of Sil Willcox of Cruisin' Music, who steered the band back into the limelight and public consciousness with the release of new recordings and a constant stream of live bookings. Here in 2009 the Wurzels are once more part and parcel of Bristolian and Somerset life and, thanks to appearances on such TV shows as *Never Mind the Buzzcocks* and *A Question of Sport*, amongst others, are back in the national

Bristol folk

psyche too. The Wurzels have been around, in one form or another, for over 43 years at time of writing and look like going on for a very long time yet. Good luck to them.

There is nothing particularly rare from the 1970s and most LPs can be found for £8 or less – the rarities began once EMI dropped the band in the early 1980s. Of the singles, the three hits should be no more than £1, though the rest could cost £5 each, with *One for the Bristol City* in picture sleeve usually costing closer to £15 - that said a copy appeared in a football memorabilia auction recently at £99.99. It remained unsold in that particular auction, but football-related memorabilia does sell for silly amounts sometimes.

Postscript: when Melanie played *Brand New Key* at Frome in 2007, she said that she was aware of where she was in the UK[253] and finished off with the Wurzels' version of the song.

Nearly made it…

Decanter, like many other semi-pro folk bands on the circuit, played the Bristol folk clubs during the early 1970s. The group was made up of Andy Hammond on guitar, Tim Brine, also on guitar, Chris Matthews on banjo, Richard Gould on bass and Sarah Bale on vocals and flute. Much like White on Black, they ploughed a folk furrow that was also at home on the cabaret circuit, with their repertoire ranging from unaccompanied singing to covering of popular American singer-songwriters, such as James Taylor. All bar one of their songs were covers, the exception being an original setting by Bale of one of Shakespeare's sonnets. Of their repertoire and the make-up of the group, Sarah Bale said:

> … it seems a pity to restrict ourselves. Our musical origins are very diverse. I played classical flute for 8 years, Tim played jazz for a long time … [there] is so much good stuff around now, we haven't needed to fall back on our own songs … we never sing the same programme two nights running, because we ourselves feel the need for a change, and because many of the people in Bristol have seen us before.[254]

The group recorded an LP in 1971, recorded by Arthur Radford of Radfords hi-fi and electronics business, which was described by Sarah Bale as, "… completely acoustic and natural … "[255] However, group members attest that the LP was not released with, apparently, no copies pressed, which is why the group appears here instead of in the main section.

The members of the group were very realistic about the ups and downs of the music business and all were noted to have kept their daytime jobs as insurance. Richard Gould later played on Fred Wedlock's *Frollicks* and Gould, Sarah Bale and Andy Hammond played on Rod Neep's two LPs, the first being recorded in mid-1973, though by this time Decanter had broken up. Gould later joined the Pigsty Hill Light Orchestra and in the 1990s was a member of the reformed Quarry Men[256], the latter along with Stonehouse Sunday afternoon session drummer, Charlie Hart. Sarah Bale married Rod Neep, whilst Tim Brine married Sue Franklin from White on Black. The Brines then formed a band called Sun along with Andy Hammond, who went on to make a cassette album.

Bristol folk

Dr. Bowser's Brown Bowel Oil Band was formed in 1976 as the Pill Pushers Band. They gigged solidly from October of that year until August 1986, playing usually with a line-up of about half a dozen, plus a caller. They didn't make their first LP until 1981, however, which is why they are not featured in the main section of the book. They released *A Good Run for Your Money* in 1981 and *Not to Be Sniffed At* in 1985, both of which were recorded by Dave Byrne from Elecampane. You can probably pick both up locally for under £10 but copies with the inserts are heading toward £20 on eBay. Beware the second LP – any sticker on the sleeve tends to leave a great, big tear when you try to remove it.

Chris Newman, despite having been active on the scene and playing on and producing other people's records in the 1970s, did not record an LP under his own name until 1981 – although, admittedly, the original version of the *The Oldest Swinger in Town* LP was credited to "Fred Wedlock and Chris Newman". Anything with his name on is well worth picking up and all, apart from the Fred Wedlock LPs, are generally around the £8 mark. *Chris Newman* and *Chris Newman Two* on the Coast label are particularly worthwhile – *Chris Newman Two* includes Fred Wedlock, on triangle, if the sleeve credits are to be believed! Read through the sections on the Pigsty Hill Light Orchestra, Fred Wedlock and White on Black for further information on Chris Newman – to be honest, he'll probably get a section to himself in the next edition.

Q. Williams is not the first person you might associate with folk music, having been a stalwart of the Bristol jazz scene since the late 1940s, playing in the Palatine Jazz Band, the Gordon Redman Wolverines, Henry's Bootblacks and Acker Bilk's Paramount Jazz Band, amongst others. However, if the book includes guitarists who played in a ragtime style, then why not those who played ragtime piano? Also, Williams played the original version of the near-legendary ballcockaphone with the Alligator Jug Thumpers. The Alligator Jug Thumpers were mistakenly put together in 1966 to back Adge Cutler and originally comprised Williams, Barry Back and Cliff Brown. However, Cutler did not need the band because he had already put the Wurzels together – nevertheless, the Jug Thumpers decided to stay together and were invited by Cutler to appear in his Scrumpy and Western shows in 1967 and the Wurzelrama shows in 1968. Both Williams and Back eventually left to be replaced by Andy Leggett and, briefly, Al Jones. When the group disbanded, the Pigsty Hill Light Orchestra formed in its wake. The Pigs went on to build a bigger ballcockaphone, but Andy Leggett paid tribute to the originator thus:

> … I'm not the originator of the Ballcockaphone. I stumbled upon it in a group called the Alligator Jug Thumpers who were predecessors of the Pigs. In that group it was played with great aplomb by a certain C. Q. Williams. I have expanded upon his model. If you compare the two models, you'll find that the Pigs' Ballcockaphones have bigger horns and more colourful balls than the Alligator's Ballcockaphone …[257]

The Alligator Jug Thumpers reformed just once in the late 1970s to perform *Sweet Miss Emmaline* in Neil Innes' BBC TV series, *The Innes Book of Records*. The Alligator Jug Thumpers didn't make any records, but Williams, whilst a member of the group, played on the 1966 Saydisc compilation LP, *Ragtime Piano*. It was subtitled *British Ragtime – Volume*

Bristol folk

One, not that a *Volume Two* was ever issued, and it also included performances by Neville Dickie and Pete 'Henry' Davies. What makes this LP worth hunting out is the fact that Williams' tracks are self-composed rather than the more usual covers. The LP was available for several years on several different label designs but is incredibly hard to find, though it tends to have a fairly low price if you find a copy: £5 to £10 should secure one.

Bristol folk

'Bonus tracks': the artists remember…

Ian Anderson remembers…

"The first couple of years after I left school I worked in an accountants' office in Bristol. I'd scraped enough A-Levels for a place at Bristol Uni to do Economics but had completely had it with formal education by then and just wanted to get on with life. The fact that I wasn't a student didn't stop me from spending most of my leisure and social time hanging out in the Student's Union though: security was pretty lax and once the staff got used to the sight of you, they never asked for a Union card[258]. Even that wouldn't have stopped me going to the Bristol University Folk & Blues Club as it was open to the public and many local folk artists used to do floor spots as well as all the student musicians.

"The academic year 1965/66 was the peak of the post-Dylan folk boom in the UK, and the University Folk Club was reportedly the biggest event society within Bristol Uni that year, with attendances that often dwarfed the Saturday night rock gigs – quite often getting audiences of over 500. That particular year they booked the biggest names on tour in the UK including Tom Paxton, Phil Ochs, Spider John Koerner (my hero, who I very proudly gave a bed to in the flat that Backwater Jook Band washboard player/ dental student Bob Summers and I shared, while I slept in the bath!), Julie Felix, Mike Seeger, Buffy Sainte Marie, Bert Jansch, Pete Stanley & Wizz Jones and The Watersons. They did so well that they kept making a profit, so they kept reducing door prices lower and lower each week in an attempt to spend their grant allocation or they wouldn't get it again the next year! Club organiser that year and 66/67 was John (or Jon?) Simmonds. [67/68 – Jim Fussell; 68/69 – Tony Stone; 69/70 Barbara ("Pebbles") Stone; 70/71 – Maggie Holland] … To get ahead of myself here, but show how all this intertwined – 69/70 University club organiser Pebbles shared a flat at 12A Royal York Crescent, and when she moved out in 1970, passed it on to John Turner and I who moved in from the flat over the Troubadour. John later moved on when Maggie Holland and I got married later that year, but we ran the early Village Thing from that address…

"At some point around [late 1965] I'd met Elliot Jackson who was learning blues harmonica. We actually met in weekly day-release accountancy lectures, both sat in the back row, bored shitless, and then discovered we were both reading copies of *Blues Unlimited* tucked inside our accountancy text books! Around Feb/March '66 we were sat in a pub in Park Row where there were regular informal jam sessions – I think it was called the Somerset then, not now – and in walked this guy in scooter gear with a guitar case slung over his shoulder. He turned out to be a) a fantastic 12-string guitar player and b) Al Jones, who had just moved to Bristol. I think we instantly decided he was too much competition so we'd better form a group together! So Anderson, Jones, Jackson arrived, Bristol's answer to Koerner, Ray & Glover.

Bristol folk

I think we got quite good quite quickly, so when the Troubadour opened in October '66 we were the first artists to play there … I chucked in my accountancy job in summer '67 – by that point I was living in the infamous "Freak House" at 2 Grove Road, off Blackboy Hill, where many of the visiting artists for the Troubadour would end up staying – Incredible String Band, Watersons, regularly Al Stewart etc – so there wasn't much sleep to be had! And anyway it was the "Summer Of Love"!

"[After Al Jones left for London,] Elliot and I kept on as a duo – as well as club stuff we did a couple of TV things for BBC's *Points West* (29th March) and the TWW's *TWW Reports* (9th April). By this time I was heavily into being heads-down authentic blues. Somewhere around then, trying to prove some long-forgotten point, we'd hauled little amplifiers, a borrowed electric guitar and a bass player down to the Ballads & Blues to do a spot of pretending to be Muddy Waters. The Ballads crowd were usually pretty broad minded, but this was too much for them and they hated it and showed it. As we snuck to the back of the room, we spotted Paul Carter (an early director of Topic Records) and his wife Angela (who had not yet become the famous novelist she would later) at the bar. They ran the (reputedly) hardline traditionalist "Folksong & Ballad" club at the Lansdowne in Clifton and if anybody was guaranteed to hate what we'd just done, it would be them. So imagine our surprise when they greeted us warmly, said how much they'd admired the integrity of what we'd just done, and invited us to do a spot at their club. To my regret now, I never dared…

"67/68 was an incredible time for the folk and blues scenes in Bristol; the Troubadour had probably been the final catalyst for lift-off. There were clubs every night of the week, huge audiences, for electric blues via a fantastic young local band The Deep Blues Band (with whom I occasionally sang) as well as the acoustic stuff. As a typical example, one Saturday in October, Al Stewart was at the Troubadour, Stefan Grossman at the Ballads & Blues and Pink Floyd at the Victoria Rooms, and all were packed! We were completely immersed in all this, with a strong axis evolved between the Bristol Troubadour and Les Cousins in London, the club at 49 Greek Street where everybody famous in folk played. As a typical example, in '68, after a packed Bristol gig with Spider John Koerner, he took Al Jones and I back to London and put us on during his allnighter at the Cousins, where Davey Graham played bongos with us! Just as John Renbourn had taken Al Jones under his wing and out on his gigs to do floor spots, Al Stewart kindly did the same with me, especially after I moved to London and Les Cousins became my regular hangout for that period.

"The Deep (a.k.a. The Deep Blues Band) … were quite young but extraordinarily talented. Whenever major blues bands came to Bristol - this was the John Mayall, Chicken Shack, Groundhogs era - they'd invariably be the support and be a hard act to follow. They also had a jammed packed regular gig at the Dugout in Park Row for a while. They were a real local cult band, and people still talk of them now in mild awe[259]. I first met them when they were in the audiences - they were mostly still at school I think - for our Folk Blues Bristol & West club at the Troubadour and then the Old Duke, and I ended up singing with them occasionally in 1968, doing 1920s country blues songs in wild early 1950s Memphis era Howling Wolf style! Anyway, eventually and in quick succession their drummer Ken Pustelnik got recruited by the Groundhogs, their astounding guitarist Adrian "Putty" Pietryga

Bristol folk

by the John Dummer Blues Band, I stole their bass player Bob Rowe for Ian Anderson's Country Blues Band when I moved briefly to London in 68/69, and their next guitarist Pete Emery also ended up in London in Jo-Ann Kelly's band (they later got married). All of them recorded in those later outfits

"We were already getting national airplay from John Peel, Mike Raven and others from the [Saydisc] EPs, and support from Alexis Korner who had written nice words in *Melody Maker*. During the first half of '68, as all the frontrunners of the UK country blues scene came down to the club at the Old Duke, we recorded them at the Meeting House, Frenchay on the Sunday afternoon, and when we had enough the compilation LP *Blues Like Showers Of Rain* went into production… With that record, everything caught fire. I spent my 21st birthday in July '68 tramping the streets of Notting Hill looking for a flat, and did my first John Peel session in August '68. The success of *Blues Like Showers Of Rain* meant that myself, Mike Cooper and Jo-Ann Kelly in particular began to get chased by major labels and producers.

"A diversion into the history of the Troubadour here. It was a very unique concept, a club on two floors (ground and basement) so when it was full, artists had to repeat their set from one floor on the other! Nobody objected, other than a very drunken John Martyn on around his third visit who became very loudly and disruptively obnoxious about it and had to be paid off and asked to leave! It opened up to seven nights a week at its peak, but was just a coffee bar, unlicensed. In spite of its strange layout, there was a period when it was easily the most successful folk venue in the UK outside London, attracting an incredible standard of resident artists – probably more who made albums than any folk club other than Les Cousins in London – and a who's who of guest artists. In October 1970, *Melody Maker* reported that more than 30,000 had taken out membership by then (it held about 180!).

"It was opened in October 1966 by Ray & Barbara Willmott (he was a Bristolian who had emigrated to Australia, then returned with his Australian wife). But by 1969 they'd had enough of the long hours for small returns and with Barbara homesick, decided to return to Australia. Somehow they produced accounts which made the Troubadour look an attractive business investment and it was bought by Peter Bush who owned the Globetrotters Club and other nightclubs/ gambling clubs. He installed local musician John Turner (who had been playing with the Downsiders and was now in at the beginning of the Pigsty Hill Light Orchestra) as resident manager.

"This was round about the point I returned from London, and for the next year John struggled to make the club earn enough to satisfy Peter Bush, who saw income so much lower than he expected that he incorrectly assumed he was being swindled. All the club's illustrious residents rallied round and often played nights for free or low door percentages to help the takings, but it still didn't add up to what Peter Bush expected. So around June '70, John was relieved of his duties and we moved round the corner to 12A Royal York Crescent. Peter Bush installed a new manager, Tim Hodgson, who came from the business world (he'd been a debt collector!), wore a suit and knew nothing about folk … The incredible happened. In a very short space of time Tim Hodgson fell in love with the

Troubadour ethos, became a devoted friend of all the musicians, changed sides, grew his hair, and continued the attempts to keep the Troubadour going by any means possible! Between us we all managed it for another year until Peter Bush finally lost his patience and closed it without notice in summer 1971."

Geoff Gale remembers…

"Although I'm a confirmed rocker – Gene Vincent and the Blue Caps, Billy Fury and the Shadows must all share some of the blame – my guitar business brought me into everyday contact with most of Bristol's folkies. I was part of Bristol's music scene from the late 1960s through to the 1980s and played in rock bands such as Screw, Wisper and Looney Tunes amongst others. I also serviced and built guitars – anything from general instrument maintenance, refretting, refinishing, general damage repair, and so on, to building guitars from my own designs – and two guitars I built ended up appearing on Top of the Pops!

"Geoff Gale Guitars (GGG) was based at several premises over the 1970s. I started working from home in Worcester Terrace in Clifton at the start of the 70s and remember having all of Shaking Stevens and the Sunsets there at one point, when their bassist needed emergency repairs – a broken machine head and nut, as I remember. A very funny and likable lot – just naturally amusing people. I also remember doing a refret for Frank Evans – Gibson 175, beautiful guitar!

"Around 1972 I moved into Bristol Musical on Horfield Road with Brian Coombs (and Willy Westlake from Wisper upstairs, dealing with amps) and a couple of years later I moved to my own workshop on Cotham Hill. Without going back and looking through my records, I couldn't say exactly when I did work for various people, though I can remember what work I did for them. I remember doing general instrument maintenance for the blues and folk set, such as Fred Wedlock, Steve Tilston, Dave Evans, Ian Hunt, John Turner, Keith Warmington, Kelvin Henderson and so on, as well as for bands, such as Macarthur Park, Stackridge, Squidd, Groundhogs, Man, Kind Hearts and English, the Climax Chicago Blues Band (I also built a guitar for their bassist, Derek Holt), Magic Muscle – and I even repaired a broken machine head on a bass for Martha Reeves and the Vandellas. I did general instrument maintenance work for the Plastic Dog people and if bands they'd booked for the Granary needed emergency guitar repairs, they generally got sent to me.

"I routinely did work for the bands I played with. Apart from the general maintenance side, when I was in the Graham Smith Combo with Huw Gower, I built guitars for both Graham and Huw. I also built a guitar for Roger Pomphrey when we were both in Looney Tunes – Roger went on to play with the Eurythmics. I also built a guitar for Ian Hunt – that had a mahogany Fender Strat body. Back to Graham Smith – he'd been in Canton Trig and played harmonica as well as guitar. He made a decent living from sessions and I drove him to a session in London for Greg Lake – must have been around 1976 or 77. Graham was booked to play harmonica and Greg Lake was generous to a fault – there was a huge supply of food and drink (etcetera!) laid on – a really nice guy.

Bristol folk

In the late 70s, when I was based in Alma Vale Road – it's still a music shop today – my guitars started to get very flattering reviews in national and international music papers and magazines after I took a stand at the London Trade Fair – a review of my Pulsar Fretless bass in Sounds in September 1978 started 'Force ten Gale takes reviewers by storm' and the photos were taken by Jill Furmanovsky. I had no idea until recently that she was such a famous rock photographer! In 1979 my guitars were showcased in Sound International – a serious trade magazine, with articles on people like Stockhausen – and the Magnum was reviewed in 'The Sounds Book of the Electric Guitar' in 1980. Guitars that I built for Andy Davies and James Warren, who I'd known since the Stackridge days, ended up on Top of the Pops during this period. Andy Davies played his on TOTP with the Korgis, but James Warren passed his on to Tears for Fears, and it was with them that it appeared on TOTP, though I can't remember which of the main two it was who played it.

"Others on the Bristol scene that I did work for over the years – admittedly nothing to do with the folk scene, though there are a fair few blues bands in there – included the Dragons, the Soul Searchers, the Korgis, Steve Payne's Paynekillers and Candy Run (and the Stan Arnold Combo before them), Fred Bloggs Band, the Fans, the Spics, the Cortinas, Uncle Po, Huggett, the Untouchables, the Explosions, Dodd's Army, Crazy Trains, Stargazer, Chantilly Lace and Eddie Martin (I remember refretting his Gibson 335). Some of these might have been in the 1980s, but they all deserve mention because they were all important parts of the vibrant local music scene.

"I moved near full-time into production of my guitars but shut the business in the early 1980s after the distributor went bust owing lots of money for guitars supplied. Nowadays I maintain, restore and supply Datsun Z Series cars and heckle the bar staff in the Hillgrove Porters Stores. The next project is to build an eco-house, hopefully in the Mendips. In the meantime, if you've got a Datsun Z you want maintained, rebuilt or restored, or if you want to buy a lovingly-restored Datsun Z, you can find me at www.auto-active.co.uk."

Andy Leggett remembers…

"The first person to hear the words "Pigsty Hill Light Orchestra" strung together in that order was Patrick Small. In 1968 he and I were a couple of folkies whiling away our unspare time helping to build the Concorde at Filton. I had bought a house adjacent to the steepish bit of the Gloucester Road at Bishopston, and thought it would be nice to keep the old name alive; (there had been pig farms there years ago, and the off-license on the corner, now part of Bristol Tools, had previously been the Pig and Whistle).

"Patrick didn't immediately share my vision for a jazz-based jug band, so it was formed as a re-invention of the Alligator Jug Thumpers, i.e. Barry Back and myself, minus that band's founder, Cliff Brown of the Chew Valley Jazz Band, but bringing in Dave Creech of the Elastic Band. John Turner was in on string bass since, being the resident compere of the Bristol Troubadour Club, he accompanied nearly everybody who played there, and knew our repertoire.

Bristol folk

"I had been getting increasingly dissatisfied with extra responsibilities being heaped onto me at the aircraft factory for no extra reward, so when the other three announced that they'd given up their jobs – "We're going on the road. How about you?" - it took me only five seconds or so to reach a decision and say "Yes".

"We didn't make much cash at first, but with Plastic Dog as our agents, things improved. Then, after an appearance at the Cambridge Folk Festival - (doesn't "Foambridge Cake Festival" sound nicer?) – a Belgian agent called Leon Lamal got us a spot on Belgian TV and for several years we could do no wrong in the Flemish-speaking parts of that fair land.

"Arriving at RAF Gütersloh to entertain in one of the messes, John wound the van window down and addressed the military policeman on the gate; "Hallo Biggles! Can you tell us where to go?" The rest of us were trying to hide under the seats.

"While making our first LP (VTS1) at Gef Lucena's house on Inglestone Common, JT was suffering with toothache. For weeks after, we were unsympathetically but gleefully singing "I ain't gonna play no second fiddle, I'm OwwwwWWWW!", and referring to him as "Toothache Turner". As Barry worked as a sound-mixer for HTV, he was able to persuade a film crew to turn out on a Sunday. A black and white film was produced of Barry, Dave, John and me, chasing each other round the shortly-to-be-demolished Thornbury railway station. The sound-track was Cushion Foot Stomp – the first track on Village Thing's first album. Unfortunately, this masterpiece was stored in HTV's archives, and at some subsequent date was cleared out and presumably destroyed.

"On the 24th May 1971, we were featured on HTV's Report West. As I coaxed melody out of the "ball-cockophone", Les Dawson stood beside me fondling its spherical component, pulling lascivious faces. Unfortunately no recording of that show exists.

"One icy evening, Dave, Barry and I had been waiting in the biting wind for John to pick us up. In the end just the three of us drove off in my Citroën Light Fifteen. The job passed off well enough with no bass, and with only three ways to split the cash, that's how we decided to stay. Just weeks later, JT astonished us with his success as Radio Bristol's new presenter, and before long he'd teamed up with Ian Hunt, to produce the Hunt and Turner "Magic Landscape" LP (VTS11). Eventually we expanded the band to include the visual hilarity of Jonathan "Wash" Hays on percussion, and the verbal wit of Dave Paskett (vocal and guitar).

"The folk clubs were good to us. We got to collaborate regularly with such characters as Fred Wedlock locally, Mike Harding around Manchester, Tony Capstick in Sheffield, Jon Isherwood in the Portsmouth area and Diz Disley in London. (He would let us camp out in his flat, and I'd put him up in Bristol. Parked outside my house, his Cadillac was a serious danger to shipping in Hatherley Road). When we played at the Edinburgh Fringe, Billy Connolly kindly took us under his then-still-alcohol-fuelled wing to show us around. He was doing the Great Northern Welly Boot Show at the time. We went straight from there via Harwich to the Tivoli Gardens, Copenhagen.

Bristol folk

"We were involved in, and helped to write, ribald pantomimes with White on Black and Fred Wedlock (Bristol Arts Centre), and with Stackridge (a national tour).

"We used to close our show with a routine called the "Water Music". Nothing to do with Handel. After my vocal – "Bye bye Brain Cells" – ingenious things were done involving kazoos, rubber tubing, bits of trumpet and lots of bubbly suds. It culminated with "Wash" singing a whole chorus with his head in a bucket of water, then coming up with a rubber fish in his teeth ... At our regular gigs in Jasper Carrott's "Boggery" folk club, Solihull – he ran it in a rugby club pavilion – this routine escalated with time into more and more of a water-fight. The audience learned what to expect, and as we approached our final number, the whole front row would don waterproof clothing and put umbrellas up. Of course the PA would be switched off and covered. Ultimately there came a night when, as we played, a window opened behind us, and there was Jasper spraying us with the groundsman's hose.

"Jasper's "Fingimigig" agency collaborated with Plastic Dog getting us work around the Midlands. One perk of this was that we got to stay in the flat Jasper shared with his long-time manager John Starkey. We had to clear little nests for our camp-beds among all the full and overflowing ash-trays, Penthouse magazines, coffee cups, old newspapers and empty bottles. Jasper's fiancée-and-eventual wife Hazel would occasionally come and attempt to tidy up, but with little hope.

"It was from here, on Jasper's phone that we were trying to telephone Barry Back one day. Barry had taken daytime work at the HTV Cardiff Studios, while in the evenings touring the Midlands folk clubs with the Piggies. News came in belatedly that our job in Kings Lynn was off. We left messages with HTV, with the Severn Bridge toll-booth and with Barry's wife Wendy. It wasn't till he was nearly into Kings Lynn that Barry phoned Wendy from a public phone box, learned the grim truth and had to drive all the way back. Not long afterwards, the stress was too much and Barry left the band. I left too after a while, wishing to do other things, but the chaps had much success in my absence, including a televised spot on the Ken Dodd Show.

"When the band was revived with Hannah Wedlock (Fred's daughter) and others in the '90s, it was Barry who, up to the time of his sad death, was the keenest organiser. We played at the Jersey Folk Festival, and Barry's second wife Melitza was in charge of selling our merchandise. As the interval arrived, Barry announced loudly into the microphone, "If you'd like a T-shirt or a tape of the band, ask my wife – she's the one sitting in the corner who looks like Myra Hindley!" If looks could kill, Barry would have been an instant victim. And, for the record, there was no resemblance between Myra Hindley and Melitza, but that was Barry's humour.

"Ironically, in the re-formed "Piggies" of the 90's, one of those involved was the same Patrick Small who so nearly could have been one of the founder-members. And a lady from Hatherley Road one day accosted me, saying "Why did you 'ave to call it the Pigsty 'Ill Light Orchestra? Lowerin' the tone! We'm tryin' to forget about all that round 'ere!'"

Bristol folk

Gef Lucena remembers…

"My most [frequently asked question] is 'how did you get into this business?', so let's start with the three strands that came together to make Saydisc. I left Chipping Sodbury Grammar School half way through science A levels sometime in 1961 to go into the retail record industry, graduating from assistant at a record shop in Broadmead to manager of the record department of the Churchill and Son Ltd music store in Park Street. This was a seminal move as Churchills was owned by Bristol piano merchant Mickleburgh Ltd ...

"Running parallel to my time in the record shop I was performing with schoolfriend Martin Pyman as The Crofters and our singing net grew wider and it was difficult keeping up the day job. We both sang, Martin played guitar and I played mandola, autoharp and a variety of other instruments rather badly. We did a lot of TV and radio work as well as guesting at folk clubs in the South West and I was commissioned to write songs on such diverse subjects as the opening of the Severn Bridge for HTV and six songs for the then Milk Marketing Board on the subject of butter, cream, cheese and milk (in my unprincipled youth, being ignorant of saturated fats). Together with students of The Old Vic Theatre School and others we formed The Bristol Poetry and Folk Club which met at The Old Duke and then The Bathurst on alternate Fridays. The Committee fell apart after someone walked off with the funds and there was general dissent about the running of the club and I took over until it folded sometime in 1967. The club had excellent residents of the ilk of young Fred Wedlock, Pat Small, Bev and Richard Dewar and many others and all were unrecorded in those early folk revival days.

"The third strand that led up to the formation of Saydisc Specialised Recordings Ltd (as it was called then) was that my father Lauri was instrumental in setting up and was Chairman of Bristol Hospital Broadcasting Service which was the first of its kind. The Crofters had their own programme ('Anything Goes') which they recorded themselves using discs and live performances and I therefore gained experience with basic recording equipment.

"To piece these strands together we go back to Mickleburgh Ltd and one of its directors, Roy Mickleburgh. Over many years Roy had assembled a kaleidoscopic collection of all things musical. Whether it was old sheet music, musical boxes, barrel organs, old brass instruments, pianolas Roy collected it and 'displayed' his amazing and chaotic collection on the leaky, cold top floor of their store in Stokes Croft. Knowing of my interest in things traditional Roy introduced me to his collection and I was instantly hooked! Here were sounds that were both beautiful to my ears but also in grave danger of decay and disappearance. And here was I with some basic recording knowledge and a need to give up the day job, but needing to have another string to my bow that wasn't 9 - 5.

"What I didn't have was money and Roy stepped in as business partner and so in May 1965 Saydisc began its 35 years of active record production in many fields of music over some 500+ albums. The first releases were EPs of Fred Wedlock live at The Poetry and Folk Club, Christmas carols on Victorian musical boxes, church bells of Bristol and LPs of 'Bristol Folks', mechanical street instruments and ragtime pianola rolls. On starting Saydisc I moved

Bristol folk

from a flat in Hampton Road, Redland back to my parent's home in Frenchay to save money, but started using the adjoining Quaker Meeting House as a studio. Quakers don't have music in their meetings but strangely the acoustic of the Meeting House was excellent. It was high ceilinged and the walls were largely pitch pine clad. To increase the reverb time, panels in the upper part of the room could be opened and the whole was heated by an archaic beetle stove in the middle of the room which became red hot and roared loudly unless the top was propped open with a poker. Maybe the room was as idiosyncratic as the company that was using it but was utilised to great effect in such diverse situations as recording The Mellstock Band, Maddy Prior with The Carnival Band, The Dartington String Quartet, Dave Evans, Frank Evans and many, many others. The Meeting House at Frenchay was still used by choice long after Saydisc moved to new studios at The Barton, Inglestone Common.

"One of The Poetry and Folk Club regulars was Genny Bultitude and we were married in 1968 and moved to our rural retreat on Inglestone Common. After a couple of years we were able to buy the adjoining cottage and converted this to a studio for the Ian Anderson brainchild, the newly formed Village Thing Records. Barry Back of The Pig Sty Hill Light Orchestra and HTV engineer helped set up the 'state of the art' equipment - actually it consisted of a Revox stereo A77 recorder and AKG C451 condenser mikes into a 4 channel Vortexion mixer with a spring reverb unit and that was all we had. I was quite a dab hand at editing so I cut between takes as required but, as I recall, a lot of the songs were complete takes and many were first takes.

"The years progressed, the Matchbox blues label came into being (another Ian Anderson inspiration) and the classical early music label Amon Ra based on Finchcocks music museum in Goudhurst, Kent began its long and successful life. Through a fortunate double booking to record an amateur group I met David Wilkins who was far more knowledgeable and interested in the technical side of recording and we joined forces. We worked together for many years recording at Frenchay, Goudhurst, Forde Abbey and then his own studios at Littleton-on-Severn. We went digital in 1983 and we were one of the first small companies to get into the CD market.

"The Company moved to bigger premises at Chipping Manor, Wotton-Under-Edge for fifteen years from about 1985 and our daughter Arwen looked after supplying distributors in some 23 countries plus a large mail order list while wife Genny did all the artwork.

"I 'retired' from active recording in 2001 but have since revamped Saydisc with 215 albums now available and am (in 2009) back folk singing (strictly not for profit) and back to The Barton. The folk scene of the early 1960s was very active and well supported and Bristol was a central hub encouraged in part by the Centre 42 movement which visited Bristol in the terrible winter of 62/63 - I don't expect many people remember that!

"PS: Pronunciation is another FAQ area, there being no CH or TH in Lucena as it is Portuguese and not Italian or Spanish. We pronounce it as a very Englishy LOOSEENA but this would be LOOSENNA in Portuguese. In with the latin blood there is a good dollop of Manx and Irish so I'm a bit of a Latinocelt."

Bristol folk

Rodney Matthews remembers…

"My involvement with the Bristol folk music scene started in 1970 when I left a steady job as a designer in an advertising agency - Ford's Creative in Fairfax Street, to join Terry Brace at Plastic Dog Graphics in Park Street. Being right next door to Plastic Dog Music Agency, Terry and me were regularly asked to design and illustrate posters for folk gigs in the area. At this time Village Thing Records … commissioned a number of album covers for their folk artistes.

"The first of these in my case, was an EP cover - 'The Great White Dap' featuring Wizz Jones, Sun Also Rises, Ian A. Anderson and The Pigsty Hill Light Orchestra, released in 1971. This was followed by Ian A. Anderson's 'A Vulture is not a bird you can trust' … 'Piggery Jokery' by the Pigsty Hill Light Orchestra, 'Magic Landscape' by Hunt and Turner [in] 1972, 'Elephantasia' by Dave Evans [in] 1972 and another for Anderson 'Singer Sleeps on as Blaze Rages' (the title comes from a newspaper article referring to a fire in Anderson's flat). Around this time I also did Fred Wedlock's 'The Folker' album cover and had some involvement in other covers by Wedlock and Anderson. My next album cover for Village Thing was 'Jonesville' by Al Jones, in 1973, thereafter I moved on to designing covers for mostly rock bands.

"During this 'golden age' I was a drummer in a succession of my own prog-rock bands, and having made the acquaintance of most of the Bristol 'folkies', I was asked to play on some of their records. For example Dave Evans had me playing congas and claves on his 'Elephantasia' and Hunt & Turner asked me to play drums on their 'Magic Landscape'. Two tracks were done at the Village Thing studio in Badminton, where I remember my hi-hat fell into a hundred pieces after the first three bars. I rushed back to Bristol at great speed to borrow a replacement. The other two tracks were recorded at Rockfield Studios near Abergavenny, where the proprietor and farmer, Kingsley Ward, had to be wrestled down from his tractor to do the session. The last of the two tracks was a spontaneous affair from Ian Hunt titled 'Rockfield Rag' which I played in one or two takes without having previously heard it! It turned out to be better than the rehearsed track in my view! Around this time I was also asked to play drums for Fred Wedlock at a Colston Hall gig. I can remember Ian Hunt played guitar, but the rest is lost in the mists of time.

"Much later in 1984, Ian Anderson emerged as the owner of a folk record label called Rogue Records, and asked me to design him an album cover for his own band 'Tiger Moth', this design won first prize at the Music Trades Association awards in 1984. Later in 1988 Anderson commissioned a second cover for Tiger Moth titled 'Howling Moth' and that was my last encounter with a Bristol 'folkie'. No – but wait, there was another. A couple of years ago I met Fred Wedlock at a birthday party for Stackridge fiddle player Mike Evans. Both Mike and Fred appeared to be in fine fettle and good for a few more years at least."

Bristol folk

Robert Stewart remembers…

"My musical career began in Bristol, for which I am ever grateful … Most Bristol folk artists, even the highly talented few, had brief evanescent performing and recording careers, before quietly tiptoeing back to mainstream life. As always, there are a few exceptions.

"One such is Ian A Anderson, who has never deviated from the path, often hewing the path himself when it was unclear to others: Ian has shown remarkable dedication to roots music, quality music journalism, and promotion of musical awareness, bringing folk blues and world music to the British public as a performer and an expert for many years. Keith Christmas, probably the best guitarist and soloist to emerge from the Bristol scene, has had a long creative and performing career. Another stalwart is Kelvin Henderson, devoted to country music and American grass roots folk music throughout his long career. Graham Kilsby (Tony Graham), is still producing recordings in Nashville. This is not a definitive list, just a few examples of those who I remember from early days in Bristol, who especially stand out as full-on in music rather than comedic entertainment. Comedy is a different world as the music is necessarily secondary to the humour: there were several Bristol folk performers who crossed over to the Other Side, such as Fred Wedlock, the Jedi master of the Farce. The few who have continued full-time in music, have done so through a combination of talent, hard work, and luck, but especially through a perverse unwillingness to do anything else even while starving …

"The folk music explosion was deeply embedded within the Consciousness Revolution of the 1960's driven by two themes: social and political activism, and the hippy peace and love movement. Some areas of Bristol, such as Clifton, Redland, and Cotham, embraced both. In the mid to late 60's, there was a naïve rumour that the seedy 18th/19th century students' and artists' enclave of Clifton was comparable to Haight Ashbury, in San Francisco. Well … I must state, with reluctance and regret, that Clifton, even with the occasional kimono or spliff, was staid and conservative by comparison. Yet, it was revolutionary within the rigid British consciousness of the day, so that naïve rumour could stand.

> Clifton Hippy 1: Hey man...check out this new folk album!
> Clifton Hippy 2: Is it dangerous? Like I mean … man … could I be busted for having it?
> Clifton Hippy 1: I don't know man, that's why I gave it to you.

"… In the mid to late 1960's, as a young musician, I shared a large ramshackle flat with singer Graham Kilsby (Tony Graham), and Wurzels' bass player Tony Bayliss. Initially I was the newbie, as both Graham and Tony were established performers at this time, having that rarest of things called Income From Music. By around 1970 or 71, however, I started to tour and do many solo gigs, also working with various singers, so things improved. We lived high up on the corner of the last house on Regent Street, Clifton, with panoramic views over the county of Somerset to the west. There were closer views of flirtatious hand-waving and smiles from the teenage convent school girls in La Retraite, who assiduously watched our back windows when they should have been studying: our shower had a large back

Bristol folk

window. I don't think any of us actually spoke to one of those lovely young ladies, as they were watched by highly trained guard-nuns who regularly patrolled the grounds swinging rosaries like nunchuks (nun-chucks?).

"In the flat downstairs lived my occasional singing partner, Albert Lightfoot, in a more civilized domestic setting, with curtains. Other musicians rented the spare room…one banjo player was asked to leave as he rehearsed Foggy Mountain Breakdown at 3 am. Everyone was involved in the burgeoning Bristol folk-scene or the broader world of entertainment, in which folk music played a significant part.

"The creaking walls absorbed British and Appalachian traditional songs sung by Albert Lightfoot, Paul Evans, and my (soon-to-be) wife Laraine. There were Woody Guthrie songs, country music, and blues, from Kelvin Henderson, Dave Gould, and Bill More. Plus the unlikely team of Fred Wedlock and myself, rehearsing traditional folksongs and his satirical numbers. Fred was a good traditional folk singer, and I was always happy to accompany him. Keith Christmas visited, and we rehearsed guitar, 73-stringed psaltery, and cittern parts for his albums. There was a jug band, The Elastic Band, founded (I think) by Kelvin, which included Dave Creech, later of the Pigsty Hill Light Orchestra, on trumpet and kazoo. As an instrumentalist I played all of the above: folk, blues, country, traditional and contemporary, and spent much time developing my solo skills and singing. I must have been very boring and over-focussed.

"In the mid to late 60's I was an occasional backing musician, playing guitar and 73-stringed psaltery for Graham Kilsby … on his night-club gigs. During a Wurzels crisis in the late 60's, Tony Bayliss, who was a fine jazz bass player, asked if I would join the band, for what was, in those days, serious money. Devoted as I was to folk music and the creation of new music and songs, the temptation to become a Wurzel, chant "ooh-aar, ooh-aar" while wearing farmer's gaiters and a straw hat, and then to have an active bank account as consolation, was short-lived. I had just married, and my wife Laraine was less than impressed by my noble artistic decision. For the record, I liked the Wurzels, and knew Adge from his early days when he sang his comic songs solo ... and unaccompanied ... at the Ballads and Blues club…I had nothing against their music, but the comic entertainment world was not the life for me.

"In the early 70's Pete Finch and Andy Leggett, both excellent musicians, Pete playing gypsy swing guitar and Andy on various wind instruments, joined me for a season in the Avon Touring Theatre Co, plus a few folk and arts-centre gigs together. Around 1974 I started a short-lived electric folk-rock band, called Sunface, which gigged at The Stonehouse club and other progressive Bristol and area venues, drawing some good reviews, or withering disapproval, depending on viewpoint. But so what…everyone tried an electric folk-rock or folk-blues band back then, except, perhaps, Ewan MacColl ...

"In 1973 I recorded my first solo album: The Unique Sound of the Psaltery, released in 1974 ... My later recordings included many songs, but this was for a series showcasing unusual instruments, produced by Decca/Argo, at their studios in Fulham Road, London. I was told

Bristol folk

that Decca UK worked closely at that time with Dolby in the development of noise reduction for studio recording, which must have involved the large Dolby A units. So we probably had good recording equipment for such a minority album. The LP included my arrangements of folk, medieval, and early music, along with my original compositions. The 73-stringed psaltery is my own design, with a unique tuning system, hence the LP title ... Signing with Decca meant international distribution: I was even paid a royalty advance, and the cheque did not bounce! USOP was one of the earliest folk/fusion albums to use an electronic analogue synthesizer, albeit primitive and low profile, blended with acoustic instruments: 73-stringed psaltery, flageolet, cittern, English concertina, guitar. I had to argue awhile with producer Kevin Daly to include the synthesizer, but in the end we agreed on it. It is difficult to grasp today ... that, back then, using a synth along with "serious" instruments was somewhat like blaspheming aloud in the Vatican. So in a small way, USOP was a ground breaking album ... and more recently has been digitally remastered for CD.

"Kevin Daly booked me for various recording sessions, including an album of traditional West Country love songs with Cyril Tawney, a major figure on the national folk scene. Cyril was also a renowned song writer: his blues-format Sally Free and Easy ... was covered by Davey Graham, Pentangle, Bob Dylan, Marianne Faithful, and many others. Not all my Argo sessions were released, and some have vanished. But I was fortunate to provide theme music for Tolkien's The Hobbit, read by Nicol Williamson, which sold for a long time on vinyl and cassette. A larger project at Decca/Argo, for Lord of the Rings around 1975, may still be in the archives (if they exist now), but was not completed.

"... I cannot reminisce over my early years in Bristol without acknowledging [Ewan MacColl and Peggy Seeger's] influence, not only on me, but on many others who still sing, perform music, or act professionally today ... Many creative people got their start at a Ewan MacColl acting or song workshop or through his and Peggy's generous influence ... MacColl and Seeger inspired some, but by no means all, aspects of my music and song-writing as a young man. In Bristol, they had originally inspired the long running Ballads and Blues club, where they performed twice a year with Ewan having a "no smoking" clause written into their contract…most unusual in those days! When MacColl and Seeger performed, the crowd reached beyond the door of the club room and down the stairs into the bar.

"While much attention was drawn to the immensely popular Troubadour club in Clifton, where everyone performed (and I was briefly an inexperienced young MC) the Ballads and Blues, a Saturday night club, also hosted national and international performers ... Commencing years before the Troubadour, the Ballads and Blues continued to run for some years after the Troubadour closed in 1971. The guest performers that we all supported as floor singers, were eclectic and numerous ... The long list included blues artists on tour such as Davey Graham (UK), Alexis Korner (UK) the godfather of British blues, and Spider John Koerner (USA), who was a substantial influence on Bob Dylan. Traditional American folk singers included Mike Seeger, Hedy West, and Tom Paley. Most of the major British traditional folk acts were booked: I met Shirley Collins, with whom I later recorded and played some wonderful concerts; Cyril Tawney, with whom I recorded and appeared on television; and the ultimate boundary breaking and stereotype-smashing coolly dressed trio

Bristol folk

of The Young Tradition. On one occasion Peter Bellamy (of the YT) and I played blues together and shocked all the traditionalists: Peter liked to sing Robert Johnson songs. Martin Carthy and Dave Swarbrick appeared often, sometimes with gypsy swing jazz guitarist Diz Disley, and the club booked many original singer-songwriters, such as the radical maestro Leon Rosselson, who is still active today.

"The Ballads and Blues also featured innovative Irish musicians such as Sweeney's Men, who, more than any other band, started the hugely successful progressive Irish/Celtic band scene. Other Irish performers included the renowned ballad singer Al O'Donnell, the old-style traditional McPeake family, and two young innovative gypsy musicians, the Furey Brothers ... Later they became hugely popular family entertainers with a larger band of Fureys, but in the early days they were iconoclastic, breaking many of the unwritten rules of folk club performing. Overall the BBB club had a broad and generous creative interpretation of "folk music", booking guest performers of high quality. The club was run by volunteers, and all monies were put into fees for future guest artists.

"... When I saw Christopher Guest's mockumentary A Mighty Wind, satirizing the 60's folk scene in New York, it brought back memories of the petty rivalries between Bristol folk acts, and, of course, some retrospective and embarrassed self-conscious laughter. Musicians used to turn to the wall to tune up, to hide their new open-guitar tunings from alert spies... but not me, no. I remember one artist satirically describing the Troubadour, saying, "I knew it was going to be tough when everyone in the front row was miming the fingering for Davey Graham's guitar solo Angie". So maybe Air Guitar really originated on the folk scene!

"Some of the creative spin-offs were surprisingly long term: it was at the Troubadour, for example, that I first met Robin Williamson (of The Incredible String Band), and many years later we wrote a book together, Celtic Bards Celtic Druids published by Cassell/Blandford Press, and did a few concerts, including the Bath Fringe Festival in the early 1990's. It was at the Ballads and Blues that I met Steve Heap, at that time in a popular vocal group called The Valley Folk, later to become director of Sidmouth International Folk Festival and other large events. Just a few years later we toured, performing together in Britain. Another musician that I gigged with in the later 70's was Pete Cooper, a versatile old-timey fiddle and mandolin player. Pete is over six feet tall, and I am short...so we sat down to perform, which made us around the same height. Although I recorded with Steve and Pete, I have no copies of anything that we did.

"In the mid-70's British sales of my first album were average, but it sold in larger numbers in French-speaking Canada and France, and was "approved" for air-play by the BBC, receiving favourable comments from John Peel. I sold more copies at gigs than in record stores! It was reviewed generously in The Gramophone ...

"There was a substantial folk audience in Europe, and a vigorous nascent music scene in Brittany, energized by Alan Stivell, who rapidly became a huge star. Suddenly the word "Celtic" was heard...no longer a Scottish football team from Glasgow, but a cultural term, and a growing musical genre. This was not the "Celtic" music that we hear today as middle

Bristol folk

of the road background pop or New Age music, but something more robust, imaginative, and less product-orientated ... For some utterly baffling reason, Breton Hell's Angels bought The Unique Sound of the Psaltery, and on my tours there I did some biker gigs at remote bar locations in the country. They sat quietly for each number, then roared approval and scrambled for drinks in the intervals. During the interval, heavy rock from the juke box pounded the walls.

"It was around 1977 that I first performed in the USA ... at the San Diego International Folk Festival, in southern California, near the Mexican border. Someone from the Festival had heard me play in Bristol, a few years before, and recommended me to the committee. My flight to LA was on a Freddy Laker plane, and took a staggering 23 hours, as we flew via Bangor, Maine. Check out the map! This first of many tours in the USA made a deep impression on me: I met, among others, some flamboyant Tex-Mex musicians, the Tacoma All-Stars blues band (my first live experience of a black American electric blues ensemble...boy, could they rock!), and the venerable American master of old-timey music on fiddle guitar and long-neck banjo, Hobart Smith, already in his 80's. Hobart generously sat down with me and showed me some licks on the banjo.

"Back in LA for a few days I played 73-stringed psaltery with Dennis Wilson of the Beach Boys playing Stick bass, at Brother Studios in Santa Monica ... and Dennis talked with me about Plato and Pythagoras ... I could write about the album that Bob Dylan recorded in the men's room of his newly built studio in LA that year (he did not like the custom sound stage)...but that would be ridiculous ...

"From the early 1970's onwards I worked in theatre in addition to folk gigs, starting at the newly built Old Vic studio theatre in King Street, which opened its doors for the first time to the sound of my acoustic folk-based music. Less glorious was our accidental soaking of the Lord Mayor, with water sprayed during a scene from the first play performed in the Studio. This musical drama about the Bristol Reform Riots of 1831, was written by Clifton playwright David Illingworth. I wrote and played the music, and Albert Lightfoot sang.

"I became a founder member of the Bristol based Avon Touring Theatre Co, which was to run for many years, starting several talented playwrights, directors, and actors, on their path to fame ... I often had to be musician, song-writer, and musical director; it was good training, and I learned about stage-craft from the more experienced actors and directors. Later my music was featured in major productions at the London Old Vic and Young Vic, Theatre Clwyd, and on various theatrical tours. I am not a great idolizer of stars, having worked with many, but a key moment for me was hearing Vanessa Redgrave and Timothy West reciting Mallory's Le Morte d'Arthur to my music.

"From theatre in the early 70's I went on to write and record music and songs for folk broadcasts and some major BBC radio dramas produced in Bristol, including two plays by poet Peter Redgrove: The Holy Sinner, and God of Glass. The first was mainly acoustic 73-stringed psaltery and flute, but for the second I wrote music for a larger rock-jazz line up, recruiting the band from folk and rock musicians on the Bristol scene.

Bristol folk

"Much of this radio music was recorded at BBC Bristol, which had a sophisticated music production studio in a converted chapel in Redland. BBC Bristol Radio was a national music recording facility, and not to be confused with local Radio Bristol, a much simpler affair held together by paper-clips ... HTV filmed some sketches with Avon Touring Co, using my music. One of our actors was briefly arrested during an HTV location shoot in Bedminster, as he was wearing a police uniform for a comedy sketch...which we were told was illegal without a special permit. Presumably it was the uniform that was illegal and not the comedy...unless our local bobbies had heard Fred Wedlock live.

"The BBC invited me to present some one-off radio specials on folk-music, and I wrote and recorded some feature items for a national BBC radio show produced by Peter Pilbeam and presented by Jim Lloyd ... Perhaps the strangest of my HTV Bristol projects in the early 70's was writing and recording music for a documentary film presented by Broadway star Elaine Stritch ...

"From 1976 onwards I created and directed music for some major feature films and television productions, occasionally with a folk music influence. Some films were with leading directors, such as Tony Richardson's Joseph Andrews, for which I booked the Gloucester Old Spot Morris Men as dancing extras, complete with clashing antlers and pounding staves. There was much musical discussion and experimentation, in London and at Crescent Studios in Bath, with Jim Henson, for The Dark Crystal. You can hear my voice as the chanting Mystics in this film, processed through a Fairlight digital synthesizer.

"... By 1974, the Bristol folk scene had declined from its frenzied heyday: I was living in Bath, only doing occasional gigs at local folk clubs, due to touring commitments. My three more traditional or Celtic based albums were recorded in Bath, by David Lord and Brian Preston, at a time when "Celtic" had not yet become the New Age franchise that it is today. David Lord went on to become a leading producer of many top artists, including Peter Gabriel ... The Crescent albums, two of which were later assigned to the Broadside label, were recorded around 1976 and 1978. They featured Bristol and Bath based musicians and singers well known on the local folk-scene, such as Phil Harrison (guitar/keyboard) and Stuart Gordon (violin) of the Shortwave Band, Albert Lightfoot (vocals), John Molineux (flute and mandolin) who at that time was in the John Renbourn Band, and Laraine Stewart (vocals), a fine singer to whom I was married for 18 years.

"I was joined on my two Celtic-based folk albums, and some wild gigs, by top-flight Irish musicians, including melodeon (Irish accordion) maestro Jackie Daley, later of Patrick Street; Finbar Furey, the leading Irish piper who mentored Davey Spillane; Finbar's youngest brother George on guitar; and cittern player and songwriter Jimmy Crowley. Fiddle on some tracks was played by Greg Smith, who had a vibrant Scottish style. Though based on traditional Celtic music, two of these albums, Tomorrow we Part, and Up like the Swallow, included many of my own original songs and instrumentals. The store sales were dismally low, due to poor distribution, but I sold large numbers at gigs, as did many musicians in those days.

"1976 was also the year that my first book was published: Where is St George?: Pagan Imagery in English Folksong (Moonraker Press UK, Humanities Press USA) ... I was asked to write this book after appearing on an HTV arts and music program, where I played the 73-stringed psaltery and talked about ancient magical ballads, singing some examples. The other guest on the program was renowned modern composer and conductor Sir Michael Tippett: why I was on the show was as much a mystery to me as it must have been to him. While I took it seriously, Fred Wedlock used to find my interest in ancient magical ballads highly amusing, often joking in a friendly manner about it at gigs where I was present, or even when I was on stage with him: it is pleasantly ironic, therefore, that HTV helped to start us both on our different professional careers.

"In recent years, much to my surprise, new artists have covered my original songs and even some instrumentals from this early 1970's period, on several CDs and on YouTube. There are several of my original Celtic-style tunes out there, heard at music sessions, that people call "traditional", though I can pinpoint when I wrote and recorded them, so they must really be "contemporary". In 2008 I received an email from Steve Henwood, of the Bath Fringe Festival, telling me that BBC radio has been playing tracks from my old recordings as weird and wonderful vintage items. I have no doubt that my touring and performing career, and my work in film television and theatre over the years, all grew from those crazy Bristol folk-scene roots. Thank you Bristol!"

Steve Tilston remembers…

"My first introduction to Bristol came at the age of 16, whilst hitchhiking with a schoolfriend – a pair of fledgling, would-be beatniks, bound for Wessex and mythical tales of sunshine and scrumpy. We ended up trudging lift-less across the town, but even then I had a feeling that one day I'd live there. It's hard to put my finger on why exactly, just a strong feeling.

"It was Ralph McTell who very kindly contacted Ian Anderson of Village Thing on my behalf. I followed it up and secured a meeting with Ian and a gig at the Troubadour Folk Club. I'd met Ralph through Wizz Jones at Les Cousins in Soho, and he'd been very complimentary about my playing and writing. At the time I was working as a trainee graphic artist in Leicester and commuting to London each weekend. By 1970 I'd become a professional musician, built up a bit of a buzz and was seriously looking to record my debut album. Although by then I'd moved to London, I never felt at ease with the place, so I liked the sound of a record company that was making alternative waves away from the ol' metropolis, and when I first clapped eyes on the magnificent Georgian crescents of the then slightly rundown and quasi bohemian Clifton village, I was be-smitten.

"At 20 I was pretty single minded in my quest to make an album, looking back, probably a bit pushy with it, but I was sitting on this powder keg of songs and it felt like I had to get them recorded or I'd explode. I remember thinking that my over eagerness had queered my pitch, but fortunately at the Troubadour gig everything came together and Ian Anderson announced to the audience that I'd be the next artist to record for Village Thing.

Bristol folk

"The album was recorded in Gloucestershire at the house belonging to one of the directors Gef Lucena, during the winter of late 70 early 71, and I wore an overcoat for some of the sessions. Nothing was overdubbed, (I don't think that facility was on offer) everything both solo and ensemble went down live. Amongst the band members was an old friend and ex musical partner of mine the fantastic guitarist Dave Evans. Although a decade older than me, Dave and I had played as a duo around the clubs of the Midlands. In fact it was after our performance at a folk concert at the Nottingham Playhouse that we met Wizz Jones. Wizz had said 'you must come down to Cousins'. I took him up on his offer and pitched up on his doorstep the following weekend. True to his word, he took me along and helped get my first booking there. At that time, Dave was trying to get a pottery business off the ground and didn't seem particularly interested in making a career in music. Ultimately his pottery folded and he moved to Devon to work for another potter. He had no telephone in Devon, so I remember travelling down to persuade him to come up to Bristol and play a bit of guitar on my debut album. I think I arrived at his place at the right moment. He didn't need much arm twisting, he came to Bristol and didn't go back.

"On harmonica and harmony vox was someone who has subsequently become a lifelong friend of mine – Keith Warmington. I still vividly remember our first meeting, it was on a zebra crossing en-route to the Splinters Coffee House in Clifton Village. He was up from Cornwall and exuded a boat load of great good humour and when in passing I asked if by any chance he played the harmonica. His eyes lit up and onto the table, like a shoal of silver pilchards, he tipped about twenty of the things, in every key imaginable. Keith only just happened to be one of the best harmonica players I've ever heard … Along with Pete Keeley, Keith was half of Strange Fruit. They became one of the most popular acts in Bristol and worked all over the country for a couple of years. Sadly, they didn't record an album, though they certainly had enough great material … Another soon-to-be friend on upright bass was John Turner, a member of the Pigsty Hill Light Orchestra and another director of Village Thing. We rehearsed a couple of days in the Troubadour and then laid it all down onto tape, almost like doing a gig.

"With hindsight I can now look back on that album fondly and pretty much realise its worth, but although it was very well received by the press and radio, I felt quite deflated and a bit embarrassed. I could only seem to focus on the defects, both in my own performance and certain technical shortcomings. Back in London, a few of my contemporaries were getting the 'full treatment,' with rhythm sections and strings, even (heaven forbid) heavenly choirs and in comparison mine seemed rough and ready. However people seemed to like it, probably for that reason amongst others and the title Acoustic Confusion seemed to sum the album up in an understated way.

"At that time I was still living in London in a shared house with a group of Scottish musicians, some of whom later became the Average White Band and I was getting exposed to a lot of new sounds and it was percolating through into the music I was writing and I was writing a lot of stuff, in fact it was pouring out of me like a nervous complaint. Acoustic Confusion had comprised of songs I'd written as an 18-year old leading up until my then age of 20, so by the time it came out, in my mind it was already out of date. Suddenly I

Bristol folk

started to get courted by other record companies. I suppose it went to my head a bit and I attempted to leave the Village Thing contract. Not surprisingly it didn't go down too well to say the very least – I don't know what I expected in my naivety. One of the labels that showed interest was Transatlantic – the then seemingly premier label for this kind of music. The owner Nat Joseph and his wife came to a gig ... at Les Cousins and later, over a pizza, he offered me a recording deal. I pointed out that there may be a bit of difficulty in getting me out of the Village Thing contract. I remember him smiling knowingly and saying "Just leave that to me!" Obviously it transpired that Transatlantic were by then distributing Village Thing, so I presume they were able to pull the right levers … I signed with Transatlantic, not least because it was the stable of a lot of acts I held in high regard – Bert Jansch & John Renbourn, Pentangle, Ralph McTell, Gerry Rafferty. However, they all seemed to leave the label around the time I joined it, which should have started some bells ringing.

"To produce the album they flew in the great American musicologist and discoverer of Joseph Spence & Furry Lewis - Sam Charters. I immediately took to Sam (not least because his wife Anne was writing a biography of Jack Kerouac) and we set to work on an album. Sam had already produced Country Joe and the Fish, and was keen to work with another songwriter both as producer and arranger. We went into Sound Techniques Studio with a host of musicians, only two of whom I knew, Hamish Stuart and Rick Kemp. Quite simply, I think for what the album was attempting to be, more time was needed in the studio. Some of the string quartet arrangements were very nice, but the horns were for the most part overblown. At the time I was like a kid let loose in a sweet shop, wanting to try a bit of everything and this being my first time in a real studio, to my ears it all sounded larger than life and fantastic.

"By the time it became vinyl I was starting to learn the lesson of 'less is sometimes more'. The worst horror was the glossy gatefold cover, over which I had no control. Although the sales in the UK were modest to say the least, Nat Joseph was able to secure an American release on MCA and a nice piece of Yankee change made its way into my bank account … Again, with hindsight, when I compare the two albums, I much prefer Acoustic Confusion and I wish I could have done things differently. Village Thing were after all trying to do the best they could for me. That said, Collection allowed me to put down a small deposit on a small house in Clifton Wood and in '73 I was delighted to finally move to Bristol.

"The acoustic music scene in Bristol by now had changed, the Troubadour had closed and The Stonehouse now became the main focal point. Clifton Village had started to become trendy and to hear 'Folk Music,' meant moving to other parts of town. Maybe this had an effect on the music, in that it seemed to develop a slightly harder edge – probably the fact that the Stonehouse was a serious drinking emporium had some influence. Some wonderful music came out of there, but not a stone was left standing after the developers moved in ... a plaque would be nice.

"In 1975, Keith Warmington and I opened a club at what was then the Bathurst Tavern overlooking Bathurst Basin. It's now called the Louisiana, but still looks pretty much the same from the outside, complete with original ironwork veranda. For the opening night we had Long John Baldry, followed by John Renbourn a week later and then in succeeding weeks, Nic Jones, Jake Thackray, The Battlefield Band, and a whole host of other top acts. With Keith, myself and Jim Reynolds as residents, it became the main acoustic club in town for a while.

"In 1976, I recorded my 3rd album 'Songs From The Dress Rehearsal'. I set up my own label Cornucopia as a flag of convenience. I'd become very frustrated by Transatlantic, particularly over their disinterest in me having one of my friends Rupert Hine as producer – they had wanted to put me with someone I regarded as totally inappropriate. Rupert subsequently went on to become a top producer and as a favour agreed to produce and play keyboards on the new album. Also roped in were Mike Giles on drums/percussion & John G Perry on bass. I think that this was my best album of the three from the 70's. It has been re-released by Market Square records, this time with the addition of 6 songs that I recorded for a proposed album for Stefan Grossman's Kicking Mule Records. The intention had been to add other instruments but due to Stefan's then wife becoming ill and his move to Italy, it was put on hold. I'm very pleased that these songs have been included, and again with hindsight that they're just guitar and vocal.

"By the late 70's I'd secured a publishing deal with a top London music publisher, (they were paying me a retainer to write a dozen songs a year) and succumbed to pressure to move back to London. Bristol was still being seen then as a bit parochial. I stood it for 3 years and then returned to Bristol in 1981. Much as I love the city, by '89 I'd had enough of cities and decided a more bucolic setting was to my liking, so I moved to the Yorkshire Pennines. I do however return to Bristol as often as possible to play gigs and see friends.

Keith Warmington remembers…

"I met Pete Keeley in the autumn of 1969 whilst I was studying in the French city of Tours … I was at a college there for a term and the French students who'd heard me blowing told me about an English guy playing at a theatre there. I went to see him and we got chatting after the gig and arranged to meet up for a play together ... he actually made me audition by playing a train blues while standing on chair in a bar he used regularly! We gelled ... Pete remains one of the best blues guitarists I've ever worked with ... at the end of term I went back to college and Pete came with me ... at the end of my studies in the summer of 1970 we got a residency at Room at the Top in Cornwall and during the summer were favourably reviewed in the Melody Maker by Andrew Means who looked after their folk pages (yes mainstream music papers carried folk pages way back then).

"We decided to move to Bristol that autumn because it had the Troubador – a fantastic club – plus Village Thing agency and record label. After pitching up in Bristol we went round to 12A Royal York Crescent and rang the door bell. Ian Anderson opens up and says ... "Ah Strange Fruit we've been expecting you." After that we were off ... it wasn't that long before we filled both floors of the "Troub" and by Christmas were travelling the country in an old Ford that cost us thirty five pounds.

"All seemed to going splendidly ... we recorded a single for Village Thing ... turned down an offer from Jo Lustig[260] (what were we thinking about?) and we were going down a storm wherever we played. At some point our relationship with VT came to an abrupt end (I think Pete and his girlfriend had a row with Ian A) and we transferred to Plastic Dog and continued gigging until June 1972 when I decided I'd had enough of being on the road ... We carried on gigging on a semi pro basis for another couple of years until Pete moved to Cornwall.

"I've always kept up gigging in a couple of great bands ... the Paynekillers and the Parole Bros. and under my own name with ace violinist Stuart Gordon. I haven't seen Pete for 15 years and last I knew he was living in Bishops Castle, Shrops. My memories of that period are all good ... for me as young man I made fantastic friends and had some wonderful musical experiences, playing on the records of Steve Tilston (a lifelong friend) and Dave Evans and enjoying life in a city that seemed at the time to have a gig on every corner."

Steve Webb and Al Read remember[261]…

"Ian Anderson ran Village Thing from the back room upstairs at 77 Park Street and as the record label began to demand more of his time he approached Al Read with an idea that he might like to take over the agency function and run it along side Plastic Dog. I was in my mid twenties at this time and part of the Granary scene playing in bands with Rod Matthews who was by then heavily involved with the graphics side of Plastic Dog.

"Al made me an offer to team up with him to run this joint agency function and I duly arrived knowing very little about the contemporary folk scene but determined to give it my best shot. Ian Anderson provided an intensive one evening induction into the vagaries of the contemporary and traditional folk scene followed by a similar session with Kelvin Henderson into the world of country music. Very different animals than the rock scene we both knew.

"The roster of artistes was impressive. The Pigsty Hill Light Orchestra and Fred Wedlock were two of the funniest acts on the folk circuit and the guitar brilliance of Dave Evans, for example, made us quickly aware that we were representing some very remarkable talent. The agency went from strength to strength adding Stefan Grossman, John Renbourn & Jacqui McShee from Pentangle, Bridget St. John, and Wizz Jones together with the Brownsville Banned from Manchester. We even discussed with Jasper Carrot the possibility of his representation before his meteoric rise to stardom. We were approached by the John Sherry Organisation, one of the largest London agencies at that time, to handle the club appearances of Tir Na Nog and Magna Carta. It all felt very impressive to a lad from Midsomer Norton – had I finally arrived?

"We were learning all the time and it was becoming clear that the artistes needed more than just bookings to promote their career. We were very aware that the likes of Jasper Carrott, Billy Connolly and Max Boyce had become major stars and along with Al Stewart and Ralph McTell, representing the singer songwriters, had broken into a much larger market and able to sell out concert tours nationwide. As an operation we needed to function at this level but we never achieved that breakthrough despite some near misses. I was convinced that Canton Trig had the song writing skills to go all the way especially with a record deal with ATV music, that Dave Evans appearance on the Old Grey Whistle Test would finally launch his career, that The Pigsty Hill Light Orchestra's guest appearance on a televised Ken Dodd Show would surely open that elusive door for them.

"In the end it was Fred Wedlock who had most success with a hit record to his credit but this was many years after our involvement. I think Al and I just about managed to make a living out of the business, as did most of the artistes, but it eventually became clear that we had "had our day" – "Right Industry wrong city". I stayed in the entertainment agency world for a few more years but it was never the same. If I had my time over would I do it all again? – you bet!"

Fred Wedlock remembers ...

"We held our Wedding Reception in the Troubadour Folk Club in Clifton. Not the usual sort of place, admittedly, but we had several good reasons. Most of our friends were Folkies; Sue and I met in the Ballads and Blues at the Bathurst; the Troub had almost become our spiritual home and, most important, thanks to the owner's generosity, it was free!

"A year or so earlier I was a regular at the Ballads and Blues – then run very efficiently by Ken Cotterell – and it was the hub of the local folk scene. One night a young business type asked me to have a look at a place in Clifton where he intended to set up a Folk Club. He said he hoped I might fancy becoming a resident. When I saw this tiny, dilapidated, half-gutted old shop in a backstreet, then realised the bloke knew next to nothing about the folk scene, actually intended to have performances going on upstairs and downstairs at the same time, and, can you believe this, wasn't going to sell alcoholic drinks, I thought what he really needed was the phone number for Barrow Gurney Mental Hospital.

"Boy, was I wrong! I'd completely underestimated the vision, determination and capacity for sheer hard work of Ray Willmott and his wife Barbara. Aided and abetted by organising types like Ian Anderson and John Turner, a whole gang of residents and comperes (which I was delighted to join) and a bevy of pretty young wenches to serve coffee, the club became a well-documented phenomenon. And the landlords of the Greyhound and the Somerset, round in Princess Victoria Street, thought it was Christmas three nights a week.

"(Actually, it nearly had to close prematurely when the Fire Officer came round one evening. He nearly wet himself when he found over 100 people packed into a basement with what amounted to not much more than a loft ladder as the only means of escape. Undaunted, Ray found a demolition site staircase and got me to help transport it from Redland. We balanced on my half-timbered Morris, with our wives desperately hanging on to stop it getting down Blackboy Hill before we did. He then cut a hole in the front wall, spent all night installing it and was legal the next day.)

Bristol folk

"In the Bristol Folk Scene we just didn't realise what a good thing we had. We were at the cutting edge of Folk Music. Everyone wanted to play here and then most of them wanted to stay in a wonderful, exciting, friendly, open and honest social scene.

"There was a party pretty much every club night. All you needed was a musical instrument, Party Four or a bottle of Anjou Rose and you were in. Sometimes you ended up dossing on the floor – as likely as not, next to the guest singer you'd been to see that night. We had a succession of performers staying in our Clifton flat and when I started travelling I could always depend on a welcome and a spare bed.

"To me the most outstanding feature of the folk scene has been the almost total artistic generosity. Performers would always share a riff, chord sequence, tuning, gag or lyric and rarely mind it being re-interpreted. And, my God, there was some talent around Bristol! Not just musicians, writers and singers but painters, poets and actors too – all cheerfully borrowing from each other and building their own acts.

"Relationships were easy – well, it was the 60's – and so were musical relationships. Solo acts abounded but you only needed enough rehearsal with a like-minded friend to make up a couple of half-hour sets, a name that nobody else had grabbed, a photograph standing under a tree and you went on the road. Then you got a record out (99 copies to avoid purchase tax) and gave up the day job. If you had a couple more friends you could call yourself a "Light Orchestra".

"Unlike Beat Groups (yes, that's what they were called!) you didn't usually carry a sound system. Many folk clubs had no amplification (and there were a couple in Bristol where microphones and guitars were looked upon as Abominations in the Sight of the Lord), so you put on heavy-gauge strings and shouted a lot.

"There was never a need to get bored bashing out the same old material. You could play virtually anything you wanted from Gaelic Mouth Music to American Blues via Ragtime and Music Hall - all in the same set - and it worked. And if you did get a bit fed up you sacked the band or went and joined somebody else's!

"I could go on waxing lyrical until I get all sentimental and misty-eyed. I could talk about the many good friends we still have from those days – and the absent ones. I'd love to tell you about the clubs and the characters just around Bristol and the experiences of the performers who ventured outside the folk scene into the Military camps and the Cabaret Clubs. I could write a whole book of anecdotes but it would take a few weeks to run most of them past the publisher's legal department … Stand by for the revelations in the next edition."

Bristol folk

Discographies and lists

UK Discography - original releases

Ian Anderson

See also: Anderson, Jones, Jackson, Mike Cooper / Ian Anderson, Hot Vultures plus **Blues Like Showers of Rain**, **The Inverted World**, **Son of Gutbucket**, **The Great White Dap**, **Matchbox Days** and **Us** in the Various Artists section.

Almost the Country Blues *(with Elliot Jackson: Saydisc SD 134, 1968, 7" EP)*
1 – Cottonfield Blues
2 – Tom Rushen Blues
1 – Big Road Blues
2 – Shake 'Em On Down

Stereo Death Breakdown *(as Ian Anderson's Country Blues Band: Liberty LBS 83242, 1969, LP)*
1 – Get In That Swing
2 – Little Boy Blue
3 – My Babe She Ain't Nothing but a Doggone Crazy Fool Mumble
4 – New Lonesome Day
5 – Short Haired Woman Blues
6 – Hot Times
1 – Stereo Death Breakdown
2 – When I Get To Thinking
3 – Way Up on Your Tree
4 – Break 'Em on Down
5 – That's Alright
6 – Baby Bye You Bye

Book of Changes *(Fontana STL 5542, 1970, LP)*
1 – Edges
2 – Internal Combustion Rag
3 – Anthem
4 – Stop and Listen
5 – Sleepy Lynne
6 – Number 61
1 – Paint It Black
2 – Mouse Hunt
3 – Put It in a Frame
4 – Book of Changes
5 – Galactic Wings (and Other Tales)
6 – De 12-Bore Blues

Royal York Crescent *(as Ian A. Anderson: Village Thing VTS, 1970, LP with lyric sheet)*
1 – No Way to Get Along
2 – Please Re-adjust Your Time
3 – Goblets and Elms
4 – Shining Grey
5 – The Worm
6 – Hero
1 – Silent Night No. 2
2 – Mr Cornelius
3 – The Maker/The Man In the High Castle/The Last Conjuring
4 – Ginger Man
5 – Working Man

Some copies on the second label design were exported to Germany for distribution by the German Autogram label: this LP had two sleeve stickers, one with Autogram catalogue number, and a poster showing, oddly, a UK music press write-up of *Book of Changes*.

A Vulture Is Not a Bird You Can Trust *(as Ian A. Anderson: Village Thing VTS, 1971, LP)*
1 – One More Chance
2 – Black Uncle Remus
3 – Policeman's Ball
4 – Edges
5 – The Survivor
1 – Well…..Alright
2 – Time Is Rife
3 – Wishing the World Away
4 – One Too Many Mornings
5 – Number 61

One More Chance / ***Policeman's Ball*** *(as Ian A. Anderson: Village Thing VTSX1002, 1972, 7")*

Bristol folk

Singer Sleeps On As Blaze Rages (as Ian A. Anderson: Village Thing VTS, 1972, LP)
1 – Hey, Space Pilot
2 – Marie Celeste on Down
3 – Spider John
4 – A Sign of the Times
5 – Paper and Smoke

1 – Paint It Black
2 – Pretty Peggyo
3 – The Western Wind
4 – Out of the Side
5 – Shirley Temple Meets Hawkwind

Anderson, Jones, Jackson
See also Ian Anderson, Hot Vultures and Al Jones.

Anderson, Jones, Jackson (Saydisc 33SD 125, 1966, 7" EP)
1 – Louise
2 – If Your Man Gets Personal

1 – Dan Scaggs
2 – I'd Rather Be the Devil
3 – Beedle Um Bum

Ray Andrews

Banjo Maestro (Folk'sle, no catalogue number, probably 1977, cassette)
1 – Banjo Vamp
2 – Kilties
3 – Minuet in G
4 – Sports Parade
5 – La Marguerite
6 – Tune Tonic

1 – Beat as you Go
2 – Bonny Scotland
3 – Sullivan Selections
4 – Annie Laurie
5 – Glitter of Steel
6 – Rugby Parade
7 – Tattoo

Stan Arnold

100 Yards / b-side unknown (Sweet Folk and Country, catalogue no. unknown, 1973, 7", existence unconfirmed)

Ladies Man (Sweet Folk All HAS RRL 01, 1973, LP)
1 – Southsea Love Song
2 – Hairy Mouse
3 – Marigold Day
4 – Deep Ellem Blues

1 – Anti-Antiseptic C&W Song
2 – Long Vulgar Introduction
3 – Short Vulgar Song
4 – 100 Yards
5 – Drunken Sailor

Ladies Man (Red Rag Recordings RRR 009, 1975, LP, reissue in same sleeve with amended label credits)

Early Red Rag-distributed copies were Sweet Folk All copies with at least one sticker added, which said, "Stan Arnold is rude vulgar, tasteless, trite & not to be missed". Some included one saying, "12 inches of COCKY": Cocky was another popular artist on the folk circuit: the sticker was included because it included Red Rag's address.

Showstoppers for the Inteljunt (Red Rag Recordings RRR 029, no year of publication included, LP)
1 – Hecklers
2 – Australian Girls (Australian Version)
3 – More Hecklers
4 – Cabaret Time
5 – Hospital
6 – Matron (and Hecklers)
7 – Anal Love

1 – Audition
2 – Here Come the Combo
3 – Australian Girls (Broadcastable Version)
4 – Rude Ending
5 – Anal Love (Disco Version)
6 – Dedication
7 – Do the Zombie

Jo Chambers

Every Woman Will Be Free (Firebrand DM 1020, 1979, LP: track listing mostly unknown)
1 – Unknown
2 – Unknown
3 – Unknown
4 – Unknown
5 – The Nights Draw In
6 – Unknown

1 – Unknown
2 – Unknown
3 – Unknown
4 – Mark the Page
5 – Unknown
6 – I Walk Down By the Floating Harbour
7 – Unknown

Bristol folk

Keith Christmas
See also **49 Greek Street**, **Clogs**, **Club Folk Volume 1** and **Club Folk Volume 2** in the Various Artists section.

Stimulus (RCA Victor SF 8059, 1969, LP)
1 – Travelling Down
2 – Bedsit Two-Step
3 – Roundabout
4 – Ice Man

1 – I Know You Can't Lose
2 – Metropolis
3 – Trial & Judgement

Fable of the Wings (B&C CAS 1015, 1970, LP)
1 – Waiting for the Wind to Rise
2 – The Fawn
3 – Lorri

1 – Kent Lullaby
2 – Hamlin
3 – Fable of the Wings
4 – Bednotch

Pigmy (B&C CAS 1041, 1971, LP)
1 – Travelling Down
2 – Timeless and Strange
3 – Evensong
4 – Spanky
5 – Poem

1 – The Waiting Grounds
2 – Song for a Survivor
3 – Forest and the Shore

Brighter Day / Sweet Changes (Manticore K 13507, 1974, 7")

Brighter Day (Manticore K 53503, 1974, LP)
1 – Brighter Day
2 – Foothills
3 – Country Farm
4 – Bargees

1 – Lover's Cabaret
2 – Robin Head
3 – Gettin' Religion
4 – Could Do Better
5 – Song of a Drifter

My Girl / Country Farm (Manticore K 13509, 1974, 7")

The Dancer / The Astronaut (Who Wouldn't Come Down) (Manticore K 13515, 1976, 7")

Songs from the Human Zoo (Manticore K 53509, 1976, LP)
1 – The Dancer
2 – The Nature of the Man
3 – 3 Golden Rules
4 – Souvenir Affair
5 – The Last of the Dinosaurs

1 – The Astronaut (Who Wouldn't Come Down)
2 – High Times
3 – Tomorrow Never Ends
4 – Life in Babylon

Mike Cooper / Ian Anderson
See also Ian Anderson, Anderson, Jones, Jackson and Hot Vultures plus **Matchbox Days** in the Various Artists section.

The Inverted World (Mike Cooper and Ian Anderson: Saydisc Matchbox, SDM 159, 1968, LP)
Side 1 by Mike Cooper
1 – One Time Blues
2 – Few Short Lines
3 – Send Me to the 'Lectric Chair
4 – The Way I Feel
5 – Good Book Teach You
6 – The Inverted World

Side 2 by Ian Anderson
1 – Cottonfield Blues
2 – West Country Blues
3 – Don't You Want To Go
4 – Big Road Blues
5 – Little Queen of Spades
6 – Tom Rushen Blues
7 – Beedle Um Bum

Bristol folk

The Crofters
See also **Bristol Folks** in the Various Artists section.

Pill Ferry and other Folk Songs (Saydisc SD 113, 1965, 7" EP in picture sleeve with insert)
1 – Pill Ferry
2 – Whip Jamboree
1 – 23rd of June
2 – The Card Song

Drink Up Thee Cider: The Crofters Sing Adge (Saydisc SD 120, 1966, 7" EP in picture sleeve with insert)
1 – Casn't Kill Couch
2 – Champion Dung Spreader
1 – When the Common Market Comes to Stanton Drew
2 – Drink Up Thee Cider

Ballad of the Severn Bridge (Saydisc SD 129, 1967, 7" EP in picture sleeve with insert)
1 – Ballad of the Severn Bridge
2 – As I Walked Out One Morn
1 – The Butter Churning Race
2 – Buttercup Meadows

Adge Cutler & the Wurzels
See also **Souvenir of the West Country** in the Various Artists section.

Drink Up Thy Zider / Twice Daily (Columbia DB 8081, 1966, 7")

Adge Cutler & the Wurzels (Columbia SX 6126, 1967, LP: issued in fake stereo circa 1972 as SCX 6126)
1 – Twice Daily
2 – Tanglefoot Twitch
3 – When the Common Market Comes To Stanton Drew
4 – Thee Cassent Kill Cooch
5 – The Champion Dung Spreader
6 – Drink Up Thy Zider
1 – Pill, Pill
2 – Mabel, Mabel
3 – The Chew Magna Cha-Cha
4 – Hark at 'Ee Jacko
5 – The Mixer Man's Lament
6 – Virtute et Industrial

Scrumpy & Western (Columbia SEG 8525, 1967, 7" EP in picture sleeve)
1 – Pill, Pill
2 – Twice Daily
1 – Hark at 'Ee Jacko
2 – Drink Up Thy Zider

The Champion Dung Spreader / When the Common Market Comes To Stanton Drew (Columbia DB 8145, 1967, 7")

Adge Cutler's Family Album (Columbia SX 6165, 1967, LP: issued in fake stereo in 1974 as SCX 6165)
1 – Easton-In-Gordano
2 – Sweet Violets
3 – The Wild West Show
4 – Barcelona Blues
5 – The Somerset Space-Race
6 – Freak-Out In Somerset
1 – Moonlight On the Malago
2 – Sniff Up Thy Snuff
3 – Drunk Again
4 – Sheriff of Midsomer Norton
5 – Avonmouth Mary
6 – The Shepton Mallet Matador

I Wish I Was Back On the Farm / Easton-In-Gordano (Columbia DB 8222, 1967, 7")

All Over Mendip / My Threshing Machine (Columbia DB 8277, 1967, 7")

Don't Tell I, Tell 'Ee / Faggots Is the Stuff (Columbia DB 8399, 1968, 7")

Cutler of the West (Columbia SX 6263, 1968, LP: issued in fake stereo circa 1972 as SCX 6263)
1 – Drink Up Thy Zider (Play-On)
2 – The Charlton Mackrell Jug Band (Interpolating: MacNamara's Band and I'm Forever Blowing Bubbles)
3 – In the Haymaking Time (Interpolating: Sing Something Simple)
4 – Five Foot Flirt
5 – Thee's Got'n Where Thee Cassn't Back'n Hassn't?
6 – Dorset Is Beautiful
7 – Up the Clump
1 – Drink Up Thy Zider (Play-On)
2 – The Chandler's Wife
3 – The Bristol Song
4 – The Marrow Song (Oh! What a Beauty)
5 – A Pub with No Beer
6 – Oh! Sir Jasper
7 – The Wurple-Diddle-I-Doo Song (The Village Band)
8 – Drink Up Thy Zider (Play-Off)

Bristol folk

Cutler of the West was reissued in the early 1980s in a different sleeve and retitled as *Vintage Cider* (Music For Pleasure MFP 50476 STEREO). This repackaged reissue is quite hard to find and can sell for up to £10.

Up the Clump / Aloha, Severn Beach (Columbia DB 8462, 1968, 7")

Ferry to Glastonbury / Saturday Night at the Crown (Columbia DB 8614, 1969, 7")

Carry On Cutler (Columbia SX 6367 [mono] / SCX 6367 [stereo], 1969, LP)
1 – Drink Up Thy Zider (Play on)
2 – All Over Mendip
3 – Down on the Farm
4 – Folk Song
5 – Aloha, Severn Beach
6 – Oom Pah Pah
7 – The Harvest of Love

1 – I Couldn't Spell !!**&@&**!!
2 – The Chewton Mendip Love-In
3 – Saturday Night at the Crown
4 – Riley's Cow-Shed
5 – Ferry to Glastonbury
6 – Willie the Shake
7 – Drink Up Thy Zider

Poor Poor Farmer / Chitterling (Columbia DB 8793, 1971, 7")

Don't Tell I, Tell 'Ee (EMI Starline SRS 5119, 1972, LP)
1 – Drink Up Thy Zider (Play on only)
2 – Don't Tell I, Tell 'Ee
3 – Oom Pah Pah
4 – Poor Poor Farmer
5 – Chitterling
6 – My Threshing Machine
7 – I Wish I Was Back On the Farm

1 – The Wild West Show
2 – I'd Love To Swim In the Zuider Zee
3 – Faggots Is the Stuff
4 – Virtute et Industrial
5 – The Wurple-Diddle-I-Doo Song (The Village Band)
6 – Drink Up Thy Zider

Little Darlin' / Mother Nature Calling (CBS CBS 8067, 1972, 7", picture sleeve)

Drink Up Thy Zider / Twice Daily (Columbia DB 9031, 1972, 7")

Little Darlin' / Mother Nature Calling (Santa Posta PNS 20, 1974, 7")

The Very Best of Adge Cutler (EMI EMC 3191, 1974, LP)
1 – Easton-in-Gordano
2 – Poor, Poor Farmer
3 – Twice Daily
4 – The Wurple-Diddle-I-Doo Song (The Village Band)
5 – Don't Tell I, Tell 'Ee
6 – Saturday Night at the Crown
7 – Riley's Cowshed
8 – Ferry to Glastonbury
9 – Up the Clump

1 – Thee's Got'n Where Thee Cassn't Back'n Hassn't?
2 – Moonlight on the Malago
3 – The Shepton Mallet Matador
4 – When the Common Market Comes to Stanton Drew
5 – The Champion Dung Spreader
6 – Aloha Severn Beach
7 – All Over Mendip
8 – I Wish I Was Back on the Farm
9 – Drink Up Thy Zider

Don't Tell I, Tell 'Ee (EMI Encore ONCR 502, 1978, LP: includes extra tracks and new sleevenotes)
1 – (Play on only) Drink Up Thy Zider
2 – Don't Tell I, Tell 'Ee
3 – Oom Pah Pah
4 – Poor Poor Farmer
5 – Chitterling
6 – My Threshing Machine
7 – I Wish I Was Back On the Farm
8 – Dorset Is Beautiful
9 – Up the Clump

1 – The Wild West Show
2 – I'd Love to Swim In the Zuider Zee
3 – Faggots Is the Stuff
4 – Virtute et Industrial
5 – The Wurple-Diddle-I-Doo Song (The Village Band)
6 – The Chandler's Wife
7 – Drink Up Thy Zider

Bristol folk

Elecampane

When God's On the Water *(Dame Jane ODJ 1, 1975, LP with insert)*
1 – The River
2 – Water
3 – The Finding of Moses
4 – The Streams of Lovely Nancy
5 – Just As the Tide Was Flowing
6 – Blue Eyed Stranger
7 – The Maid of Australia

1 – The Bold Fisherman
2 – Marrowbones
3 – The Water of Tyne
4 – Our Ship Is Ready
5 – Well Met
6 – A Sailor's Life

Further Adventures of Mr Punch *(Dame Jane ODJ 2, 1978, LP with booklet)*
1 – The story so far
2 – Mr Punck is carried off to hell
3 – Punch finds he's not alone
4 – Jack Ketch
5 – Mr. Plod
6 – Judy
7 – Punch pleads for mercy
8 – The ghost is willing to listen
9 – Mr. Punch's philosophy
10 – The ghost takes pity
11 – Enter Old Nick
12 – The ghost pleads for Punch
13 – Mr Punch becomes a soldier

1 – The Army's worse than hell
2 – Punch is terrified of the coming battle
3 – On arrival at the battlefield
4 – Punch has a terrible dream
5 – Punch wanders into the enemy camp
6 – Dutch courage
7 – A chance meeting
8 – What the Devil!
9 – A terrible fight
10 – Mr. Punch the hero
11 – Revels and dancing
12 – Punch makes a pledge
13 – Finálè

Dave Evans

See also **Us**, **Contemporary Guitar Workshop** and **Jigs and Reels** in the Various Artists section.

The Words In Between *(Village Thing VTS 6 1971, LP)*
1 – The Words In Between
2 – Rosie
3 – Grey Lady Morning
4 – Insanity Rag
5 – Magic Man

1 – Now Is the Time
2 – Doorway
3 – City Road
4 – Circular Line
5 – Sailor

Elephantasia *(Village Thing VTS 14, 1972, LP)*
1 – Only Blue
2 – Elephantasia
3 – Lady Portia
4 – That's My Way
5 – On the Run

1 – St. Agnes Park
2 – Beauty Queen
3 – Ten Ton Tasha
4 – Earth, Wind, Sun & Rain
5 – Take Me Easy

Sad Pig Dance *(Kicking Mule SNKF 107, 1974, LP: a tablature booklet was available for this LP)*
1 – Stagefright
2 – Chaplinesque
3 – The Train and the River
4 – Veronica
5 – Captain
6 – Knuckles and Buster
7 – Medley: Mole's Moan (The Gentle Man Trap)

1 – Sad Pig Dance
2 – Raining Cats and Doga
3 – Braziliana
4 – Sun and Moon
5 – Steppenwolf
6 – Morocco John
7 – Sneaky

Take a Bite Out of Life *(Kicking Mule SNKF 122, 1976, LP: a tablature booklet was available for this LP)*
1 – Keep Me from the Cold
2 – Whistling Milkman
3 – Illustrated Man
4 – You and Me
5 – Insanity Rag
6 – Every Bad Dog

1 – Take a Bite Out Of Life
2 – Willie Mae
3 – You're Wrong
4 – Sunday Is Beautiful
5 – Tear Away
6 – Lucky Me
7 – I'm All Right

Bristol folk

Take a Bite Out of Life / *Sad Pig Dance (Kicking Mule SOK 37, 1976, 7")*

Keep Me from the Cold / *Shebag an Shemor (Kicking Mule SOK 42, 1979, 7")*

Frank Evans
See also **Jazz Tête à Tête** in the Various Artists section

Mark Twain Suite (77 SEU 12/37, 1970, LP)

Side 1 (The Suite)
1 – Big Missouri
2 – Lazy Afternoon
3 – Hymn for the Minister
4 – Ballad to Becky
5 – Huckleberry's Thing
6 – The Pipe of Peace and Reprise

Side 2 (Ballads and Blues)
1 – Whose Bloos
2 – Con Alma
3 – Waltz for Django
4 – Days of Wine and Roses
5 – Longing for Baia

Stretching Forth (Saydisc SDL 217, 1971, LP: track listing unavailable)

In an English Manner (as The Frank Evans Consort: Saydisc SDL 233, 1972, LP)
1 – Summer Song
2 – Greensleeves
3 – Ayre by Purcell
4 – In An English Manner
5 – Pavane – "Lady Long of Wraxall"
6 – Bourée

1 – Bach Double Violin Concerto, 1st Movement transcribed for 2 Guitars
2 – Scarborough Fair
3 – The Girl With the Flaxen Hair
4 – Longing for Baia
5 – Bach 2 Part Invention in D minor
6 – A Pastoral Scene
7 – Air From the Suite No 3 in D

Noctuary (Blue Bag BB 101, no year of publication, LP)
1 – Nuages
2 – A Child Is Born
3 – Send In the Clowns
4 – Wave
5 – What Are You Doing the Rest of Your Life?

1 – Gymnopedies
2 – Round Midnight
3 – The Song Is You
4 – Body and Soul

Soiree (Blue Bag BB 102, no year of publication, LP)
1 – Waltz for Django
2 – Andalucia
3 – Dear Bill
4 – Soirée

1 – Autumn Leaves
2 – What's New?
3 – Angel Eyes
4 – Misty
5 – Manoir de Mes Reves
6 – All the Things You Are

…for Little Girls (Blue Bag BB 104, no year of publication, LP)
1 – My Funny Valentine
2 – I've Grown Accustomed to Her Face
3 – Sweet Lorraine
4 – Little Girl Blue
5 – Laura

1 – Sophisticated Lady
2 – Pavane pour une Infante Defunte
3 – Waltz for Debbie
4 – Lil' Darlin'
5 – Mary

Pavane pour une Infante Defunte is miscredited as "Pavane pour Enfante Princess Defunct" on the sleeve, though is correctly credited on the label.

Blue Bag releases did not include year of publication, though these can generally be inferred from various sleeve credits: *Noctuary* was recorded 9th November 1975 and the sleevenotes were written 17th June 1976, so 1976 is assumed; *Soiree* was recorded on the 5th, 6th and 7th May 1977, so 1977 is assumed; *For Little Girls* date-checks a session with George Benson in 1978 and my assumption is that the record was issued in either late 1978 or 1979.

Bristol folk

Flanagan's Folk Four
See also **Troubadour Folk** in the Various Artists section.

No title *(Gosport Sound Services acetate, 1967, LP in plain brown paper bag sleeve, 4 copies only)*
1 – Star of the County Down
2 – Henry Joy
3 – Mason's Apron
4 – The Rocky Road to Dublin
1 – The Wandering Tinker
2 – Kilgarry Mountain
3 – The Valley of Knockanure
4 – Harvest Home & the Sunshine Hornpipe

Folkal Point
See also **Folk Heritage** in the Various Artists section.

Folkal Point *(Midas 003, 1971, LP)*
1 – Twelve Gates into the City
2 – Scarborough Fair
3 – Sweet Sir Galahad
4 – Lovely Joan
5 – Circle Game
6 – Cookoo's Hollerin'
1 – Edom O'Gordon
2 – Victoria Dines Alone
3 – You Ain't Going Nowhere
4 – Anathea
5 – National Seven
6 – Once I Knew a Pretty Girl

Kelvin Henderson

Kelvin Henderson Country Band *(Westwood, WRS 045, 1974, LP: track listing unknown)*

Slow Movin' Outlaw *(Windmill WMD 250, 1975, LP)*
1 – Why You Been Gone So Long
2 – A Restless Wind
3 – Help Me Make It through the Night
4 – Jeannie's Afraid of the Dark
5 – Games People Play
6 – Mona
1 – Joe, Don't Let Your Music Kill You
2 – In the Shelter of Your Eyes
3 – We Had It All
4 – Song of Hickory Hollers Tramp
5 – Slow Movin' Outlaw
6 – Sundown

Black Magic Gun *(Checkmate CMLS 1016, 1977, LP)*
1 – Sweet Mama
2 – Pamela Brown
3 – Black Magic Gun
4 – Big Wheel
5 – He Went To Paris
6 – West Texas Country-Western Dance Band
1 – Memphis Gene
2 – L.A. Freeway
3 – Sad Songs and Waltzes
4 – Western Union Wire
5 – Winonah
6 – Victim of Life's Circumstances

Kelvin Henderson *(GMP, catalogue number unknown, 1978, LP: track listing unknown)*

Sunday School to Broadway */ b-side unknown (Chopper CHOP 2, 1979, 7")*

Country Comes West *(Chopper, catalogue number unknown, 1979, LP: track listing unknown)*

The Door is Always Open */ b-side unknown (Buffalo BUFF 1001, 1979, 7")*

Slow Movin' Outlaw *(Chevron CHV 036, 1979, LP: reissue in same sleeve design with altered label credits)*

Hot Vultures
See also Ian Anderson, Anderson, Jones, Jackson and Mike Cooper / Ian Anderson.

Carrion On *(Hot Vultures: Red Rag RRR 05, 1975, LP)*
1 – Low Down Dog
2 – The Sky
3 – I Love the Life I Live
4 – So It Goes
5 – Pretty Polly
6 – Baby What's Wrong/ Shame Shame Shame
1 – The Midnight Special
2 – Another Normal Day
3 – Bound to Lose
4 – You Can't Judge A Book by The Cover
5 – The Road to Marazion
6 – We Got Hard Times Now

Bristol folk

The East Street Shakes *(Hot Vultures: Red Rag RRR 015, 1977, LP)*
1 – Put Your Money in Your Shoes
2 – Southern Cannonball
3 – Handful of Rain
4 – Charley Patton
5 – The Blues Got the World By the Balls
6 – John the Revelator
7 – Hello Stranger Blues
1 – Takin' My Time
2 – Mail Order Mystics
3 – Hobo Bill's Last Ride
4 – Just Allow Me One More Chance
5 – London Blues
7 – Aloha, Aloha, What's All This 'Ere Then
8 – Can't Be Satisfied

Up the Line *(Hot Vultures: Plant Life PLR 018, 1979, LP)*
1 – Preachers Blues
2 – Pontchatrain
3 – Black Dog Blues
4 – Mistreated Mama
5 – The Spring of 65
6 – Going Across the Mountains
7 – Corinna Corinna
1 – The TB Blues
2 – South Coats Bound
3 – Bonny Light Horseman
4 – Black Snake Moan
5 – Chattanooga Papa
6 – Write Me a Few of Your Lines

Hunt and Turner

See also **Us** in the Various Artists section.

Magic Landscape *(Village Thing VTS 11, 1972, LP)*
1 – Hold Me Now
2 – Silver Lady
3 – We Say We're Sorry
4 – Magic Landscape
5 – Mr. Bojangles
1 – Living Without You
2 – Man of Rings
3 – Older Now and Younger Then
4 – Morning for Eve
5 – Rockfield Rag

Erik Ilott

See also **The Shanty Men** in the Various Artists section.

Ship Shape and Bristol Style *(Folk'sle, 1973, LP)*
1 – Lash Up and Stow
2 – Aboard the 'Kangaroo'
3 – Haul on the Bowline
4 – Little Fishes
5 – Bristol Channel Jamboree
6 – A Sailor Coming Home on Leave
7 – 'The Fu Fu Band'
8 – Old Horse
9 – Blow the Man Down
1 – O'Riley's Daughter
2 – Jock Paton
3 – Sally Brown
4 – Last Piece of Pudding
5 – Paddy Doyle's Boots
6 – Bristol Hornpipes
7 – Bristol Town
8 – Titanic

Sounds of the Sea *(Ribena/Lyntone LYN 3249, no year of publication, 7" flexidisc: double-sided flexidisc pressed at 33⅓ rpm with 12 page booklet – narrated by Michael Aspel with sound effects: shanties by Ilot)*

Independent Folk

Independent Folk *(GWR DM 015, 1978, LP with insert)*
1 – Albion Sunrise
2 – High Germany
3 – Waters of Tyne
4 – South Australia
5 – Across the Hills
6 – Early Morning Rain
7 – Peat Bog Soldiers
8 – Graham's Tunes
1 – Marco Polo
2 – The Drover's Song
3 – Liverpool Lullaby
4 – Swinton May Song
5 – Lord of the Dance
6 – Peter's Tunes
7 – Liverpool Lou
8 – Down in the Coalmine

Bristol folk

Al Jones

See also Anderson, Jones, Jackson plus **49 Greek Street**, **Club Folk Volume 1**, **Club Folk Volume 2**, **Us** and **Matchbox Days** in the Various Artists section.

Alun Ashworth Jones (Parlophone PMC/ PCS 7081, 1969, LP)
1 – Siamese Cat
2 – Come Join My Orchestra
3 – Ire and Spottiswood
4 – Tramp
5 – Sarah in the Isle of Wight

1 – What Was I Thinking
2 – Riverbend
3 – Railway Lines
4 – Big City

Jonesville (Village Thing VTS 19, 1973, LP)
1 – Jeffrey Don't You Touch
2 – Get Out of My Car
3 – Tell the Captain
4 – Bernard's Exit
5 – High and Dry
6 – Earthworks

1 – Ice Age
2 – Time to Myself
3 – To London with You
4 – Most Chickens are Mild and Friendly or Would Like to Be
5 – Caught In a Storm
6 – Black Cat
7 – The Wild Rover

Graham Kilsby

See also **Bristol Folks** and **Troubadour Folk** in the Various Artists section.

In a Folk Mood (Saydisc SD 126, 1967, 7" EP in picture sleeve)
1 – Chastity Belt
2 – She's Like the Swallow

1 – Man of Constant Sorrow
2 – Keep the Willow

Kind Hearts and English

Call Me Darling / I Still Believe In You (DJM DJS 615,1976, 7")

Kareen (Thank You for the Way You Are) / A Wish for a Season (DJM DJS 657, 1976, 7")

A Wish for a Season / Call Me Darling / Kareen (Thank You for the Way You Are) (DJM DJP 10001, 1976, 7" *promotional EP in picture sleeve, which miscredits Kareen as "Karen", though the label gets it right*)

A Wish for a Season (DJM DJF 20490, 1976, LP)
1 – Kareen
2 – Call Me Darling
3 – For the Better
4 – A Wish for a Season

1 – Wake in the Morning
2 – Everything
3 – Somehow We've Been Here Before
4 – I Still Believe in You
5 – Viking Invasion

The sleeve credits "Kareen" but the label credits "Kareen (Thank You for the Way You Are)".

Beachcomber (DJM DJF 20512, 1977, LP)
1 – Beachcomber (Intro)
2 – I See Her
3 – Love Walked In
4 – 1000 Years
5 – Beachcomber (Reprise)

1 – Can You Remember?
2 – Experiences
3 – The Music's Reaching
4 – Sky Full of Red
5 – Caught in a Crossfire

Siobhan Lyons

Patriot Games (accompanied by John C. Edwards: Saydisc SD 116, 1966, 7" EP)
1 – Patriot Games
2 – She Moved Through the Fair

1 – Every Night
2 – Slean Libh

Bristol folk

Shelagh McDonald
See also **Dungeon Folk**, **Clogs**, **Club Folk Volume 1**, **Club Folk Volume 2** and **Rave On** in the Various Artists section.

Album (B&C CAS 1019, 1970, LP)
1 – Mirage
2 – Look Over the Hill and Far Away
3 – Crusoe
4 – Waiting for the Wind to Rise
5 – Ophelia's Song

1 – Richmond
2 – Let No Man Steal YourThyme
3 – Peacock Lady
4 – Silk and Leather
5 – You Know You Can't Lose

Stargazer (B&C 1043, 1971, LP with inner sleeve)
1 – Rod's Song
2 – Liz's Song
3 – Lonely King
4 – City's Cry
5 – Dowie Dens of Yarrow

1 – Baby Go Slow
2 – Canadian Man
3 – Good Times
4 – Odyssey
5 – Stargazer

Mudge and Clutterbuck
See also **Troubadour Folk** in the Various Artists section.

Sheep (as Dave and Tim: Saydisc 33SD 156, 1968, 7" EP in picture sleeve, pressed at 33⅓ rpm)
1 – Robert E. Lee
2 – For the Evening

1 – Joe Collett
2 – Memory Book

Rod Neep

Heading for the Sun (Folk Heritage FHR 052, 1973, LP, track listing unknown)

I Give You the Morning (Label and catalogue number unknown, 1974, LP)
1 – The Last Thing On My Mind
2 – Annie's Song
3 – I've Got Nothing but Time
4 – I Give You the Morning
5 – Leaving London
6 – Can't Help but Wonder Where I'm Bound

1 – My Lady's a Wild Flying Dove
2 – Outward Bound
3 – Jimmy Newman
4 – Peace Will Come
5 – Rambling Boy
6 – Wish I Had a Troubadour

Old Pete and John Christie

Isambard Kingdom Brunel (Saydisc 33SD 279, 1977, 7" mini LP in picture sleeve)
1 – Isambard Kingdom Brunel (John Christie)
2 – The Great Britain Saga (Old Pete)
3 – The Cabot Song (John Christie)

1 – Silvery Pools (Old Pete)
2 – Inventions (John Christie)
3 – Gardening for Gran (Old Pete)

Record is subtitled "and other comical saga'ls from our area'l with Old Pete & John Christie". Old Pete is Peter Lawrence.

Sally Oldfield
See also Sallyangie.

Water Bearer (Bronze BRON 511, 1978, LP, first issue with lyric insert)
1 – Water Bearer
2 – Songs of the Quendi: Night Theme; Wampum Song; Nenya; Land of the Sun

1 – Weaver
2 – Night of the Hunter's Moon
3 – Child of Allah
4 – Song of the Bow
5 – Fire and Honey
6 – Song of the Healer

Mirrors / *Night of the Hunter's Moon* (Bronze BRO 66, 1978, 7")

Bristol folk

Water Bearer (Bronze BRON 511, 1978, LP, second issue with stickered sleeve and updated lyric insert)
1 – Water Bearer
2 – Songs of the Quendi: Night Theme; Wampum Song; Nenya; Land of the Sun
3 – Mirrors

1 – Weaver
2 – Night of the Hunter's Moon
3 – Child of Allah
4 – Song of the Bow
5 – Fire and Honey
6 – Song of the Healer

After the success of the single, *Water Bearer* was hurriedly repressed with *Mirrors* added with a sticker on the sleeve stating the track's inclusion. The repress was heavily re-promoted with conspicuous in-store displays.

You Set My Gypsy Blood Free / *Water Bearer* (Bronze BRO 79, 1979, 7")

Easy (Bronze BRON 522, 1979, LP with lyric sheet)
1 – The Sun In My Eyes
2 – You Set My Gypsy Blood Free
3 – Answering You
4 – The Boulevard Song
5 – Easy

1 – Sons of the Free
2 – Hide and Seek
3 – First Born of the Earth
4 – Man of Storm

The Sun in My Eyes / *Answering You* (Bronze BRO 83, 1979, 7" in picture sleeve)

Dave Paskett

I Still Dream About Your Smile (Thinks! THINK 1, 1975, LP)
1 – Telephone Blues
2 – Fairies at the Bottom of Her Garden
3 – I Could Not Take My Eyes Off Her
4 – Oh Dear! What Can The Chatter Be?
5 – Ditty
6 – I Still Dream About Your Smile

1 – The Truckdriver and the Highwoman
2 – Business Executive
3 – Evening Class Rose
4 – Just My Way
5 – Trotty Feet the Pig
6 – Constable Love

Pasketry (Thinks! THINK 2, 1979, LP)
1 – Johnny Went to London
2 – The Wicked Grocer
3 – Hummin' to Myself
4 – The Butcher and His Wife
5 – Don't You Be Foolish Pray
6 – I Could Have Felt More

1 – Trim Rigged Dozy
2 – Falling In Love Again
3 – Come Back
4 – The Wages of Skin
5 – The Washing Line
6 – What'll I Do
7 – I Loved a Lass

Lindsay Peck with the Friary Folk Group

Reality From Dream (Saydisc contract press CP 109, 1975, LP in wraparound sleeve with PVC outer)
1 – Dawn
2 – Destiny
3 – Careless World
4 – Vagabonds Cry
5 – Arthur Guitar
6 – Floating
7 – Whistling Man
8 – Lovesick Pinks
9 – Forever Farewell

1 – Do You Want To Sing
2 – One Hit Wonder
3 – And It's No Good
4 – Who Can We Blame
5 – Born Traveller
6 – What's Life
7 – Night Child
8 – Free To Dream

Bristol folk

Pigsty Hill Light Orchestra
See also **The Great White Dap** and **Us** in the Various Artists section.

Pigsty Hill Light Orchestra Presents! (Village Thing VTS 1, 1970, LP)
1 – Cushion Foot Stomp
2 – Funny Side of the Street
3 – Silk Pyjamas
4 – Company Policy
5 – On Sunday
6 – Second Fiddle
1 – T'Ain't No Sin
2 – Sleepy Time Blues
3 – My Pet
4 – Nothing Else Will Do Babe
5 – Sporting Life Blues
6 – Men of Harlech

Piggery Jokery (Village Thing VTS 8, 1971, LP)
1 – Sadie Green
2 – Motorway Song
3 – High Society
4 – The Wiltshire Plumbers Saga
5 – Sweet Miss Emmaline
6 – Let Your Linen Hang Low
1 – Basin Street Blues
2 – Meet Me Where They Play the Blues
3 – Desperate Dan
4 – The Silly Organ Story
5 – Shim Sham Shimmy
6 – Royal Garden Blues

The Pigsty Hill Light Orchestra (Pigsty Hill Light Orchestra PHLO 001, 1976, LP)
1 – High Society
2 – Buddy Is Not a Sweetheart
3 – Coney Island
4 – Jazzbo Green
5 – Everybody's Making It Big
6 – Motorway
1 – You're Always Welcome
2 – Five Foot Two
3 – Short of the Line
4 – D.I.V.O.R.C.E.
5 – Taking My Oyster for Walkies
6 – Roland the Roadie

Pat Purchase

Blues and Gospel (Private release, no catalogue number, 1998, CD)
1 – Thinking Blues (accompanied by Gerry Bath)
2 – Take Me for a Buggy Ride (with the Pearce Cadwaller Stompers)
3 – When I Move To the Sky (with the Pearce Cadwaller Stompers)
4 – On Revival Day (with the Yarra Jazz Band)
5 – Just a Closer Walk with Thee (with the Yarra Yarra Jazz Band)
6 – In the Sweet Bye and Bye (with the Yarra Yarra Jazz Band)
7 – See See Rider (with the Bayou Blue Five)
8 – Honey Where You Been So Long? (with the Bayou Blue Five)
9 – Pleading for the Blues (with the Bayou Blue Five)
10 – Misery Blues (with the Bayou Blue Five)
11 – In the Wee Midnight Hour (with the Bayou Blue Five)
12 – Journey to the Sky (with Shine)
13 – Step By Step (with Shine)
14 – Swing Low Sweet Chariot (with Shine)

Although releasing records in Australia and the US, Purchase did not issue any records in the UK. The CD is iincluded because it represents the only available UK recordings made by Purchase during the 1960s and 1970s.

Sallyangie
See also Sally Oldfield plus **Listen Here!** in the Various Artists section.

Children of the Sun (Transatlantic TRA 176, 1968, LP)
1 – Strangers
2 – Lady Mary
3 – Children of the Sun
4 – A Lover for All Seasons
5 – River Song
6 – Banquet on the Water
1 – Balloon
2 – A Midsummer's Night's Happening
3 – Love In Ice Crystals
4 – Changing Colours
5 – Chameleon
6 – Milk Bottle
7 – The Murder of the Children of San Fransisco
8 – Strangers

Bristol folk

Two Ships */ Colours of the World (Transatlantic/Big T BIG 126, 1969, 7")*

Child of Allah */ Lady Go Lightly (Philips 6006 259, 1972, 7")*

Children of the Sun *(Transatlantic TRA 176, 1978, LP: reissue with the same track listing as the original but in different sleeve design)*

Pat Small
See also The West Country Three plus **Bristol Folks** in the Various Artists section.

A Man of Bristol */ Sand in My Shoes (label and catalogue number unknown, 1976, 7")*

Stackridge

Dora the Female Explorer */ Everyman (MCA MKS 5065, 1971, 7")*

Stackridge *(MCA MDKS 8002, 1971, LP)*
1 – Grand Piano
2 – Percy the Penguin
3 – Three Legged Table
4 – Dora, the Female Explorer
5 – Essence of Porphry

1 – Marigold Conjunction
2 – West Mall
3 – Marzo Plod
4 – Slark

Label credits "West Mall", but sleeve credits "32 West Mall". Original copies are on a black and blue label design whilst a few later copies are on a short-lived red and orange label design. It is possible that there are copies on a short-lived black label design[262]. LP later redistributed as MCG 3505 on the post-1973 black/rainbow label design.

Slark */ Purple Spaceships Over Yatton (MCA MKS 5091, 1972, 7")*

Anyone for Tennis? */ Amazingly Agnes (MCA MKS 5103, 1972, 7")*

Friendliness *(MCA MKPS 2025, 1972, LP)*
1 – Lummy Days
2 – Friendliness (1)
3 – Anyone for Tennis
4 – There Is No Refuge
5 – Syracuse the Elephant

1 – Amazingly Agnes
2 – Father Frankenstein Is Behind Your Pillow
3 – Story of My Heart
4 – Keep on Clucking
5 – Friendliness (2)
6 – Teatime

No insert was issued with the LP, but confusion exists because many people slipped the *Friendliness* tour programme into the album sleeve and these copies are occasionally offered for sale with text such as, "includes rare booklet insert". Just to add to the confusion, this tour programme was reprinted in 1999 for the second Granary reunion, at which the reformed Stackridge played (and Mutter Slater was the support act). The original tour programme has four pages, with adverts for both the LP and the Rhubarb Thrashing Society & Fan Club on the rear, whilst the facsimile is a single sheet with only one side printed.

Do the Stanley */ C'est la Vie (MCA MUS 1182, 1973, 7")*

The Galloping Gaucho */ Fundamentally Yours (MCA MU 1224, 1973, 7")*

Dangerous Bacon */ The Last Plimsoll (MCA MCA 124, 1974, 7")*

The Man in the Bowler Hat *(MCA MCG 3501, 1974, LP)*
1 – Fundamentally Yours
2 – Pinafore Days
3 – The Last Plimsoll
4 – To the Sun and Moon
5 – The Road to Venezuela

1 – The Galloping Gaucho
2 – Humiliation
3 – Dangerous Baco
4 – The Indifferent Hedgehog
5 – God Speed the Plough

Spin Round the Room */ Pocket Billiards (Rocket PIG 15, 1975, 7")*

Bristol folk

Extravaganza *(Rocket PIGL 11, 1974, LP)*
1 – Spin Round the Room
2 – Grease Paint Smile
3 – The Volunteer
4 – Highbury Incident (Rainy July Morning)
5 – Benjamin's Giant Onion
6 – Happy In the Lord

1 – Rufus T. Firefly
2 – No One's More Important than the Earthworm
3 – Pocket Billiards
4 – Who's That Up There with Bill Stokes?

Hold Me Tight / *Breakfast with Werner von Braun (Rocket ROKN 507, 1976, 7")*

Mr. Mick *(Rocket ROLL 3, 1976, LP)*
1 – Hold Me Tight
2 – Breakfast with Werner von Braun
3 – Steam Radio Song
4 – The Dump
5 – Save a Red Face

1 – The Slater's Waltz
2 – Coniston Water
3 – Hey Good Looking
4 – Fish in a Glass

Hey, trivia fans! The girl on the sleeve of *Mr. Mick* appeared on another record sleeve – *Between the Poppy and the Snow*, by Robert MacCleod, released on Charisma in March 1976 (CAS 1114).

Do the Stanley *(MCA MCF 2747, 1976, LP)*
1 – Dora the Female Explorer
2 – Everyman
3 – Percy the Penguin
4 – Slark
5 – Anyone for Tennis
6 – Amazingly Agnes
7 – Purple Spaceships Over Yatton

1 – Do the Stanley
2 – The Road to Venezuela
3 – Dangerous Bacon
4 – Lummy Days
5 – The Galloping Gaucho
6 – C'est la Vie
7 – Let There Be Lids

Let There Be Lids was previously unissued.

Strange Fruit

Cut Across Shorty / *Shake That Thing (Village Thing VTSX 1001, 1971, 7")*

Bob Stewart

The Rollright Ritual + Magical Songs of Britain *(Helios Occult Cassette Club, catalogue number unknown, 1974, cassette)*
Side one by W. G. Gray and others
1 – The Rollright Ritual

Side two by Bob Stewart
1 – The Weaver's Song
2 – The Stone Chant
3 – The Song of the Mother
4 – The Cursing Song
5 – The Cutty Wren

The Unique Sound of the Psaltery *(Argo ZDA 207, 1975, LP)*
1 – Sulis Music
2 – The Leaves of Life
3 – Seasons of the Year
4 – Lord Inchquin
5 – Spring Dance
6 – Seven Singing Gypsies
7 – Moorish Dance
8 – Uncourtly Music

1 – Greensleeves
2 – The Castle Ballad, and the Ivory Pipes
3 – Processional
4 – Music of the Middle Pillar
5 – The Autumn Dance
6 – A Romantic Moonlit Drive through the Shady Whispering Orange Groves of Barber-Haunted Old Seville
7 – The Candlemass Carol

Bristol folk

The Wraggle Taggle Gypsies O *(Crescent ARS 105, 1976, LP)*
1 – The Wraggle taggle Gypsies O/Gypsy Davy
2 – The Wife of Usher's Well
3 – Searching For Lambs – 1
4 – Saint James Hospital
5 – Marta's Gone

1 – Give the Fiddler a Dram/Liza-Anne
2 – Long Langkin
3 – Edward
4 – Searching For Lambs – 2
5 – Jackson and Johnson
6 – The Two Magicians
7 – Wraggle-Tag

Tomorrow We Part *(Bob Stewart & Finbur Furey: Crescent ARS 110, 1976, LP)*
1 – Bird in the Tree
2 – Anach Chuain/Brian Barou's March
3 – The Chance/The Old Pipe on the Hob/The Mad Cat
4 – A Ramble to the West
5 – Kiss the Maid Behind the Barrel
6 – Slievenamon/Garret Barry's Jig

1 – La Volta
2 – Morning on a Distant Shore
3 – The West Wind
4 – Over the Cliff/Denver the Dancer
5 – Down by the Glenside/Cork City
6 – Regulation Reel
7 – Tomorrow We Part

Up Like the Swallow *(Broadside BRO 131, 1978, LP)*
1 – Up Like the Swallow
2 – The Farewell March/The Craw Kilt the Pussy
3 – Young Beichan
4 – Pipe on the Hob
5 – The Hawk of May
6 – Fair of Face

1 – The Weaver's Song
2 – Pretty Polly
3 – The Waterfall
4 – The Song of the Green Man
5 – How Come that Blood?
6 – Slieve Russell
7 – The Traveller's Song

Tomorrow We Part *(Bob Stewart & Finbur Furey: Broadside BRO 133, 1979: reissue in different sleeve design)*

Stewart's music was also used as incidental music on Argo's 4-LP box set of *The Hobbit* (Argo ZPL1196/9, 1974, 4-LP set in box). *Tomorrow We Part* was again reissued in the early 1980s in the same sleeve design as the Broadside reissue but credited to "The Furey's and Bob Stewart" complete with inappropriately-placed apostrophe.

Steve Tilston
See also **A Stereo Introduction to the Exciting World of Transatlantic**, **The Best of British Folk**, **Us**, **The Transatlantic Valentine** and **Guitar Workshop** in the Various Artists section.

An Acoustic Confusion *(Village Thing VTS 5, 1971, LP)*
1 – I Really Wanted You
2 – Simplicity
3 – Time Has Shown Me Your Face
4 – It's Not My Place to Fail
5 – Train Time

1 – Sleepy Time On Peel Street
2 – Prospect of Love
3 – Green Toothed Gardener
4 – Normandy Day
5 – Rock & Roll Star

White label test pressings exist with two extra tracks as well as with the above track listing. First issue on original Village Thing label design in non-laminated sleeve. Later issues in laminated sleeve with second label design.

Collection *(Transatlantic TRA 252, 1972, LP)*
1 – Falling
2 – Mind How You Go
3 – City Life
4 – All in a Dream
5 – Highway

1 – One Man Band
2 – I'm Coming Home
3 – Reaching Out
4 – All in Her Time
5 – Don't Let It Get You Down

Songs from the Dress Rehearsal *(Cornucopia CR 1, 1977, LP)*
1 – Coming Into Love Again
2 – Face of a Friend
3 – Fairground Rock 'N' Roll
4 – Do What You Please
5 – The Greening Wind
6 – Impressions

1 – Liberated Ladies
2 – In the Light Tonight
3 – Make Time for Love
4 – She's the Woman
5 – Rain All Around
6 – Help Yourself to This Song

Bristol folk

Aj (Adrienne) Webber
See also **Troubadour Folk** in the Various Artists section.

Power of Prayer / That's Life *(Anchor ANC 1022, 1976, 7")*

Aj Webber *(Anchor ANCL 2007, 1976, LP)*
1 – Rhythm and Time
2 – Here Comes That Feeling
3 – The Gardener
4 – That's Life
5 – Witchi-Tai-To
6 – The Moon's a Harsh Mistress

1 – Broken Pieces
2 – Jam Jars
3 – Movie Queen
4 – The Carpenter
5 – Power of Prayer

Fred Wedlock
See also **Sounds of Bristol** and **Us** in the Various Artists section.

Volume One *(Saydisc, no catalogue number assigned, 1965, 7" EP in picture sleeve with insert)*
1 – Silbury Hill
2 – Si Mi Quieres Escribir

1 – Franklin
2 – Hey Nelly Nelly

Virtute et Industrial *(as Fred Wedlock, Bev and Richard Dewar: Saydisc SD 124, 1966, 7" EP in picture sleeve)*
1 – Virtute et Industrial
2 – Broomfield Hill (Bev and Richard Dewar only)
3 – Racing Pigeon

1 – Sovay (Bev and Richard Dewar only)
2 – Maid of Clifton (Fred Wedlock only)
3 – Bi-psychedlic Tandem (B. & R. Dewar only)

The Folker *(Village Thing VTS 7, 1971, LP)*
1 – The Folker
2 – British Bobby
3 – Moreton Bay
4 – Thees Got'n Wur Thee Casn't Back'n, Asn't

1 – Spencer the Rover
2 – Skinheads
3 – Bristol Buses
4 – Bruton Town
5 – Lurn Theeself Fawk

White label test pressings exist with *The National Anthem*, which includes a lyric about the Queen being Prince Philip in drag, which was removed from the released version. Originally issue on the first label design.

Frollicks *(Village Thing VTS 20, 1973, LP)*
1 – The Vicar and the Frog
2 – Robin Hood
3 – Handier Household Help
4 – Salvation Army Lassie
5 – Examinations Rag
6 – Oh Sha La La La

1 – Vatican Rag
2 – Robin Head
3 – Lovely Like Me
4 – Superman
5 – Talking Folk Clun Blues
6 – Wild Rover

White label test pressings exist in wraparound proof sleeve.

Fred Wedlock's Homemade Gramophone Record *(Pilluck Produckshun PPS 1, 1975, LP issued with an 'apology' insert)*
1 – Vet
2 – The Bantam Cock
3 – Mississippi Sawyer
4 – Secret Agent
5 – The Widow and the Fairy
6 – A Song of Patriotic Prejudice

1 – The Teacher
2 – Side By Side
3 – The Two Magicians
4 – Mini Cooper
5 – John Barleycorn
6 – British Rail
7 – Flasher

Greatest Hits *(Pillock Produckshuns PPS 17, 1977, LP)*
1 – British Bobby
2 – Handier Household Help
3 – Donkey Reel
4 – Bristol Buses

1 – Skinheads
2 – Football Song
3 – Talking Folkclub Blues
4 – Robin Hood

Bristol folk

Out of Wedlock *(EMI One-Up OU 2217, 1978, LP)*
1 – I Couldn't Spell ****
2 – English Urban Garden
3 – The Gnome
4 – Three Drunken Nights
5 – The Riddle Song
6 – The Threshing Machine

1 – Clevedon Cowboy
2 – The Plumber
3 – The Great Fish Finger Disaster
4 – Early One Evening
5 – Inter-City
6 – British Rail Pies
7 – Ten Inch Reel
8 – Mini-Cooper.

The Oldest Swinger in Town *(Fred Wedlock and Chris Newman: Pilluck Produckshuns PPS 271, 1979, LP)*
1 – The Oldest Swinger in Town
2 – The Union Psalm
3 – American Trilogy Part II
4 – Boxes
5 – The Jogger's Song
6 – Nuages/I Got Rhythm
7 – Tits and Bums

1 – The Hippies and the Hairies-O
2 – Soldiers Joy
3 – Breathalysed
4 – Teddy Bears Rave Up
5 – Sweet Sue
6 – An Old Somerset Poem
7 – The Weather
8 – Songs

The Oldest Swinger in Town / *The Jogger's Song* (Coast, CODS 1, 1979, 7")

The West Country Three
See also **Pat Small**.

The West Country Three Play the Hits of Peter Paul, and Mary *(Marble Arch MALS 1195, 1969, LP)*
1 – Blowing in the Wind
2 – The Last Thing on My Mind
3 – When I Die
4 – Single Girl
5 – Six White Horses
6 – To Be Free

1 – Jesus Met the Woman
2 – If I Had a Hammer
3 – Early Morning Rain
4 – Old Coat
5 – Weep for Jamie
6 – Leaving on a Jet Plane

White on Black

White on Black *(Saydisc SDL 251, 1974, LP)*
1 – Country Roads
2 – Snowbird
3 – Big Yellow Taxi
4 – Scarborough Fair
5 – Bitter Green
6 – Meet Me on the Corner

1 – Carey
2 – Nowhere Man
3 – Bramble Cottage
4 – Together Forever
5 – Norwegian Wood
6 – I Don't Know How to Love Him

The Wurzels
See also **Souvenir of the West Country** in the Various Artists section.

I'm the Captain of a Dredger *(planned as a single, but not issued: 7" test pressings exist)*

The Wurzels Are Scrumptious! *(EMI One-Up OU 2087, 1975, LP)*
1 – Drink Up Thy Zider – Play-on
2 – Don't Tell I, Tell 'Ee
3 – Look at 'Ee, Looking At I
4 – Who Needs Summer?
5 – The Verger (interpolating City Girl and Somewhere My Love)
6 – Speedy Gonzales
7 – Twice Daily

1 – The Shepton Mallet Matador (interpolating Y Viva Espana)
2 – A Drinking Man's Life
3 – I'm the Captain of a Dredger
4 – Cheddar Cheese
5 – Gotta Have Tenderness
6 – The Market Gardener
7 – Drink Up Thy Zider

Combine Harvester (Brand New Key) / *The Blackbird* (EMI 2450, 1976, 7")

Bristol folk

Combine Harvester *(EMI One-Up OU 2138, 1976, LP: some copies included a sticker on the sleeve, which said "Includes the No. 1 hit single")*
1 – The Blackbird
2 – Somerset Born and Proud
3 – Keep Your 'And On Your 'Alfpenny
4 – Crabapple Hill
5 – Middle for Diddle

1 – The Combine Harvester(Brand New Key)
2 – Let There Not Be Light
3 – Down In Nempnett Thrubwell
4 – Call of the Wild
5 – My Somerset Crumpet Horn

I Am a Cider Drinker */ Back of My Old Car (EMI 2520, 1976, 7")*

Morning Glory */ Rock Around the A38 (EMI 2568, 1976, 7")*

Golden Delicious *(EMI Note NTS 122, 1977, LP)*
1 – Drink, Drink Yer Zider Up
2 – Cabot Song (Big 'Ead)
3 – Good Old Somerset
4 – Rock Around the A38
5 – I Keep Smilin'
6 – Pheasant Plucker's Son

1 – Morning Glory
2 – There's a Spider In the Bathtub
3 – Base Over Apex
4 – Short Time Livin'
5 – School Days, Young Days
6 – I Am a Cider Drinker (Una Paloma Blanca)

Farmer Bill's Cowman */ Springtime (EMI 2637, 1977, 7")*

Give Me England! */ Speedy Gonzales (EMI 2677, 1977, 7")*

One for the Bristol City */ Chedder Cheese (EMI 2686, 1977, 7")*

Give Me England! *(EMI Note NTS 138, 1977, LP)*
1 – Give Me England!
2 – Willie Friese-Greene
3 – Sally-Army Teacher
4 – Tremble On
5 – The Mixer Man's Lament
6 – Speedy Gonzales

1 – Farmer Jonesies' Travellin' Disco Show
2 – Sousaphone Sam
3 – The Jubilee Day
4 – Hey, Come With Me
5 – Nellie the Bionic Cow
6 – Haggis Farewell
7 – Farmer Bill's Cowman (I Was Kaiser Bill's Batman)

The Tractor Song */ Funky Farmyard (EMI 2792, 1978, 7")*

I'll Never Get a Scrumpy Here */ I Got My Beady Little Eye On Thee (Columbia DB 9051, 1978, 7")*

I'll Never Get a Scrumpy Here *(EMI Note NTS 160, 1978, LP)*
1 – Funky Farmyard
2 – The Tractor Song (The Pushbike Song)
3 – Down Our Street
4 – I'll Never Get a Scrumpy Here
5 – Mevagissey
6 – Somerset Jigolo

1 – Our Village Band
2 – Two Milk Churns
3 – Ferry To Glastonbury
4 – I Got My Beady Little Eye On Thee
5 – Wish I'd Stayed a Bachelor
6 – Drunk On a Saturday Night

I Am a Cider Drinker *(EMI Encore ONCR 523, 1979, LP)*
1 – I Am a Cider Drinker (Paloma Blanca)
2 – Down Our Street
3 – Springtime
4 – Back of My Old Car
5 – I Keep Smilin'
6 – Cabot Song (Big 'Ead)
7 – Sousaphone Sam
8 – Sally-Army Teacher
9 – Nellie the Bionic Cow
10 – Farmer Jonesie's Travellin' Disco Show

1 – The Shepton Mallet Matador
2 – Who Needs Summer
3 – Gotta Have Tenderness
4 – My Somerset Crumpet horn
5 – Crabapple Hill
6 – Mevagissey
7 – Drunk on a Saturday Night

Bristol folk

Greatest Hits *(EMI Note NTS 190, 1979, LP)*
1 – I Am a Cider Drinker (Paloma Blanca)
2 – Morning Glory
3 – Rock Around the A38
4 – School Days, Young Days
5 – Speedy Gonzales
6 – Give Me England!
7 – One For the Bristol City
8 – Farmer Bill's Cowman (I Was Kaiser Bill's Batman)

1 – Drink Up Thy Zider
2 – Don't Tell I, Tell 'Ee
3 – Funky Farmyard
4 – The Tractor Song (The Pushbike Song)
5 – Our Village Band
6 – I Got My Beady Little Eye On Thee
7 – The Blackbird
8 – I'll Never Get a Scrumpy Here
9 – Combine Harvester (Brand New Key)

Various Artists (in release order)

Shipshape and Bristol Fashion *(Port of Bristol Authority, 1964, one-sided 7" EP)*

No track listing included. This one-sided EP was issued to commemorate the 1964 film of the same name and comprised spoken word and shanties from the film soundtrack. If rumour is true, it is narrated by Sir Lawrence Olivier – it sounds like him and he was at the Bristol Old Vic around the time that the film was made. Apart from spoken word sections, talking about the history and the then current plans of the port, there are also shanties, though these are uncredited and the artists remain unknown, as do the dates of recording – so these may not be either Bristolian singers and the shanties may not have been recorded in the 1960s, but the record is included just to be on the safe side. As to value, these tend to sell for around £15 each.

Bristol Folks *(Saydisc, no catalogue number, 1965, LP, limited edition of 99 copies)*
1 – Fiddle Medley (Bev and Richard Dewar)
2 – She Moved Through the Fair (Anne Mavius)
3 – Man of Constant Sorrow (Patrick Small)
4 – Tramps and Hawkers (The Crofters)
5 – Dona, Dona, Dona (Graham Kilsby)
6 – Across the Hills (Paul Evans)

1 – He Was My Brother (Paul Evans)
2 – Fare Thee Well (Bev and Richard Dewar)
3 – Dirty Streets (Anne Mavius)
4 – Geordie (The Crofters)
5 – Flora (Patrick Small)
6 – Farewell (Graham Kilsby)

The artists featured on *Bristol Folks* were regular performers at either the Bristol Ballads and Blues Club or the Bristol Poetry and Folk Club (or both). Graham Kilsby, Patrick Small and the Crofters have their own write-ups elsewhere in this book and of the others, only Bev and Richard Dewar made further recordings, those being backing Fred Wedlock on his *Virtute et Industrial EP*, also on Saydisc. The Dewar brothers were from Clevedon and played fiddle (Bev) and Guitar (Richard). Anne Mavius was a schoolteacher and *Dirty Streets* on the album is one of her own compositions. Paul Evans was fairly new to the Bristol folk scene and he favoured modern folk songs, his songs on the album being by Leon Rosselson and Paul Simon respectively. The LP is unknown on the collectors' scene and only 99 copies were pressed.

Ragtime Piano *(Saydisc SD 118, 1966, LP)*
1 – Original Rags (Neville Dickie)
2 – Daintiness Rag (Neville Dickie)
3 – Rosotio (Quentin Williams)
4 – The Cowcatcher (Quentin Williams)
5 – Paragon Rag (Neville Dickie)
6 – Rag-Time Dance (Neville Dickie)

1 – The Nailbreaker (Quentin Williams)
2 – Ceonothus Rag (Quentin Williams)
3 – Hilarity Rag (Pete Davis)
4 – Maple Leaf Rag (Pete Davis)
5 – Weeping Willow (Neville Dickie)
6 – The Thriller! (rag) (Neville Dickie)
7 – Grace and Beauty (Neville Dickie)

Jazz Tête à Tête *(77, 1966, LP)*
1 – Freedom Monday (Tubby Hayes and the Les Condon Quartet)
2 – When My Baby Gets Mad - Everybody Split (Tubby Hayes and the Les Condon Quartet)
3 – Jeep Is Jumpin' (The Tony Coe Quintet)
4 – Blues We Played Last Night (The Tony Coe Quintet)
5 – Blues for Sunday (The Frank Evans Trio)
6 – Polka Dots and Moonbeams (The Frank Evans Trio)

Track listing taken from the CD reissue (Progressive PCD-7079), which may not include the tracks as originally sequenced, so exact order of tracks is currently unknown (CD bonus track not listed above).

Bristol folk

Troubadour Folk *(Kernow Records, 1967, LP, limited edition of 99 copies)*
1 - Whistling Kettle Blues (Mudge and Clutterbuck)
2 - The Ballad of Amy MacPherson (Adrienne Webber)
3 - Bendigo ("Big Brian" Webb)
4 - Hear the Wind Blow (Flanagan's Folk Four)
5 - The Old Man of the Sea (Graham Kilsby)
6 - Cooley's Reel & the Mason's Apron (Flanagan's Folk Four)

1 - Joe the Carrier Lad (Roger White)
2 - Suzanne (Graham Kilsby)
3 - The Star of the County Down (Flanagan's Folk Four)
4 - Sleep in My Bed Once Again (Adrienne Webber)
5 - How Long, Baby, How Long? (Mudge and Clutterbuck)
6 - Chicken on a Raft ("Big Brian" Webb)

Andy Leggett's memories of the album (email dated 12th November 2008):

> "It was recorded live by Derek Burgoygne in the Troubadour on an evening (or two) in November 1967. Roger White … [is] still in circulation, but not on the folk scene. Like me, he eventually morphed into a jazz musician, playing a very tasty New-Orleans-style string bass. "Big Brian" - a large shanty-singer from Cornwall - has been dead a long time now. "Chicken on a Raft", as you probably know, is seamen's slang for egg on toast Graham Kilsby … changed his stage name to Tony Graham and made a successful new career for himself in Nashville Tennessee. "The Old Man of the Sea" is a tribute to (Sir) Francis Chichester, who had recently sailed round the world in "Gypsy Moth"."

Blues Like Showers of Rain *(Saydisc Matchbox, SDM 142, 1968, LP)*
1 – A Few Short Lines (Dave Kelly)
2 – Going to Germany (The Panama Limited Jug Band)
3 – Nothin' In Ramblin' (Jo-Ann Kelly)
4 – Dealing with the Devil (Simon & Steve)
5 – Meeting House Rag (Mike Cooper)
6 – Friday Evening Blues (Ian Anderson [with "Putty" and Elliot Jackson])
7 – Dark Road Blues (The Missouri Compromise)

1 – Say No to the Devil (Simon & Steve)
2 – Black Snake Moan (Mike Cooper)
3 – If I Had Possession (The Missouri Compromise)
4 – Rowdy Blues (Ian Anderson)
5 – Black Mary (Jo-Anne Kelly)
6 – Travelling Blues (Dave Kelly)
7 – Cocaine Habit (The Panama Limited Jug Band)

"Putty", who played on Anderson's *Friday Evening Blues*, was the nickname for Adrian Pietryga, guitarist with Bristol's The Deep Blues Band. Mike Cooper's *Meeting House Rag* is named after the venue at which the LP was recorded, The Quaker Meeting House, in Frenchay, Bristol.

Listen Here! *(Transatlantic TRA SAM 2, 1968, LP)*
1 – Travellin' Song (The Pentangle)
2 – Eight Frames a Second (Ralph McTell)
3 – In Love with a Stranger (Gordon Giltrap)
4 – Tie Tocative (Bert Jansch & John Renbourn)
5 – Song (John Renbourn)
6 – The Circle Game (The Ian Campbell Group)

1 – Urge for Going (The Johnstones)
2 – Harvest Your Thoughts of Love (Bert Jansch)
3 – Love in Ice Crystals (The Sallyangie)
4 – Blues for Dominique (Bob Bunting)
5 – Certainly Random (Ron Geesin)
6 – Granny Takes a Trip (The Purple Gang)

Dungeon Folk *(BBC REC 35S, 1969, LP)*
1 – Big Mon (Orange Blossom Sound)
2 – Homestead on the Farm (Orange Blossom Sound)
3 – Hullo Stranger (Shelagh McDonald)
4 – Long About Now (The Crown Folk)
5 – Maybe Someday (The Crown Folk)
6 – Nothing But Time (Dana Stirk)
7 – Kentucky (The Big Timers)
8 – C.C. Rider (Cliff Aungier)
9 – Nicolette (Cliff Aungier)

1 – Marble Town (Orange Blossom Sound)
2 – Big Sandy River (Orange Blossom Sound)
3 – Street Walking Blues (Shelagh McDonald)
4 – The Dancing Bear (The Crown Folk)
5 – Suzanne (Dana Stirk)
6 – Gold Watch and Chain (The Big Timers)
7 – Hickory Wind (The Big Timers)
8 – The Last Thing on My Mind (Cliff Aungier)

Bristol folk

Son of Gutbucket *(Liberty LBX 4, 1969, LP)*
1 – Bootleg (Creedence Clearwater Revival)
2 – My Babe She Ain't Nothing but a Doggone Crazy Fool Mumble (Ian Anderson's Country Blues Band)
3 – I Got Love If You Want It (Johnny Winter)
4 – Preparation G (T.I.M.E.)
5 – Walking Down Their Outlook (High Tide)
6 – Oh Death (Jo-Ann Kelly & Tony McPhee)
7 – Don't Mean a Thing (Floating Bridge)
8 – Sergeant Sunshine (Roy Harper)
9 – Mistreated (Groundhogs)

1 – Sic 'Em Pigs (Canned Heat)
2 – Hard Headed Woman (Andy Fernbach)
3 – T. B. Blues (McKenna Mendelson Mainline)
4 – Sunshine Possibilities (Famous Jug Band)
5 – Hurry Up John (Idle Race)
6 – I'm So Tired (Brett Marvin & The Thunderbolts)
7 – Leavin' My Home (T.I.M.E.)
8 – Sugar on the Line (Aynsley Dunbar Retaliation)

49 Greek Street *(RCA Victor SF 8118, 1970, LP)*
1 – Running Shoes (Al Jones)
2 – Untitled Piece (Andy Roberts)
3 – Strange Fruit (Tin Angel)
4 – Shifting Sands (Synanthesia)
5 – Robin Head (Keith Christmas)

1 – Red Road Digger (Robin Scott)
2 – Persuasion (Tin Angel)
3 – Spread Your Carpet (Nadia Cattouse)
4 – Elsie Straw's Saga (Mike Hart)
5 – It Takes a Lot to Laugh, It Takes a Train to Cry (Al Jones)

The Great White Dap *(Village Thing VTSX 1000, 1970, 7" EP pressed at 33⅓ rpm and issued in a picture sleeve)*
1 – Time is Flying (Wizz Jones)
2 – Tales of Jasmine & Suicide (Sun Also Rises)

1 – Silent Night No. 2 (Ian A. Anderson)
2 - Taint No Sin (Pigsty Hill Light Orchestra)

Men and the Sea *(credited to Stan Hugill and the Folk Tradition: City Museum Bristol, no catalogue number assigned, 1971, LP)*
1 – Can't You Dance the Polka (Paul Evans)
2 – William Taylor   (Paul Evans)
3 – Rounding the Horn (Paul Evans)
4 – Chief O'Neil's Favourite
5 – Haul Away for Rosy (Dave Searle)
6 – The Lime Juice Ship (Stan Hugill)
7 – Andrew Rose (Dave Byrne)
8 – Santiano (John Colley)
9 – Kishmull's Galley (Rosemary Musters)

1 – Hog's Eye Man (Kevin Standring)
2 – John Kanaka (John Colley)
3 – Hanging Johnny (Nigel Hallett)
4 – Row, Bullies, Row (Dave Searle)
5 – Lord Franklin (Lorraine Stewart)
6 – Bound for South Australia (Stan Hugill)
7 – Admiral Benbow (Dave Byrne)
8 – The Old Man and the Afterguard (John Shaw)
9 – The Ship that Never Returned (Rosemary Musters)

Artist credits are for solo singer. No credit is given for *Chief O'Neil's Favourite* as this is an instrumental, though the line-up was Nigel Hallett, fiddle, Bob Stewart, mandolin, and Paul Evans, spoons. John Shaw has the following to say about the LP (email, dated 21st July 2009):

> The recording was first conceived as background sound effects to a Bristol Museum exhibition about marine archaeology. At the request of museum staff, various regular and occasional singers and players from the Folk Tradition song club ... recorded a selection of sea songs and shanties for this purpose. The "star" on the recordings was Stan Hugill ... the only non-local performer on the record. The museum people were pleased with the results, and decided to press it as a record to sell to tie in with the exhibition ... The recording was all done one Saturday morning at the HTV Studios at Arnos Vale ... the recording was very rushed, with virtually everything being (often unrehearsed) a first take. Generally speaking the view ... was that it was OK for a background atmosphere tape, but we were very surprised when the Museum people decided to put it out as a record ... Still it had a certain amount of cult success. I think the Museum sold out of its initial pressing of 1000 (?) copies, and did a second run.

Clogs *(Peg PS 1, 1972, LP; included 99p sticker & gatefold insert)*
1 – Captain Coulston (Steeleye Span)
2 – Richmond (Andy Roberts)
3 – The Irish Washerwoman/The Ash Plant (Martin Carthy & Dave Swarbrick)
4 – The King (Steeleye Span)
5 – Poem (Keith Christmas)
6 – Murder of Maria Marten (Shirley Collins)

1 – Rave On (Steeleye Span)
2 – I Live Not Where I Love (Tim Hart and Maddy Prior)
3 – Captain's Log (Spirogyra)
4 – Rod's Song (Shelagh McDonald)
5 – Lord Randall (Martin Carthy)
6 – Yarrow (Marc Ellington)
7 – Welcome Home (Andy Roberts)

Bristol folk

Club Folk Volume 1 *(Peg PS 2, 1972, LP)*
1 – The Sailor (Robin Scott)
2 – Red and Green Christmas (Nadia Cattouse)
3 – Blue Railway Fields (P.C. Kent)
4 – The Barley Straw (Martin Carthy & Dave Swarbrick)
5 – Autumn to May (Andy Roberts)
6 – Travelling Down (Keith Christmas)
1 – Rolling and Tumbling (Synanthesia)
2 – Sweet Sunlight (Shelagh McDonald)
3 – Our Captain Cried All Hands (Martin Carthy & Dave Swarbrick)
4 – Come Join My Orchestra (Al Jones)
5 – Disbelief Blues (Mike Hart)
6 – Jello (Andy Roberts)

Club Folk Volume 2 *(Peg PS 3, 1972, LP)*
1 – Rainy Night Blues (Shelagh McDonald)
2 – What Was I Thinking (Al Jones)
3 – Trafalgar Square (Synanthesia)
4 – Broadened (P.C. Kent)
5 – The Sound of Rain (Robin Scott)
6 – B.C. People (Nadia Cattouse)
1 – Domeama (Martin Carthy)
2 – Where the Soul of Man Never Dies (Andy Roberts)
3 – All Around My Grandmother's Floor (Nadia Cattouse)
4 – Bed-Sit Two Step (Keith Christmas)
5 – Yawny Morning Song (Mike Hart)
6 – Ire and Spottiswood (Al Jones)

A Stereo Introduction to the Exciting World of Transatlantic *(Contour 2870 315, 1972, LP; included foldout advertising poster)*
1 – Will the Circle Be Unbroken (Pentangle)
2 – Streets of London (The Johnstones)
3 – Shoeshine Boy (The Humblebums)
4 – P.F. Sloan (Unicorn)
5 – Blues Jumped the Rabbit (Stefan Grossman)
6 – Nature's Way (Stray)
1 – Springtime Promises (Pentangle)
2 – Elvira Madigan (Mr Fox)
3 – Rosemary Lane (Bert Jansch)
4 – Willy O Winsbury (John Renbourn)
5 – Original Rags (John James)
6 – Falling (Steve Tilston)

The Best of British Folk *(Contour 2870 313, 1972, LP)*
1 – Lord Franklin (Pentangle)
2 – I'm Reaching Out (Steve Tilston)
3 – The Gay Goshawk (Mr Fox)
4 – Needle of Death (Bert Jansch)
5 – John Barleycorn (The Young Tradition)
6 – Westron Wynde (John Renbourn)
1 – Ye Jacobites By Name (The Johnstones)
2 – To Meet You I Hurry Down (John James)
3 – Paddy Lay Back (The Ian Campbell Folk Group)
4 – Tom All Alone (Dave Cartwright)
5 – The Lonesome Boatman (Finbur & Eddie Furey)
6 – History of Football (Hamish Imlach)

Matchbox Days *(Village Thing VT-SAM 16, 1972, LP)*
1 – Bulldog Blues (Mike Cooper)
2 – Stop Breakin' Down (Prager, Rye & Hall)
3 – Nothin' In Ramblin' (Jo Ann Kelly)
4 – Searchin' The Desert (Al Jones)
5 – Maybelle Rag (John James)
6 – Dark Road Blues (The Missouri Compromise)
1 – Travellin' Blues (Dave Kelly)
2 – Cocaine Habit (Panama Ltd. Jug Band)
3 – Cottonfield Blues (Ian A. Anderson)
4 – Rambling Man (Frances McGillivray)
5 – The Inverted World (Mike Cooper & Ian Anderson)
6 – Spoonful (Wizz Jones)

This was a compilation of tracks from the two *Blues Like Showers of Rain* volumes (SDM 142 and SDM 167) and Cooper and Anderson's *The Inverted World* LP (SDM 159). *Stop Breakin' Down* was originally credited to "Simon and Steve" on SDM 167; *Cottonfield Blues* was originally credited to "Ian Anderson" (without the "A") on SDM 159; *The Inverted World* was originally credited to "Mike Cooper" on SDM 159 (though with a credit to say that Anderson played on it); Dave Kelly's *Travellin' Blues* was originally credited as "Travelling Blues" on SDM 142. Mike Cooper's *Bulldog Blues*, John James' *Spoonful* and Al Jones' *Searchin' the Desert* were previously unreleased.

Us *(Village Thing VT-SAM15, 1972, LP)*
1 – Only Blue (Dave Evans)
2 – West End Rag (Tight Like That)
3 – Beggerman (Wizz Jones)
4 – The Folker (Fred Wedlock)
5 – I Really Wanted You (Steve Tilston)
1 – One More Chance (Ian A. Anderson)
2 – Another Normal Day (Tucker Zimmerman)
3 – Sweet Miss Emmaline (The Pigsty Hill Light Orchestra)
4 – Fafnir and the Knights (Sun Also Rises)
5 – Hold Me Now (Hunt & Turner)

Bristol folk

Fafnir and the Knights was previously unreleased. As Ian Anderson says (email dated 5th May 2009), "... we discovered that you can't print blue ink over silver without a laminate to seal it, as it quickly rubs off - a mint, completely unscuffed copy of that cover must be a very rare thing." Copies should cost somewhere around £20.

The Transatlantic Valentine *(Transatlantic MMS 101, 1973, 7" EP, no picture sleeve, custom label design)*
1 – Falling (Steve Tilston)
2 – Kicking Up the Dust (John James & Pete Berryman)
3 – Queen of the Sea (Stray)
1 – Didn't I? (Gerry Rafferty)
2 – P.F. Sloan (Unicorn)
3 – Continental Trailways Bus (The Johnstones)

This promotional EP was either given away at gigs or record shops or was given away with a music paper or girl's magazine – my wife can't remember where her copy came from now, just that it was a freebie. The record plays at 33⅓ rpm.

Sounds of Bristol *(Saydisc, 33SD, 1973, 7" LP)*
Side one narrated by Geoffrey Woodruff
1 – Virtute et Industrial (Fred Wedlock with Bev and Richard Dewar)
2 – Fanfare from the City Trumpeters (courtesy of City & County of Bristol)
3 – The Bells of St Mary Redcliffe
4 – Peacocks at Clifton Zoo
5 – "Harry Brown" under Clifton Suspension Bridge
6 – Quarter Jacks of Christ Church with St Ewan in Broad Street

1 – An illustrated exposition of Bristol, dialect and humour by the recognized master of those arts (Geoffrey Woodruff)

Subtitled, *A Portait of Bristol in Sounds, Dialect & Song*, this record was issued in a sepia tone sleeve, though there is a rare variation with black and white sleeve (worth approximately £5 and £10 respectively). This was the first of four 7" LPs, which were basically EP's pressed to play at 33⅓ rpm, generally presenting about 20 minutes of content per record. This particular record was well-marketed with local record shops being provided with special Saydisc-branded cardboard plinths to hold ten or so copies, with these plinths designed to be placed on the shop counter. The plinth proudly proclaimed that the records sold for the bargain price of 65p (if memory serves after all this time), which, along with their prime position on the shop counter next to the till, provoked both speculative and impulse purchasing. Even better, the record was released to coincide with the Bristol 600 celebrations, which commemorated six hundred years of Bristol's status as both a City and County. Bristol's County status was removed less than a year later and, similarly, this record presented much else of Bristol, such as the ceremony at the Pie Poudre Court, whose days were numbered. The Harry Brown lasted into the early 1980s and has been immortalised both on an Arnolfini postcard of the late 1970s, which described the ship as "River Avon driftwood", and by the shanty group, The Harry Browns.

Folk Heritage *(Windmill WMD 179, 1973, LP)*
1 – October Song (Folkways)
2 – Rawtenstall Annual Fair (Combine Harvester)
3 – Matt Highland (Blue Water Folk)
4 – Maid of the Mill (Horden Raikes)
5 – Willie's Gone (Blue Water Folk)
6 – Sweet Sir Galahad (Folkal Point)
7 – Lancashire Fusilier (The Yardarm)

1 – Whitby Smuggler's Song (Parke)
2 – Staten Island Harvest Home (Gallery)
3 – A Beggin' (Paul and Glen)
4 – Queen of the Night (Mike Raven and Joan Mills)
5 – Johnny Lad (The Jovial Crew)
6 – Dancers of Stanton Drew (Parke)
7 – I Never Will Marry (The Blue Horizon)

Guitar Workshop *(Transatlantic TRA(D) 271, 1973, double LP with booklet inside the gatefold sleeve)*
Side one
1 – Trout Joins the Cavalry (Simon Boswell)
2 – Nefarious Doings (Chris Hardy)
3 – Black Scrag (Philip John Lee)
4 – One Blue Guitar (Pete Berryman)
5 – The Loneliness of the Long Distance Acoustic Traveller (Willy Barrett)
Side three
1 – Stalks and Seeds (Philip John Lee)
2 – The Entertainer (John Rogers)
3 – Kenneth's Riverbank song (Davey Murrell)
4 – Hair Across the Frets (Willy Barrett)
5 – Brother Nature (John & Mike Rogers)

Side 2
1 – Ferdinand the Spider (Davey Murrell)
2 – Rock Salmon Suite (Steve Tilston)
3 – South Devon Atmosphere (Mike Rogers)
4 – Mica (Chris Hardy)
5 – Trout Sundae (Simon Boswell)
Side 4
1 – Eighteen Bricks Left on April 21 (Mark Warner & Graeme Taylor: David Bedford composition)

Bristol folk

Rave On *(Mooncrest CREST 17, 1974, LP)*
1 – Rave On (Steeleye Span)
2 – The Ploughboy and the Cockney (Tim Hart and Maddy Prior)
3 – Western Wynde (Tim Hart and Maddy Prior)
4 – Banks of the Bann (Shirley Collins)
5 – Cold Haily Windy Night (Steeleye Span)
6 – Let No Man Steal Your Thyme (Shelagh McDonald)
7 – Lovely on the Water (Steeleye Span)

1 – Just As the Tide Was Flowing (Shirley Collins)
2 – Cannily, Cannily (Tim Hart and Maddy Prior)
3 – Matt Hyland (Martin Carthy)
4 – Of All the Birds (Tim Hart and Maddy Prior)
5 – The Bank (Martin Carthy & Dave Swarbrick)
6 – Marrowbones (Steeleye Span)

Original, matt-sleeved copies have artist photos on the rear. Later, gloss-sleeved reissues have no artist photos.

Souvenir of the West Country *(EMI One-Up OU 2174, 1977, LP: track listing unknown)*

Amusingly, the sleeve shows all the places after which songs on the LP are named. The only problem is that the sleeve shows Salisbury Cathedral, but the song included on the LP is *Winchester Cathedral* (as covered by Mrs. Mills, if memory serves), which isn't quite in the area covered by the LP. There are many more compilations with tracks by Adge Cutler's Wurzels and the later Wurzels, though these LPs are mostly of little interest to a folk audience. This particular LP is included in the discography because there is a lot more material that is of interest to folk or West Country audiences. Between them, Adge Cutler's Wurzels and the post-Adge Wurzels have nine tracks on the album.

Contemporary Guitar Workshop *(Kicking Mule SNKF 143, 1978, LP: included tablature booklet)*
1 – Silver Bells (Duck Baker)
2 – Jessica (Dave Evans)
3 – Flopped Ear Mule (Leo Wijnkamp Jr.)
4 – Walking My Baby Back Home (Duck Baker)
5 – Dickie's Blues No. 2 (Jim McLennan)
6 – Cold Feet (Dave Evans)
7 – The Chrysanthemum (Jim McLennan)
8 – Grey Hills (Dave Evans)

1 – Mardi Gras Dance (Duck Baker)
2 – The Elephant March (Leo Wijnkamp Jr.)
3 – Fisher's Hornpipe (Duck Baker)
4 – Ugly Duckling (Dave Evans)
5 – The Easy Winners (Jim McLennan)
6 – Charles O'Connor (Duck Baker)
7 – Jolymont (Dave Evans)

The Shanty Men *(Greenwich Village GVR 201, 1978, LP)*
1 – Rio Grande (Jim Mageean)
2 – Reuben Ranzo (John Goodluck)
3 – Bay of Mexico (Matt Armour)
4 – Whisky Johnny (Erik Ilott)
5 – Hob-y-Derri-Dando (Mick Tems)
6 – Hanging Johnny (Johnny Collins)
7 – Paddy Doyle's Boots (Joe Stead)
8 – Do Me Johnny Bowker (Jim Mageean)
9 – Lowlands (Don Shepherd)

1 – Sally Brown (Johnny Collins)
2 – Where Am I to Go (Jim Mageean)
3 – A Hundred Years Ago (John Goodluck)
4 – Put Yer Shoulder Next to Mine (Erik Ilott)
5 – Blow the Man Down (Matt Armour)
6 – Haul on the Bowline (Johnny Collins)
7 – Sally Rackett (Joe Stead)
8 – Tom's Gone to Hilo (Alex Campbell)
9 – Leave Her Johnny Leave Her (Mick Tems)

Irish Reels, Jigs, Hornpipes & Airs *(Kicking Mule SNKF 153, 1979, LP: included tablature booklet)*
1 – The Galtee Hunt (Dave Evans)
2 – Medley: The West Wind / The Blackbird (Duck Baker)
3 – The Sunny Bank (Dan Ar Bras)
4 – Lagan Love (Davy Graham)
5 – Medley: Old Hag You Have Killed Me / The Hag with the Money (Davy Graham)
6 – Hewlett (Dave Evans)
7 – Irish Washerwoman (Duck Baker)
8 – Leaving Brittany, Going to Ireland (Dan Ar Bras)

1 – The March of the King of Laoise (Duck Baker)
2 – Shebcg an' Shemor (Dave Evans)
3 – The Fisherman's Lilt (Dan Ar Bras)
4 – Medley: Carrickfergus / The Water is Wide (Davy Graham)
5 – Miss McLeod's Reel (Duck Baker)
6 – The Donegal Pilgrim (Dave Evans)
7 – Boys from Blue Hill (Dan Ar Bras)
8 – Mawgan Magan (Dave Evans)

CD discography

The focus of the book is on vinyl record releases during the 1960s and 1970s, so no attempt has been made to make this CD discography 'definitive' in any way. It is merely a listing of those (mostly UK) CDs known to be more or less generally available at the time of publication. Most are still commercially available or otherwise are still fairly easy to find.

Currently in preparation: a Village Thing compilation is planned for release by Weekend Beatnik in 2010 to mark the 40th anniversary of the launch of the label. The CD will include some previously unreleased tracks.

Ian Anderson

Stereo Death Breakdown *(as Ian Anderson's Country Blues Band: Fledg'ling FLED 3073, 2008: reissue of the Liberty label LP plus two tracks from "Book of Changes")*

Ray Andrews

Classic English Banjo *(Musical Traditions MTCD 314, 2001: includes tracks from the "Banjo Maestro" cassette plus otherwise unreleased material from the 1970s and early 1980s; also includes a comprehensive booklet)*

Keith Christmas

Brighter Day *(Voiceprint VP220CD, 2004: reissue of the Manticore LP – in the US sleeve design – plus 5 otherwise unreleased bonus tracks)*

Stories from the Human Zoo *(Voiceprint VP219CD, 2004: reissue of the Manticore LP)*

Timeless and Strange *(Castle CMRDC 786, 2004: compilation of tracks from RCA Victor and B&C LPs with an otherwise unreleased bonus track)*

Adge Cutler and the Wurzels
See also the Wurzels.

The Wurzels & Adge Cutler & the Wurzels *(EMI Ideal IDL 114, 1991: compilation of Adge Cutler and the Wurzels single and LP tracks from 1966 to 1969 plus Wurzels single and LP tracks from 1975 to 1979)*

The Finest 'Arvest of the Wurzels Featuring Adge Cutler *(EMI Gold 527 0462, 2000: compilation of Adge Cutler and the Wurzels single and LP tracks from 1966 to 1972 plus Wurzels single and LP tracks from 1975 to 1979)*

The Finest 'Arvest of the Wurzels Featuring Adge Cutler *(EMI Gold 534 4102, 2002: reissue of the 2000 CD with one track replaced and one track added)*

Cutler of the West *(EMI Gold 584 8072, 2003: reissue of the 1968 LP)*

Dave Evans

The Words In Between *(Weekend Beatnik WEBE 9039, 2001: reissue of the Village Thing LP with 5 tracks from "Elephantasia")*

Frank Evans

In an English Manner *(as The Frank Evans Consort: Saydisc CD-SDL 233: reissue of the Saydisc LP)*

Ballade *(Blue Bag, 2003: reissue of the early 1980s compilation LP of Blue Bag recordings from 1975 to 1979)*

Bristol folk

Hot Vultures

Vulturama (Weekend Beatnik WEBE 9031, 2001: compilation of tracks from the Red Rag and Plant Life LPs)

Hunt & Turner

Magic Landscape (Village Thing VTS 211: reissue of the Village Thing LP)

Al Jones

Alun Ashworth Jones (Mooncrest CRESTCD 068, 2001: reissue of the Parlophone LP plus 17 of bonus tracks, including a live set recorded in 1969 and tracks made for an abortive Trailer label LP in 1971)

All My Friends Are Back Again (Castle CMEDD 1403, 2007: 2-CD compilation of "Alun Ashworth Jones" and "Jonesville" with bonus tracks)

Shelagh McDonald

Stargazer (Mooncrest CRESTCD 040, 1999: reissue of the B&C LP plus 5 bonus tracks)

Album (Mooncrest CRESTCD 059, 2000: reissue of the B&C LP plus 8 bonus tracks)

Let No Man Steal Your Thyme (Sanctuary CMDDD 1065, 2005: 2-CD compilation of "Album" and "Stargazer" with bonus tracks)

Old Pete and John Christie

Old Pete (Saydisc CD-SDL 255: compilation of two Saydisc 7" LPs, "Old Pete" and "Isambard Kingdom Brunel" ; Old Pete's humorous, Bristolian monologues plus John Christie's songs.

Sally Oldfield

The Collection (Castle Communications CCSCD 125: long-deleted compilation of Bronze label material from 1978 to 1981)

Mirrors Remixes 2001 (Vale VLCDMX 292-4, Spain, CD single: original version plus six remixes)

Water Bearer (Sanctuary CMRCD989, 2004: reissue of the 2nd press Bronze LP with "Mirrors")
Mirrors (The Bronze Anthology) (Sanctuary CMDDD1324, 2007: 2-CD compilation of Bronze label material from 1978 to 1981)

Pat Purchase
See the main discography for details of the Pat Purchase retrospective CD.

Sallyangie

Children of the Sun (Castle/Sanctuary, 2002: 2-CD reissue of the Transatlantic LP plus 15 bonus tracks, including the Transatlantic single and BBC session)

Stackridge

BBC Radio 1 Live In Concert (Windsong WINCD 019, 1992: three complete sessions from 1972, 1973 and 1975)

The Radio 1 Sessions (Strange Fruit SFRSCD 40, 1997: complete Radio 1 session from [probably] 1973)

The Original Mr Mick (Dap DAP103CD, 2000: the final Rocket LP as the band originally wanted the LP issued)

Bristol folk

Purple Spaceships Over Yatton *(The Best Of) (Angel Air SJPCD228, 2006: compilation of MCA and Rocket-era material with a 2007 re-recording of "Purple Spaceships Over Yatton")*

Stackridge *(Angel Air SJPCD230: remastered reissue of the MCA LP plus the single version of "Slark" and "Let there Be Lids")*

Friendliness *(Angel Air SJPCD231: remastered reissue of the MCA LP plus "Everyman", "Purple Spaceships Over Yatton", "C'Est la Vie" and "Do the Stanley")*

The Man in the Bowler Hat *(Angel Air SJPCD232: remastered reissue of the MCA LP)*

Extravaganza *(Angel Air SJPCD233: reissue of the Rocket LP)*

Mr Mick *(Angel Air SJPCD234: 2-CD remastered reissue of the Rocket LP plus the album as originally intended)*

Bob Stewart

The Rollright Ritual *(details unknown, available from www.rjstewart.net. "The Unique Sound of the Psaltery" is also available, from the same source, as a digitally-remastered cassette)*

Steve Tilston

An Acoustic Confusion *(Village Thing VTS 205: reissue of the Village Thing LP with 2 bonus tracks)*

Songs From the Dress Rehearsal *(Market Square MSMCD132, 2005: reissue of the Cornucopia LP with 6 bonus tracks from an unfinished LP for Stefan Grossman's Kicking Mule label)*

Fred Wedlock

Geoffrey Woodruff Entertains *(Saydisc CD-SDL 322: reissue of "Sounds of Bristol", including Fred Wedlock's version of "Virtute et Industrial", plus "Geoffrey Woodruff Live", which comprises a humorous exposition of the Bristol dialect)*

The Folker *(Village Thing VTS 207: 2-CD reissue of The Folker and Frollicks, plus all four tracks from the 1965 "Volume One" EP and "Virtute et Industrial" from the 1966 EP of the same name)*

The Wurzels
See also Adge Cutler and the Wurzels

The Wurzels *(EMI Ideal CD IDL 22, 1988: compilation of tracks from singles and LPs from 1975 to 1979. Includes one more track than the 1981 LP equivalent)*

The Wurzels Collection *(HMV Easy 5 32071 2, 2001: compilation of Wurzels single and LP tracks from 1975 to 1979 plus one track by Adge Cutler and the Wurzels)*

Various Artists

Jazz Tete a Tete *(Progressive PCD-7079, US, 1993: reissue of the 1967 LP featuring the Frank Evans Trio, with bonus track by the Tony Coe Quintet)*

Matchbox Days *(Ace/Big Beat CDWIKD 168, 1997: remastered and expanded version of the Village Thing label LP, "Matchbox Days", plus tracks from the two Matchbox label "Blues Like Showers of Rain" complations. Includes comprehensive sleeve notes)*

Most of the above artists have more recent releases available via their websites. Website details are available on p. 193 and links are also provided to these at www.bristol-folk.co.uk.

Bristol folk

Artists booked as guests at the Bristol Troubadour, 1966-1971

Mike Absalom
Adrienne (a.k.a. Aj Webber)
Pete Airey
Alligator Jug Thumpers
Ian Anderson
Ian Anderson & Elliot Jackson
Anderson Jones Jackson
Harvey Andrews
Harvey Andrews & Chris Rohmann
Cliff Aungier
Norman Beaton
Dominic Behan
Peter Bellamy
Patrick Benham
Jon Betmead
Big Brian
Derek Brimstone
Bob (Stewart) & Albert (Lightfoot)
Martin Carthy
Martin Carthy & Dave Swarbrick
Jasper Carrott
Alex Campbell
Michael Chapman
Keith Christmas
Shirley Collins
Mike Cooper
Mike Cooper & Jerry Kingett
The Crofters
Crownfolk (a.k.a. 1812)
Arthur 'Big Boy' Crudup
Adge Cutler & The Wurzels
Decameron
Sandy Denny
Bev & Rich Dewar
Diz Disley
The Downsiders
Robin Dransfield
Rob Edwards
Dave Evans
Paul Evans
The Exiles
The Famous Jug Band
Flanagan's Folk Four
The Flint Hill Three
John Foreman
Jackson C. Frank
Gasworks
Tim Greenwood
The Hooters
Gothic Horizon
Stefan Grossman
The Halliard
Tim Hart & Maddy Prior
Dorris Henderson
The Incredible String Band
Jackie & Bridie
John James
Bert Jansch
Al Jones
Wizz Jones
Wizz Jones & Clive Palmer
Johnny Joyce
Dave Kelly
Jo-Ann Kelly
Louis Killen
Graham Kilsby
Jack & Margaret King
Gerry Lockran
Trevor Lucas
Mac (Tresler) & Mick (Strode)
John Martyn
Liz MacKinlay
Ian McCann & The Roan County Boys
Shelagh McDonald
Paul McNeil & Linda Peters
Ralph McTell
(Dave) Mudge & (Tim) Clutterbuck
Michael-Claire (Mike Milner & Claire Hart)
Noel Murphy
Noel Murphy & Shaggis
Noel Murphy & Draught Porridge
The New Modern Idiot Grunt Band
Dave Nixon
Sally Oldfield
Orange Blossom Sound
John Pearse
Piccadilly Line
Pigsty Hill Light Orchestra
Duffy Power
John Renbourn
John Renbourn & Jacqui McShee
Leon Rosselson
Ian Russell
Sally (Oldfield) & Ian (Bray)
Colin Scot(t)
Johnny Silvo
Simon (Prager) & Steve (Rye)
Pat Small
The Southern Ramblers
Pete Stanley & Brian Golbey
Al Stewart
Bob Stewart
Strange Fruit
The Strawbs
Sun Also Rises
Cyril Tawney
Allan Taylor
Jeremy Taylor
Steve Tilston
The Tinkers
Tir na Nog
Dave Travis
Dave Turner
Chas Upton
Dave Waite & Marion Segal
The Watersons
Deena Websters
Fred Wedlock
The West Country Three
The Westlanders
Alan White
White On Black
Roger White
Colin Wilkie & Shirley Hart
Brenda Wootton & John The Fish
Martyn Wyndham Read
The Yetties
The Young Tradition

List typed up from a handwritten copy that had been on the wall of the Troubadour. This was rescued from the dustbin outside the club the day the venue was unceremoniously closed. Courtesy Ian Anderson.

Bristol folk

Artists booked as guests at the Folk Blues Bristol & West, 1967-1969

Mike Absalom
Ian Anderson's Country Blues Band
Duster Bennett
Michael Chapman
Mike Cooper
Paul Darby
Dharma Blues
Champion Jack Dupree
Andy Fernbach
John James

Curtis Jones
Dave Kelly
Dave Kelly & Putty
Jo-Ann Kelly
Jo-Ann Kelly & Bob Hall
Spider John Koerner
Alexis Korner
Alexis Korner & Nick South
Mac & Mick
Brett Marvin & the Thunderbolts

Mississippi Fred McDowell
Ralph McTell
Steve Miller
The Missouri Compromise
Mark Newman
The Panama Limited Jug Band
Simon Prager & Steve Rye
Gordon Smith
Smooth & Lump
The Titanic Jug Band

List courtesy of Ian Anderson

Websites

Ian Anderson and fRoots
fRoots website - www.frootsmag.com/
Ian Anderson's MySpace site - www.myspace.com/vulturama

Keith Christmas
Official website - www.kcblues.co.uk/

Adge Cutler and the Wurzels/Wurzels
Official website - www.thewurzels.com/
Wurzelmania - www.wurzelmania.co.uk/
Scrumpy and Western - www.scrumpyandwestern.co.uk/

Dave Evans
Official website - http://users.swing.be/devans/

Dave Fuller
Dave Fuller's MySpace site –
www.myspace.com/davefullermusic

Dave Griffiths
Official website - www.mandolinexpress.co.uk/

Maggie Holland
Official website - www.maggieholland.co.uk/

Ian Hunt
Official website - www.ianhunt.net/

Andy Leggett
Official website - www.andyleggett.com/

Rod Neep
Official website - www.rod-neep.com/

Plastic Dog
Official Granary website - www.thegranaryclub.co.uk/
Rodney Matthews official website - www.rodneymatthews.com/

Saydisc and Village Thing
Official Saydisc website - http://www.saydisc.com/
Official Village Thing website - http://www.myspace.com/villagething
VinylAttic's comprehensive Saydisc and Village Thing discography website - www.vinylattic.com

Stackridge
Official website - www.stackridge.net/
Mutter Slater's website - www.mutterslater.com/
Angel Air website (official outlet for Stackridge CDs/DVDs) – www.angelair.com/

Robert John Stewart
Official website - www.rjstewart.org/
Official website - www.rjstewart.net/
Dreampower website - www.dreampower.com/

Steve Tilston
Official website - www.steve-tilston.co.uk/

Fred Wedlock
Official website - www.fredwedlock.com/

References

[1] Originally published by Fiducia, 2000 and reprinted with some new content as a limited run of 500 in 2009.
[2] Well, almost. The Big Bill Broonzy version goes thus: "One day, radio-announcer Studs Terkel asked Big Bill Broonzy if the song he'd just presented was a "Folk Song". "Well," answered Big Bill, "I never heard a cow singing it". Quoted from the sleeve notes for the Various Artists LP, *The Folk Scene* (1963) Golden Guinea/Elektra. The horse version seems to be the one that has stuck, though.
[3] Long-established, Bristol-based, second-hand record shop.
[4] The Electric Muse (Dave Laing, Robin Denselow, Karl Dallas & Robert Shelton) Methuen, 1975.
[5] The closest that Sharp got to Bristol in his song collecting visits were the Harptrees, Compton Martin, Ubley, Blagdon, Bishop's Sutton, Temple Cloud, Farrington Gurney, Nempnett Thrubwell, Chew Magna and Chew Stoke, those on the edge of Mendip being particularly bike-unfriendly
[6] Sleeve notes from *Somerset Sisters* by the Roots Quartet (2000) RQ Records.
[7] Whilst major UK label catalogues of the 1930s and 1940s include many folk records, these are mainly instrumental arrangements for folk dance orchestras/bands of various descriptions or military bands, either that or folk songs sung by popular recording stars of the day. There is no mention in any UK label catalogue issued by Parlophone, Regal Zonophone, Columbia, HMV, MGM, Brunswick or Decca between 1933 and 1948 of any recording by what we would now term a 'folk singer'.
[8] Discuss!
[9] Email dated 15th November 2008.
[10] Email dated 25th June 2009.
[11] Email dated 15th November 2008.
[12] This moved briefly in 1971 to the Crown and Dove, in Bridewell Street, before moving to its long-term home in the Nova Scotia, on the Cumberland Basin.
[13] Folk Blues Bristol and West later moved again to The Full Moon, on Stokes Croft.
[14] Op. cit.
[15] Email dated 8th December 2008.
[16] Ibid.
[17] Ibid.
[18] Email dated 10th November 2008.
[19] Email dated 21st December 2008.
[20] Email dated 26th June 2009.
[21] Email dated 9th December 2008.
[22] The emergence of a white blues sound (Tony Wilson), Melody Maker, 28th December 1968.
[23] Country Blues Comes To Town (Tony Wilson), Melody Maker, 31st August 1968.
[24] Email dated 8th December 2008.
[25] Death of a folk club – whose fault? (Dave Berry) Pre-View, August 1971.
[26] Folk (Andy Leggett) Pre-View, March 1972.
[27] Club Spot (Colin Irwin) Melody Maker, 10th August 1974.
[28] The May 1972 edition of Pre-View also mentions that the Folk Tradition Club was approaching its 5th anniversary and that the Ballads and Blues Club was approaching its 10th anniversary.
[29] The only other recording from the Ship Inn to come to light is a private EP by Henry's Bootblacks c. 1967.
[30] Ian Anderson, quoted in In Session Tonight (Ken Garner) BBC, 1993.
[31] This was Simon Prager and Steve Rye, the latter of whom joined the original Groundhogs.
[32] David Wilkins 'proper job' was as an anaesthetist.
[33] Email dated 7th November 2007.
[34] Ian Anderson, quoted in Focus On Folk: Bristol's cream (Andrew Means) Melody Maker, 1st January 1972.
[35] Email dated 9th December 2008.
[36] Melody Maker, 18th April, 1970.
[37] Email dated 9th December 2008.
[38] Keith Christmas and Shelagh McDonald were signed to the Village Thing agency but not to the label.
[39] Op. cit.
[40] From explanatory notes accompanying Plastic Dog memorabilia for use in this book.
[41] Soon to be renamed Squidd after a line-up change.
[42] Village Dog's Plastic Thing (no author attributed) Dogpress, October 1971.
[43] Email dated 9th December 2008.
[44] Ibid.
[45] Ibid.
[46] Folk News (no author attributed) Melody Maker, 6th July 1974.
[47] Albums (Colin Irwin) Melody Maker, 27th July 1974.
[48] For the full story, see The Granary Club (Al Read) Broadcast Books, 2003.

Bristol folk

[49] In Search of Forever (Rodney Matthews), Dragon's World, 1985.
[50] Webb was guitarist with Rodney Matthews' groups, Originn and Squidd.
[51] Op. cit.
[52] Ian's back with a vulture (Jerry Gilbert) Sounds, edition unknown.
[53] Email dated 9th December 2008.
[54] Ibid.
[55] Ibid.
[56] Ibid.
[57] Ibid.
[58] LP Supplement – Blues (no author attributed) Melody Maker, 7th June 1969.
[59] Ian's back with a vulture (Jerry Gilbert) Sounds, edition unknown.
[60] Then home of Pink Floyd, Edgar Broughton Band, Kevin Ayers, Al Stewart, Third Ear Band, etc.
[61] Email dated 9th December 2008.
[62] Ian revises the gospel (Jerry Gilbert) Melody Maker,15th November 1969.
[63] Theories, rants, etc. (letter from Ian Anderson) Mojo, August 1994.
[64] Ibid.
[65] Sounds Reviews (Roscoe Byfleet) Pre-View, January 1972.
[66] Focus On Folk: Bristol's cream (Andrew Means) Melody Maker, 1st January 1972.
[67] Email dated 9th December 2008. It was the lunchtime edition of the Bristol Evening Post for 11th March 1968 that ran the story.
[68] Op. cit.
[69] Both Dave Peabody and Dave Griffiths recorded LPs for Village Thing and Matchbox, first as part of Tight Like That and later on Peabody's solo LPs. Both continue to play, with Griffiths now a long-term Bristol resident, most often to be heard playing with Jim Reynolds.
[70] Probably: no publication date is included, but this is most likely when copies arrived at his agency.
[71] Email dated 25th April 2009.
[72] Sleeve notes from *Isambard Kingdom Brunel* by Old Pete and John Christie (1975) Saydisc.
[73] Bath University's School of Architecture was confusingly based at Kings Weston House near Shirehampton – five miles outside Bristol on the opposite side of the city to Bath!
[74] *Examinations Rag* was part of Christmas' repertoire, but was not recorded by him – he had a selection of 'funnies' though these mostly ended up unrecorded.
[75] September's Rich Harvest (Jerry Gilbert) Sounds, 10th October, 1970.
[76] Al Jones found himself in the company of the Beatles on Parlophone – Roberton did not yet have a single outlet for records by his artists.
[77] www.martin-kingsbury.co.uk/christabeldetail061269.htm.
[78] Not the Bristol-based Mike Evans.
[79] Miscredited on the sleeve as 'autoharp'.
[80] September's Rich Harvest (Jerry Gilbert) Sounds, 10th October, 1970.
[81] Magic Muscle did not release any records during their lifetime.
[82] Christmas Spirit (Pete Graham-Brown) Preview, May 1972.
[83] Email dated 5th January 2009.
[84] Christmas time in hard rock (Jerry Gilbert) Sounds, date unknown, probably summer 1971.
[85] As a Shirehampton lad, it was a rare treat in the 1960s and early 1970s to cross the Avon on the Pill Ferry.
[86] Email dated 15th November 2008.
[87] Ibid.
[88] As commemorated at the end of the live recording of *Up the Clump* included on the LP, *Cutler of the West*. Len Thomas was in the audience the night that the LP was recorded.
[89] Recollections of Jazz in Bristol: My Kind of Town (compiled by Dave Hibberd) Fiducia Press, 2000.
[90] http://www.johnmilesorganisation.org.uk/page2.htm.
[91] Now these are rare.
[92] Are these recordings still in the vaults?
[93] *Recollections of Jazz in Bristol: My Kind of Town* (compiled by Dave Hibberd) Fiducia Press, 2000.
[94] Nicknamed after the character from the Goons. Davis had also recorded several piano rags for a Saydisc LP – see the Q. Williams section for further details.
[95] An early hypothesis for an uncanny similarity between versions of some of the songs was that a well-rehearsed band should be able to sound the same on two recordings. You should, however, have seen the look on Henry Davies' face when I used the words "well-rehearsed" and "Adge and the Wurzels" in the same sentence. In this instance, however, the single and later LP versions of *Aloha Severn Beach*, although uncannily similar, are different recordings.
[96] Recollections of Jazz in Bristol: My Kind of Town (compiled by Dave Hibberd) Fiducia Press, 2000.
[97] If so, they still miscredited *Drink Up Thy Zider* with a publishing date of 1967 instead of 1966.
[98] I'd love to swim in the cider, see?

Bristol folk

[99] Flipback sleeves are those where (usually) three flaps have been folded over from the front sleeve and glued in place along the top, bottom and side edges on the back of the sleeve. Later pressings had, initially two flaps (top and bottom only), then no flaps at all.
[100] Email dated 21st May 2009.
[101] 1978 promotional pack.
[102] http://www.archive.org/stream/englishfolkplay027958mbp/englishfolkplay027958mbp_djvu.txt
[103] Op. cit.
[104] The sleeve of which was designed by Peter Lord, who is now with Aardman.
[105] Arthur Radford was the owner of Radford's, the highly-regarded Bristol-based hi-fi and electronics business.
[106] Email dated 21st July 2009.
[107] Email dated 21st May 2009.
[108] http://www.fromefestival.co.uk/2005/reviews.html
[109] http://users.swing.be/devans/Lutherie.htm - Dave Evans' website.
[110] Focus On Folk: Good Evans (Andrew Means) Melody Maker, 8th January 1972.
[111] Anecdotal evidence suggests that Airey later joined Gryphon, though this is unconfirmed.
[112] Sounds Reviews (Mike Morrish) Pre-View, November 1971.
[113] Email dated 4th June 2009.
[114] Ibid.
[115] Ibid.
[116] Quoted in Focus On Folk: Good Evans (Andrew Means) Melody Maker, 8th January 1972.
[117] Graham Smith played bass and harmonica, amongst other instruments. He had recently played on Magna Carta's *Lord of the Ages* LP along with drummer, Alan Eden, who ended up running one of Bristol's long-term drum shops.
[118] Al Stewart had a habit of coming to Bristol to find backing bands for tours – a couple of years later he got Ian Hunt, Tony Bird and Graham Smith together as his backing band. Well, nearly.
[119] The Granary Club (Al Read) Broadcast Books, 2003.
[120] Ibid.
[121] At the time of writing, the OGWT performance of *Stagefright* can be seen on YouTube.
[122] http://users.swing.be/devans/Ambr%E9e.htm.
[123] Email dated 4th June 2009.
[124] http://www.allaboutjazz.com/php/news.php?id=12672, posted 16th February 2007.
[125] http://www.frankevansmusic.co.uk/biography.html.
[126] Email dated 2nd May 2009.
[127] http://www.allaboutjazz.com/php/news.php?id=12672, posted 16th February 2007.
[128] If you don't get the joke, think of Maurice Chevalier.
[129] http://www.frankevansmusic.co.uk/biography.html.
[130] Folk Spot (Gertrude) Western Daily Press, 20th July 1967.
[131] Email dated 12th November 2008.
[132] Ibid.
[133] Email dated 11th November 2008.
[134] Op. cit.
[135] http://time-has-told-me.blogspot.com/2006/09/folkal-point-uk-folk-1971-review-by.html.
[136] Folk (Andy Leggett) Preview, June 1972.
[137] Further research indicates that it is possible that one or both of the Polydor LPs may have later been issued in the UK, but this has not been confirmed.
[138] Kelvin Henderson Stamping an Individual Mark on the British Scene (Alan Cackett) Country Music Review, January 1978.
[139] Ibid.
[140] www.Saydisc.com.
[141] Quoted in Hunt and Turner (Barbara Keith) Preview, October 1972.
[142] The next year it changed its name to Glastonbury Fayre before becoming globally well-known as the Glastonbury Festival.
[143] Hunt and Turner (Barbara Keith) Preview, October 1972.
[144] (No title or auther credited) Melody Maker, 8th April 1972.
[145] Some Slade recordings from the 1940s were made briefly available by the late Peter Kennedy in the early 2000s. HMV arranged to record a Slade LP in 1950, but he died a week or so before the recording date.
[146] Bones are set between the fingers and clicked together, sounding a little like castanets.
[147] Roger Digby, quoted in sleeve notes from the booklet accompanying *Shipshape & Bristol Fashion* by Erik Ilott (1973) Folk'sle.
[148] From a transcription of a John Maher interview from 1975, which is included in the accompanying booklet to *Classic English Banjo* by Ray Andrews (2007) Musical Traditions Records.
[149] This was supposed to be the first of a new type of destroyer, but thanks to defence cuts became a one-off.

Bristol folk

[150] Email dated 15th November 2008.
[151] Email dated 9th December 2008.
[152] Although Beatles records appeared on their own Apple label design the group was still contracted to Parlophone, hence Parlophone catalogue numbers for all non-solo releases.
[153] Op. cit.
[154] The address of Les Cousins club in London.
[155] (Title and author unknown) Melody Maker, 20th December 1969.
[156] Ibid.
[157] The Folk singer's Christmas treat (no author attributed) Bristol Weekly News, 2nd December, 1970.
[158] Email dated 1st June 2008. This email galvanised me into finally starting work on this book.
[159] Email dated 17th November 2008.
[160] Ibid.
[161] Email dated 9th December 2008.
[162] Ibid.
[163] Ibid.
[164] Ibid.
[165] Ibid.
[166] Just in case you are wondering about the various spellings, John Tippet does only have one 't' at the end. Keith's name is really 'Tippetts' but he removed the final 's' because of the inability of the music press to cope with putting the apostrophe in the right place when writing about his band. Julie Tippetts, née Driscoll, kept the correct spelling of her married name throughout.
[167] Looney Tunes, with an impeccable sense of timing, broke up just as Warner Brothers asked them for a demo. Guitarist, Roger Pomphrey, later went on to record and tour with bands such as the Eurythmics.
[168] Focus on Folk - Shelagh: the new Sandy Denny? (Karl Dallas) probably Melody Maker, around early November 1970.
[169] March 1971, though exact date unknown.
[170] September's Rich Harvest (Jerry Gilbert) Sounds, 10th October 1970.
[171] Focus on Folk - Shelagh: the new Sandy Denny? (Karl Dallas) probably Melody Maker, November 1970.
[172] Op. cit.
[173] The Village Dog's Plastic Thing (no author attributed) Dogpress, May 1971.
[174] This test pressing would sell for a hefty amount, its existence having been previously unknown.
[175] Recorded 1st December 1971, *Lonely King*, *For You* and *Odyssey* were broadcast on 16 December, but the final song of the session, *Spin*, wasn't broadcast until 27th January 1972.
[176] Quoted in sleevenotes by David Wells for *Let No Man Steal Your Thyme* by Shelagh McDonald (2005) Castle.
[177] Back from the wilderness (Grace Macaskill) Scottish Daily Mail, 19th November 2005.
[178] Ibid.
[179] Email dated 9th December 2008.
[180] It's moving for Mudge and Clutterbuck (Jerry Gilbert) Melody Maker, 23rd May 1970.
[181] Oddly the 8-track cartridge version was issued on the Reprise label – presumably this was a mistake.
[182] Email dated 8th December 2008.
[183] The unlikely Mudge and Clutterbuck (Jerry Gilbert) Sounds, 7th November 1970.
[184] Ibid.
[185] M and C are leaving the clubs (Andrew Means) Melody Maker, 6th February 1971.
[186] Email dated 9th December 2008.
[187] Email dated 5th May 2009.
[188] Email dated 14th July 2009.
[189] http://archivecdbooks.org/
[190] Changeling (Mike Oldfield) Virgin Books, 2008.
[191] Ibid.
[192] Ibid.
[193] Mike Oldfield: A Man and His Music (Sean Moraghan) Britannia Press, 1993.
[194] Op. cit.
[195] Email dated 9th December 2008.
[196] These gigs can be approximately dated because they coincided with the French student riots of 1968.
[197] In Session Tonight (Ken Garner) BBC Books, 1993.
[198] According to Losing My Virginity (Richard Branson) Virgin, 1998. If this is accurate, what was being recorded is unknown, but it is possible that the recordings were for Sally's *Child of Allah* single as the dates near enough fit. On the other hand, there is no confirmation of Mike's involvement on this single.
[199] http://www.mdjnet.dk/discog.html.
[200] National Rock/Folk Contest (no author attributed) Melody Maker, 3rd June 1972. Bristol rock band, Kiasma also made the semi-finals: again you may ask 'who?' as they do not seem to be included in any local listings.

Bristol folk

[201] The Pump House Trio included the ex-Stackridge violinist, Mike Evans, at this point.
[202] With whom Andy Leggett later played.
[203] The Alligator Jug Thumpers reformed for a performance on The Innes Book of Records TV series.
[204] Compiled by Dave Hibberd (2000) Fiducia Press.
[205] From an article in the British Aircraft Corporation's house newspaper, Airframe, October 1969.
[206] Sounds Reviews (Roscoe Byfleet) Pre-View, January 1972.
[207] Focus On Folk: Piggery Jokery (Andrew Means) Melody Maker, 5th February 1972.
[208] Email from Ian Anderson dated 9th December 2008.
[209] Email dated 9th April 2009.
[210] Except for Dr. Crock and His Crackpots.
[211] Email dated 9th April 2009.
[212] Fennell had left East of Eden offshoot band, Barnaby Goode, in July of this year.
[213] Record Reviews (Steve Chadwick) Pre-View, August 1971.
[214] http://www.stackridge.net/imagine.htm.
[215] Squidd was the new name, following a line-up change, for Originn. Squidd's track from the TV show, is available on CD from Rodney Matthews at www.rodneymatthews.com.
[216] Email dated 19th February 2009.
[217] The December 1972 Preview oddly lists both the 15th and 16th for this for-one-night-only-extravaganza.
[218] Billy Bent had legally changed his name to Billy Sparkle.
[219] Except for the *Do the Stanley* compilation and the *BBC Radio Live In Concert* CD, the latter of which was briefly available on the Windsong label in 1992. The live CD comprised concerts form 21st July 1972, 15th February 1973 and 7th January 1975. The CD is very rare and the few copies that appear tend to get snapped up at around the £20 mark or higher.
[220] http://www.dreampower.com/rjbio.html.
[221] Email dated 9th December 2008.
[222] The sleeve notes erroneously state that Stewart played autoharp.
[223] Email dated 14th April 2009.
[224] Ibid.
[225] Email dated 10th November 2008.
[226] Yes, "Hats".
[227] The Electric Muse: The Story of Folk into Rock (Dave Laing, Robin Denselow, Karl Dallas & Robert Shelton) Methuen, 1975.
[228] Op cit.
[229] Ibid.
[230] (No title or author attributed) Melody Maker, June 17th, 1972.
[231] Folk (Andy Leggett) Preview, June 1972.
[232] Tilston: glossy cover poet (Karl Dallas) Melody Maker, 8th April 1972.
[233] Email dated 25th February, 2009.
[234] Op. cit.
[235] (No title or author attributed) Melody Maker, 15th April, 1972.
[236] The folk singer's Christmas treat (no author attributed) Bristol Weekly News, 2nd December 1970.
[237] Ibid
[238] Article title unknown (Jerry Gilbert) Sounds, 1st September 1973.
[239] At least, those that weren't cancelled when Justin Hayward lost his voice for two days.
[240] Email dated 4th December 2008.
[241] Quoted from Fred Wedlock: Interview (Barbara Keith) Preview, September 1972.
[242] The *Sounds of Bristol* 7" LP did very well, probably because it was issued to coincide with the Bristol 600 celebrations: Saydisc had a stall at the fair that was held on the Downs and one of the nearby stallholders (for the shop, What Katy Did Next, trivia fans) remembers that the Saydisc stall seemed to incessantly play recordings of steam locomotives at full volume – probably a selective memory!
[243] Sleeve notes from *In a Folk Mood* by Graham Kilsby (1967) Saydisc.
[244] It was these same ladies that refused to have anything to do with Roy Harper's *Flashes from the Archives of Oblivion* (until a certain part of Harper's anatomy had been blacked out on the sleeve) and who also refused to press Monty Python's *Live at Drury Lane* because of certain swear words of Germanic origin and the mention of a certain part of the female anatomy – with a dagger up it. Hm, they may have had a point!
[245] Wedlock goes full time (Colin Irwin) Melody Maker, 15th June 1974.
[246] Ibid.
[247] Unholy state of Wedlock (Colin Irwin) Melody Maker, 10th August 1974.
[248] Ibid.
[249] Email dated 15th December 2008.
[250] Folk (Andy Leggett) Pre-View, February 1972.
[251] Disc made by Bristol (author, source and date unknown).

Bristol folk

[252] Albums (Colin Irwin) Melody Maker, 18th May 1974.
[253] Though she confused a few by referring to Frome and environs as "Hobbitland" and "The Shire".
[254] Decanter (no author attributed) Preview, June 1972.
[255] Ibid.
[256] Yes, the band that used to include John Lennon, Paul McCartney and George Harrison.
[257] The Plain Man's Guide to the Ballcockaphone: An Interview with the Pigsty Hill Light Orchestra (no author attributed – though probably Andy Leggett) Preview, December 8th 1972 to January 4th 1973.
[258] Nothing changes … I used to regularly get into the Bristol Students Union in the mid-1980s on a four year-old card from Exeter University, which was only ever asked for once.
[259] They reformed briefly in the late-1980s or early 1990s and again took Bristol by storm, almost literally in my recollection of one of their gigs at the Kings Arms at the top of Blackboy Hill.
[260] Jo Lustig was an extremely influential and successful national agent and promoter of the time.
[261] Written by Steve Webb following an evening of conversation and beer with Al Read and the author at the Golden Lion, Bishopston, Bristol, which is the venue for the regular Granary reunion nights.
[262] MCA went through a bewildering set of label design changes during 1972/73 and no-one yet seems to have definitively stated during which dates specific labels were current. In fact a couple of the label designs seem to have been concurrent!